THE GUITARIST'S PICTURE CHORD ENCYCLOPEDIA

Compiled by John Pearse.
Photographs by Roger Perry.

Amsco Music Publishing Company

New York · London · Sydney

International Standard Book Number: 0.8256.2199.2
Library of Congress Catalog Card Number: 77-81867

Exclusive Distributors:
Music Sales Corporation
24 East 22nd Street, New York, N.Y. 10010 USA
Music Sales Limited
8/9 Frith Street, London W1V 5TZ England
Music Sales Pty. Limited
120 Rothschild Street, Rosebery, Sydney, NSW 2018, Australia

Printed in the United States of America by
Vicks Lithograph and Printing Corporation

Contents

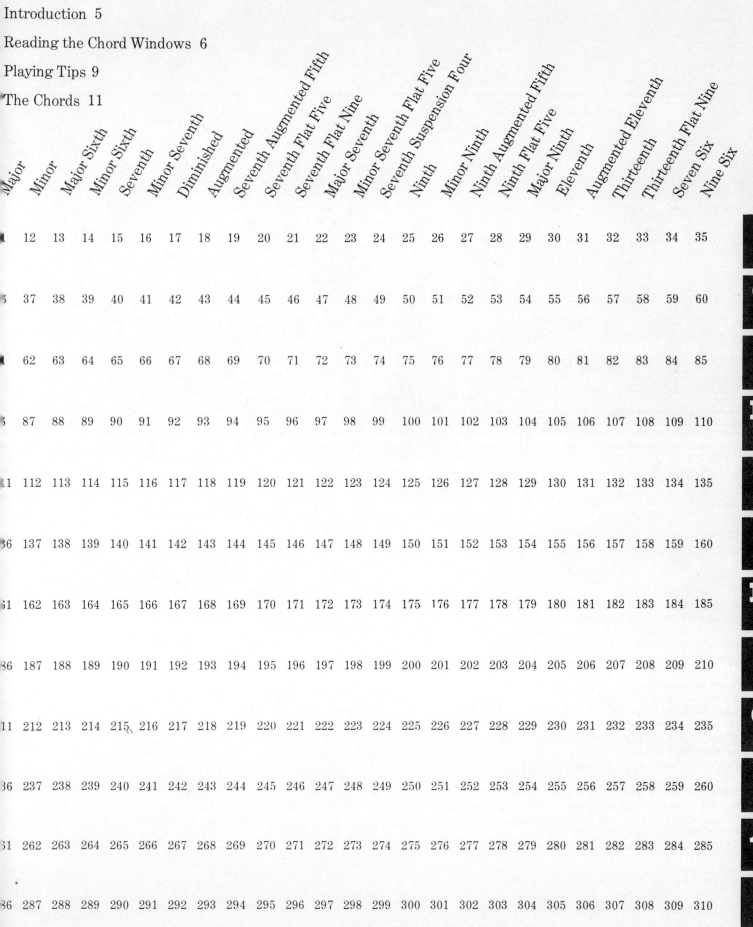

Root	Major	Minor	Major Sixth	Minor Sixth	Seventh	Minor Seventh	Diminished	Augmented	Seventh Augmented Fifth	Seventh Flat Five	Seventh Flat Nine	Major Seventh	Minor Seventh Flat Five	Seventh Suspension Four	Ninth	Minor Ninth	Ninth Augmented Fifth	Ninth Flat Five	Major Ninth	Eleventh	Augmented Eleventh	Thirteenth	Thirteenth Flat Nine	Seven Six	Nine Six
C	11	12	13	14	15	16	17	18	19	20	21	22	23	24	25	26	27	28	29	30	31	32	33	34	35
C#/Db	36	37	38	39	40	41	42	43	44	45	46	47	48	49	50	51	52	53	54	55	56	57	58	59	60
D	61	62	63	64	65	66	67	68	69	70	71	72	73	74	75	76	77	78	79	80	81	82	83	84	85
D#/Eb	86	87	88	89	90	91	92	93	94	95	96	97	98	99	100	101	102	103	104	105	106	107	108	109	110
E	111	112	113	114	115	116	117	118	119	120	121	122	123	124	125	126	127	128	129	130	131	132	133	134	135
F	136	137	138	139	140	141	142	143	144	145	146	147	148	149	150	151	152	153	154	155	156	157	158	159	160
F#/Gb	161	162	163	164	165	166	167	168	169	170	171	172	173	174	175	176	177	178	179	180	181	182	183	184	185
G	186	187	188	189	190	191	192	193	194	195	196	197	198	199	200	201	202	203	204	205	206	207	208	209	210
G#/Ab	211	212	213	214	215	216	217	218	219	220	221	222	223	224	225	226	227	228	229	230	231	232	233	234	235
A	236	237	238	239	240	241	242	243	244	245	246	247	248	249	250	251	252	253	254	255	256	257	258	259	260
A#/Bb	261	262	263	264	265	266	267	268	269	270	271	272	273	274	275	276	277	278	279	280	281	282	283	284	285
B	286	287	288	289	290	291	292	293	294	295	296	297	298	299	300	301	302	303	304	305	306	307	308	309	310

For Pres Rishaw and Bob Johnson...

Introduction

When I was a young guitar student, many years ago, I spent a large proportion of each week's pocket money on chord dictionaries. Every Saturday evening I'd unwrap my latest 'find' and spend many painracked hours trying to force my fingers into positions only possible to an eight-fingered, double-jointed giant. Dispirited, the next Saturday would find me once again haunting the music stores in search of a chord dictionary that didn't make me feel like a cripple! It wasn't until much later, when I was writing tutor methods myself, that I discovered that a great many chord books for the guitar are written by keyboard players; people with no idea what is – and, more important, what is not – possible on a guitar fingerboard. I decided then that one day I would make the time to write a dictionary of <u>playable</u> guitar chords. Here it is.

I only wish that someone had written it when I was learning to play!

John Pearse, London 1977.

Reading the chord 'windows'

The six **vertical lines** represent the six **strings** of your guitar.

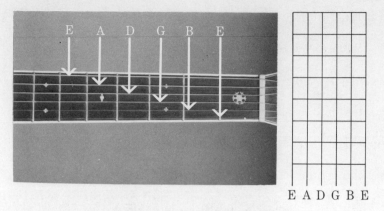

The **horizontal lines** represent the **fretbars** or **frets** which are inlaid into the fingerboard.

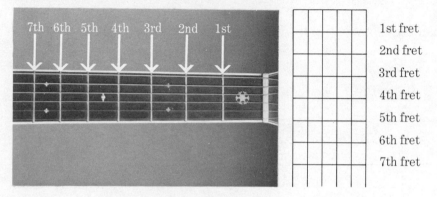

We take the **top line** to represent the **nut** or **top fret**...

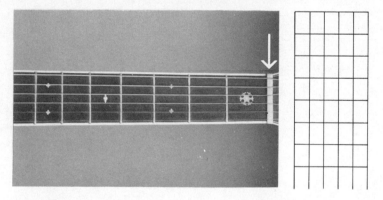

...unless a different fret value is marked on the 'window'.

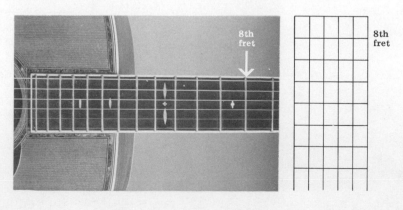

On the **vertical lines** (the string lines) are marked **numbers** which show you just where the strings should be held down in order to produce a note or notes wanted for a **chord**.

e.g. The first finger holds down the second string immediately behind the first fret.

Any string marked with a **X**

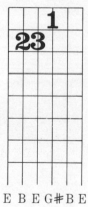

...is **not** part of the chord and **should not be sounded.**

Written out **beneath** each fingering are the **notes which together make up the chord.**

E B E G# B E

A **bowed line** linking two **or more** notes is called a **barré**.
This just means that all the strings contained in the bow are held down by the same finger.

e.g. The first finger holds down both the first and second strings immediately behind the first fret.

7

A bowed line across **all six strings** is called a **grand barré**.

Playing Tips

Whenever possible, keep your left thumb pressed firmly against the back of the guitar neck.

This acts rather like the tightening up of a carpenter's vise, and exerts equal pressure on both the back of the neck and the fingerboard. This makes it much easier to hold down your chords, especially barré chords, firmly.

Always try to hold a string down immediately behind the fret.

If you're too far away...

...the string will not ring clearly.

When you think that you've got a chord fingered correctly, play it over slowly–one string at a time.

If one or more strings sound muffled, check that your fingers haven't wandered away from the fret.

If your chord still sounds dampened, try bracing your thumb more firmly.

If this still doesn't solve the problem, check that one of your other fingers isn't falling over and touching the muffled string.

Finally, perhaps the most important tip of all.
Never practise until your hands ache or you begin to feel tired. It's much better to quit whilst you're still feeling good and full of enthusiasm. It will make it easier to get your guitar out of its case for tomorrow's practise. As your hands get used to forming chords, and as your mind begins to think in note formations, you'll find that your sessions will become longer. Let this happen naturally. Remember, it is better to have a fifteen minute practice session that you enjoy than a painful hour that leaves you inclined to give the guitar a miss for a week.
Happy Playing!

If you look down the table of contents in the front of the book you'll see that some keys have more than one name. $C^{\#}$, for instance, is also called $D^{\flat}$.

Notes or keys that sound the same although they have different names are said to be 'enharmonic'..... and when I was planning just how the book should be layed out I decided to include any enharmonically equivalent keys in the headings.

If you turn to the section on $F^{\#}$ you'll see that it is also known as $G^{\flat}$. This posed a problem, however, when I came to set out the notes which appear beneath each fingering. Should I structure them as a sharpened—or a flattened key? Obviously, to put both names for each note would be both clumsy and rather confusing. I have, therefore, set out all enharmonic keys using sharps. The notes of the flattened equivalent, should you need them, can be instantly worked out in your head.

e.g. $D^{\#}$ $G^{\#}$ C F   would convert to $E^{\flat}$ $A^{\flat}$ C F

C Major

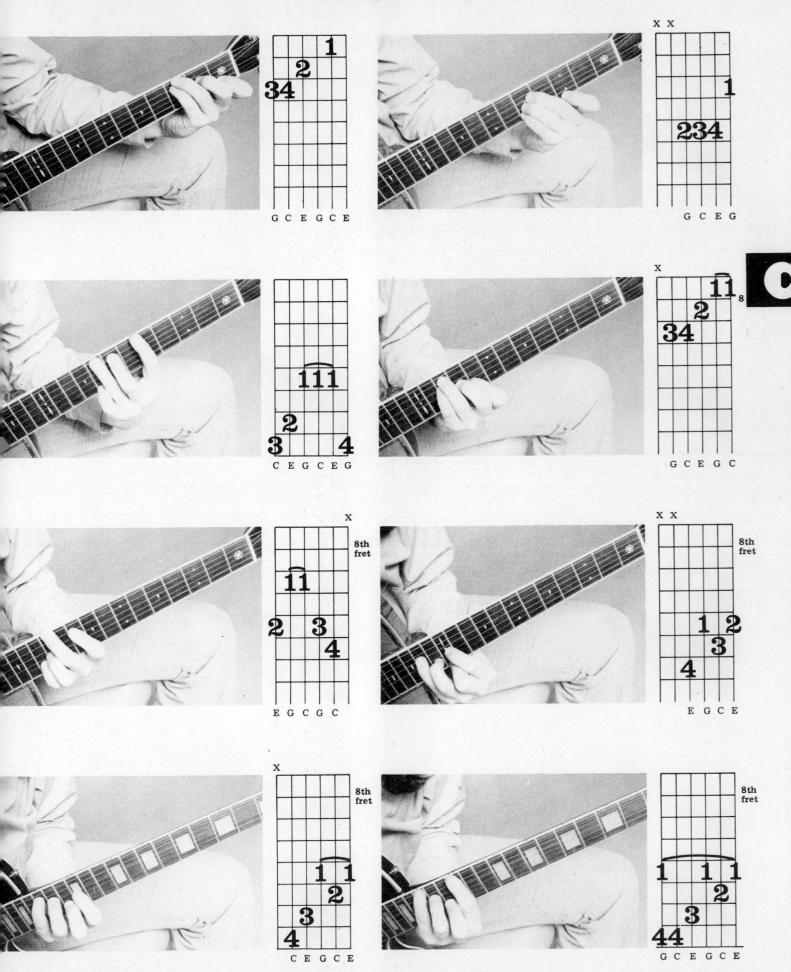

11

C Minor

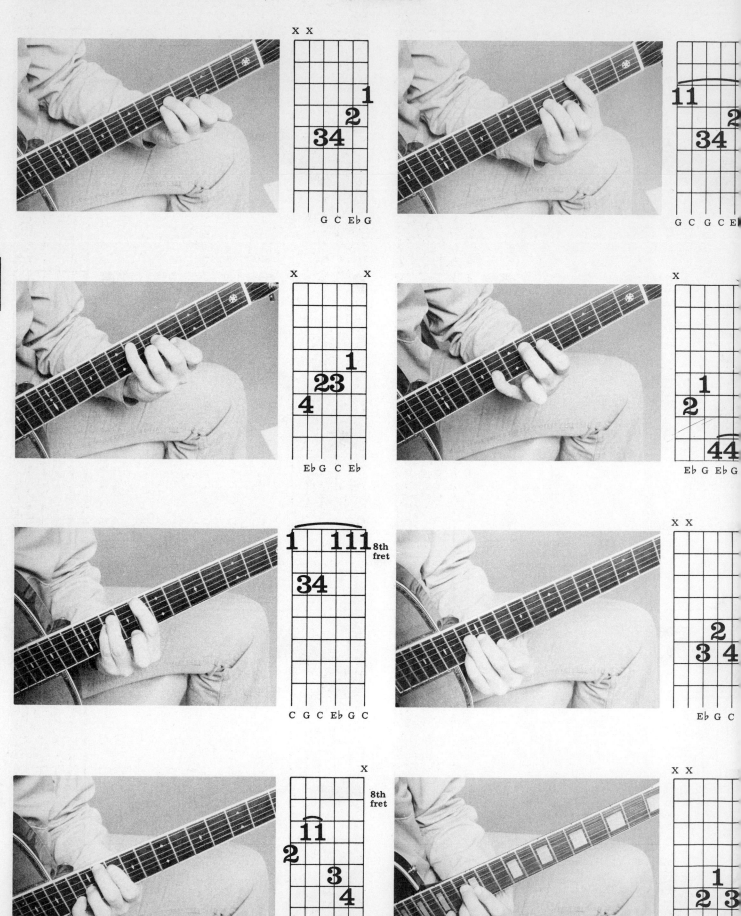

12

C Major Sixth

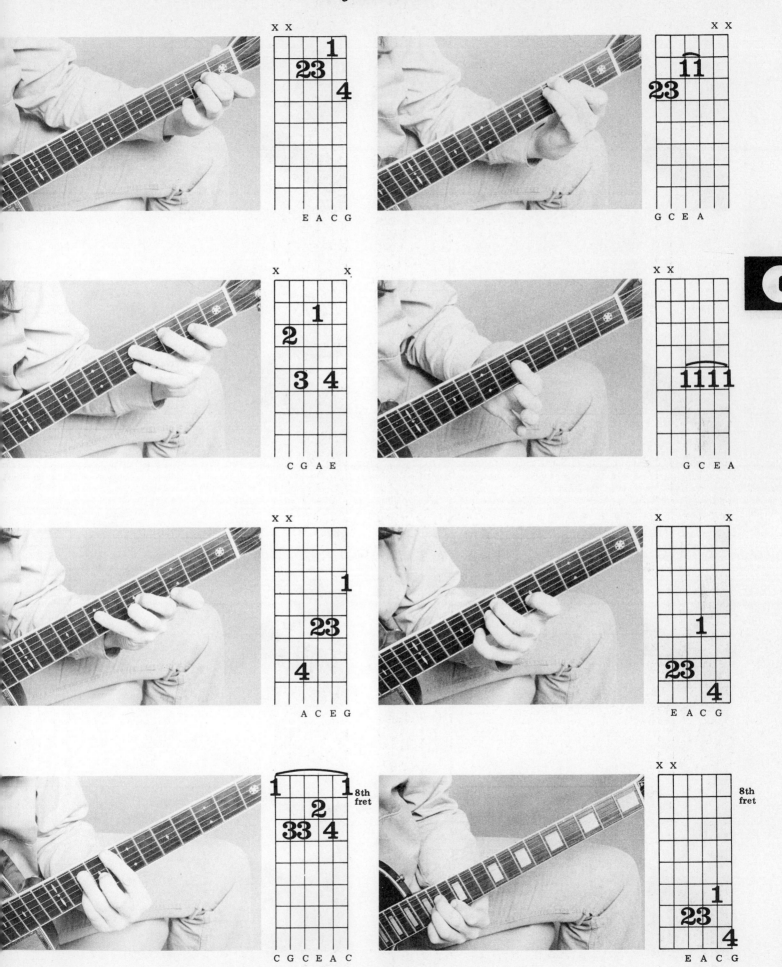

C Minor Sixth

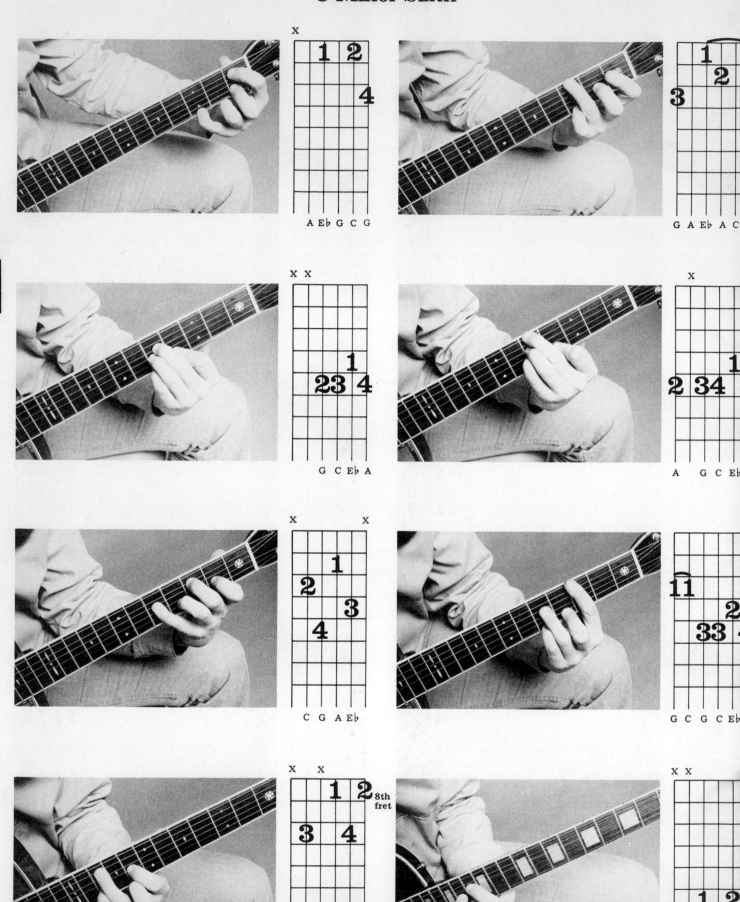

C Seventh

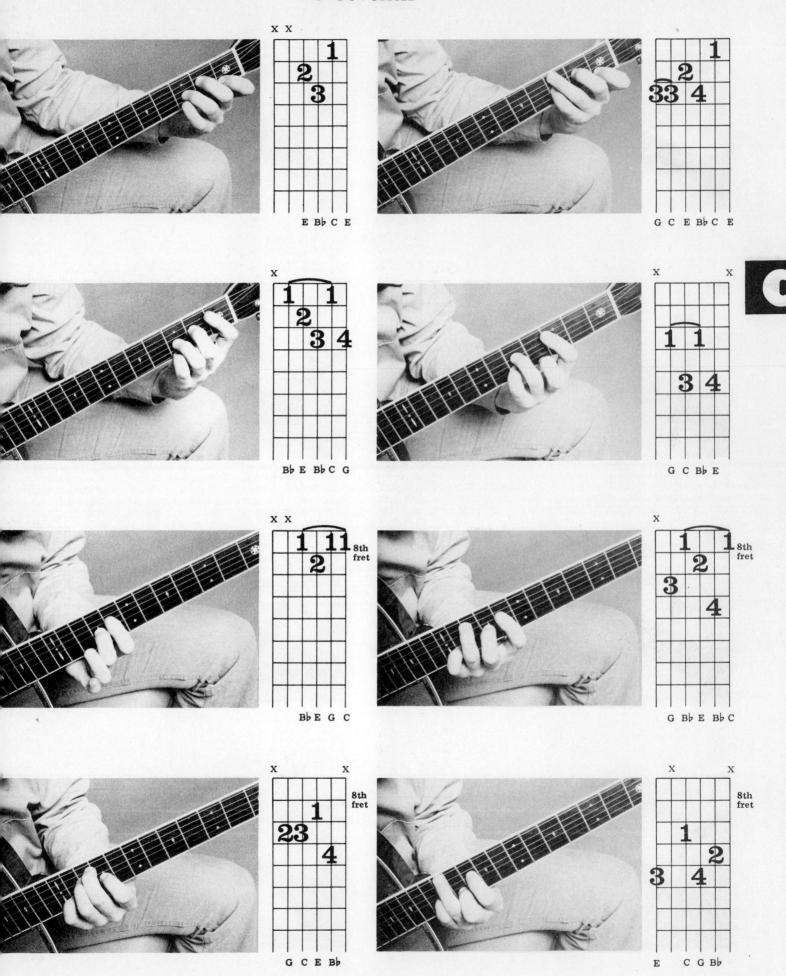

15

C Minor Seventh

16

C Diminished

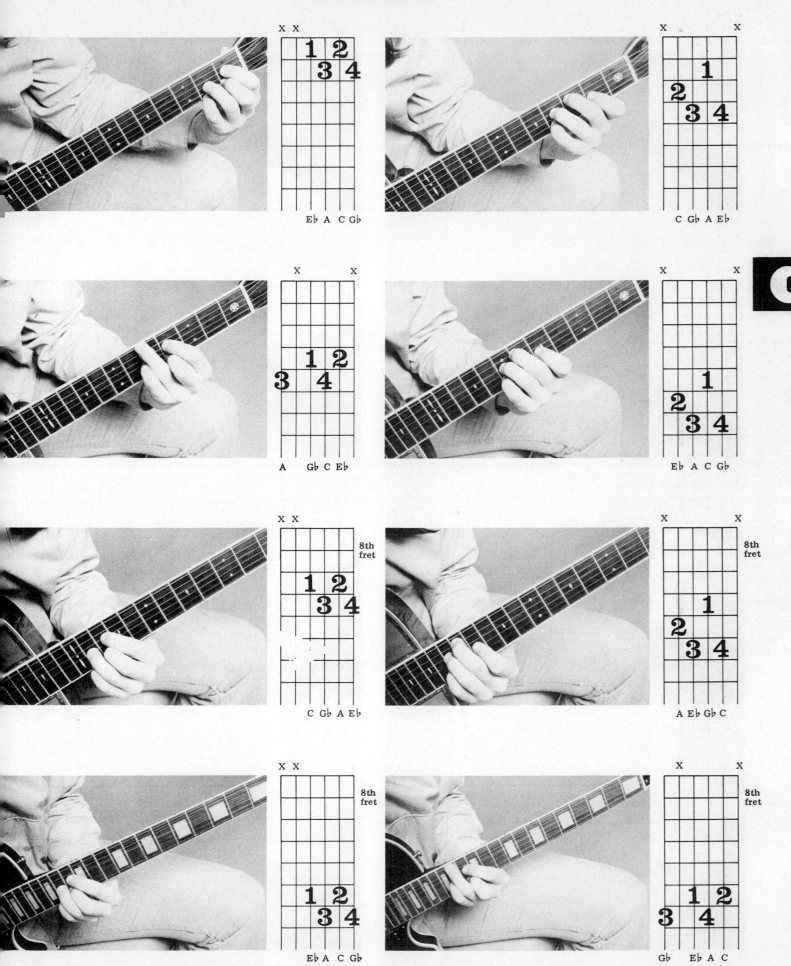

C Augmented

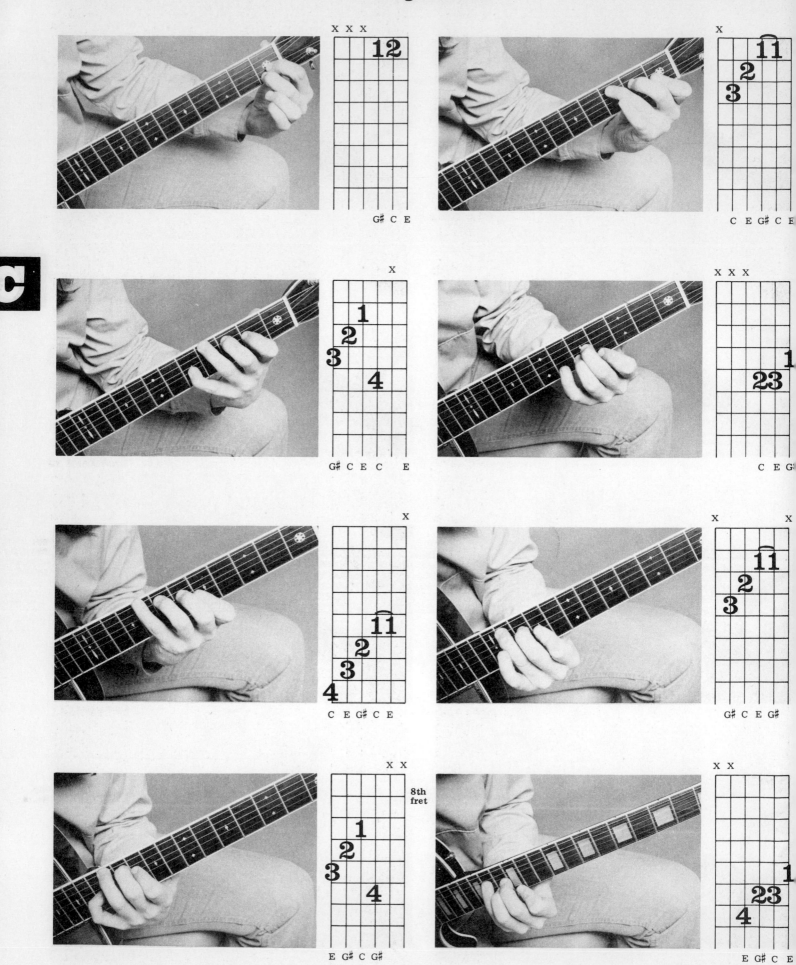

18

C Seventh Augmented Fifth

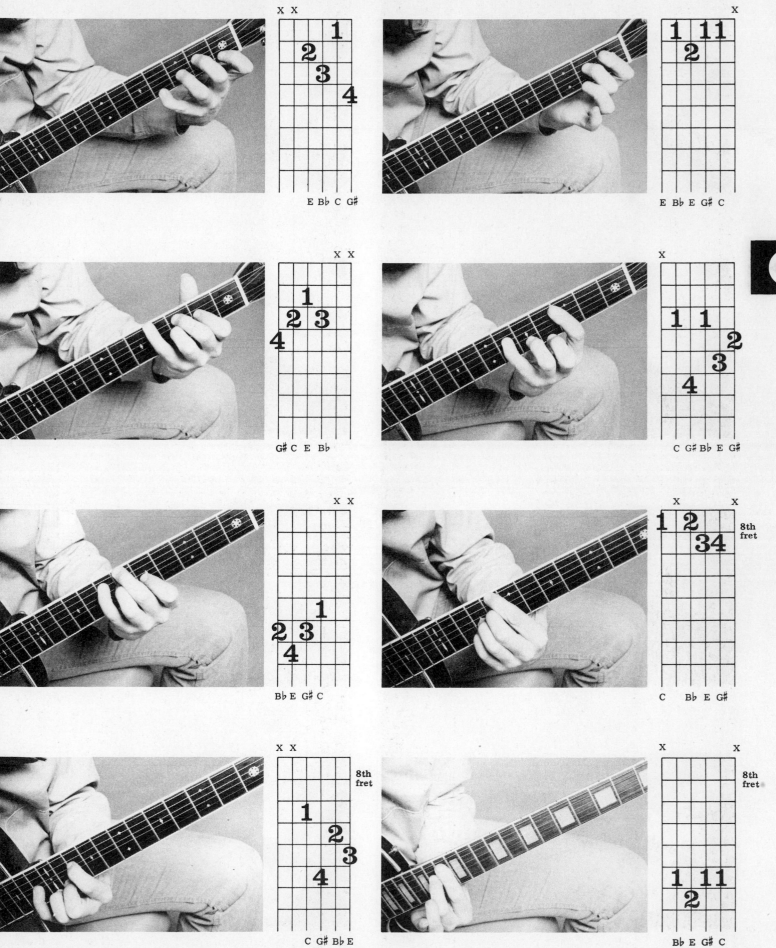

E Bb C G#

E Bb E G# C

G# C E Bb

C G# Bb E G#

Bb E G# C

C Bb E G#

8th fret

C G# Bb E

8th fret

Bb E G# C

8th fret

19

C Seventh Flat Five

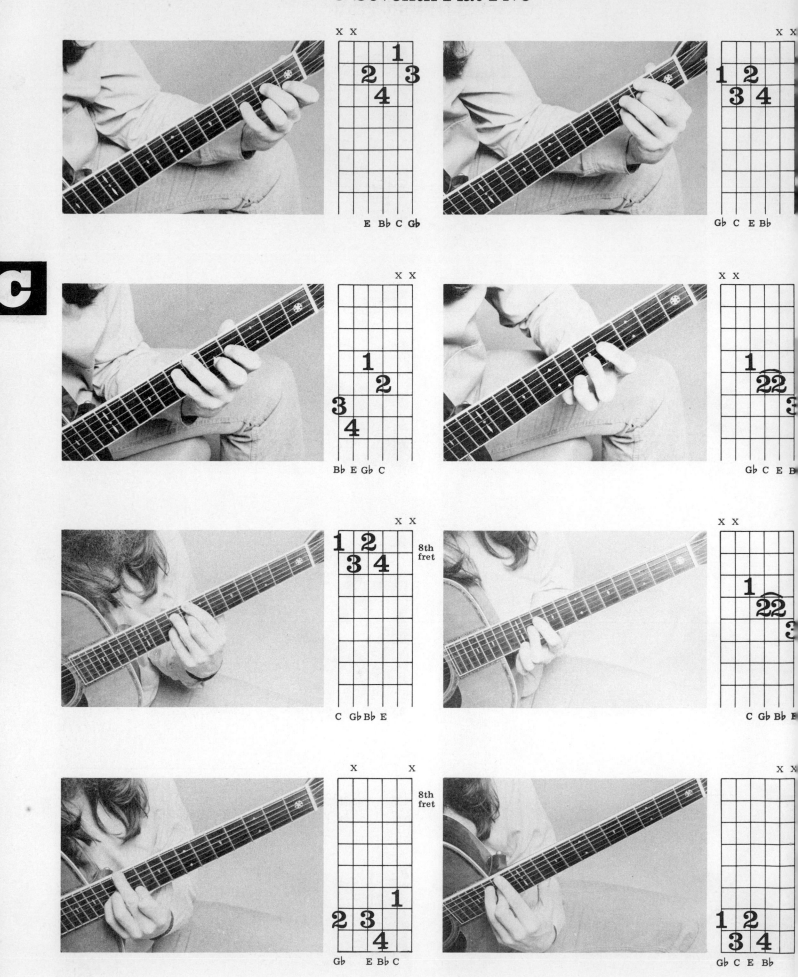

C Seventh Flat Nine

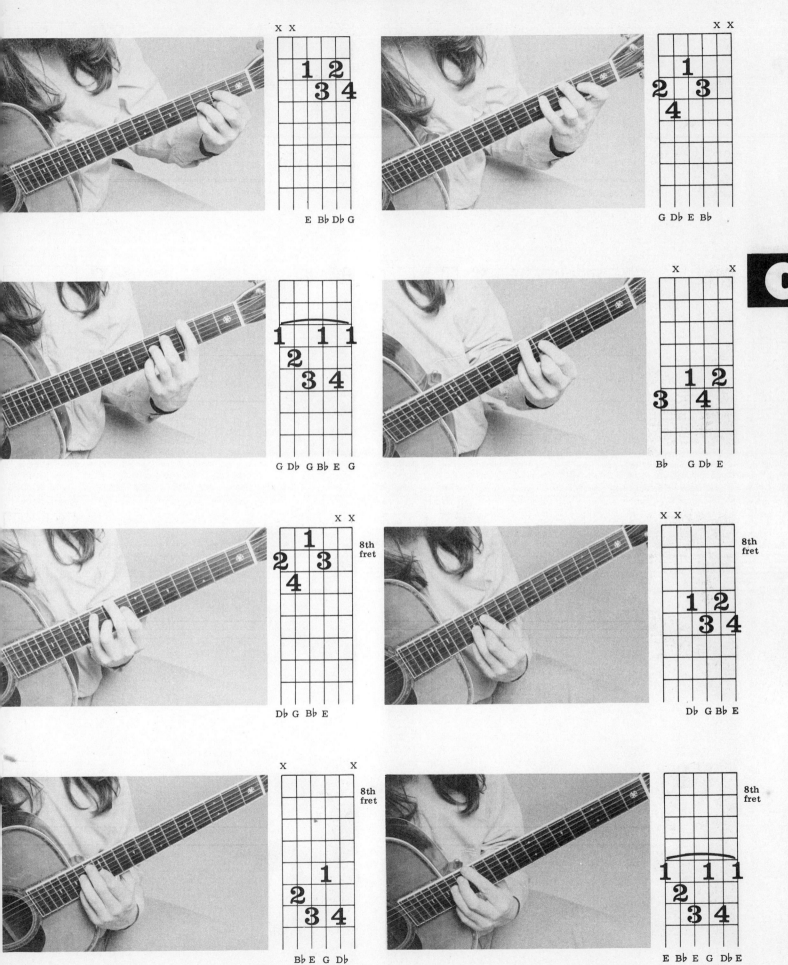

21

C Major Seventh

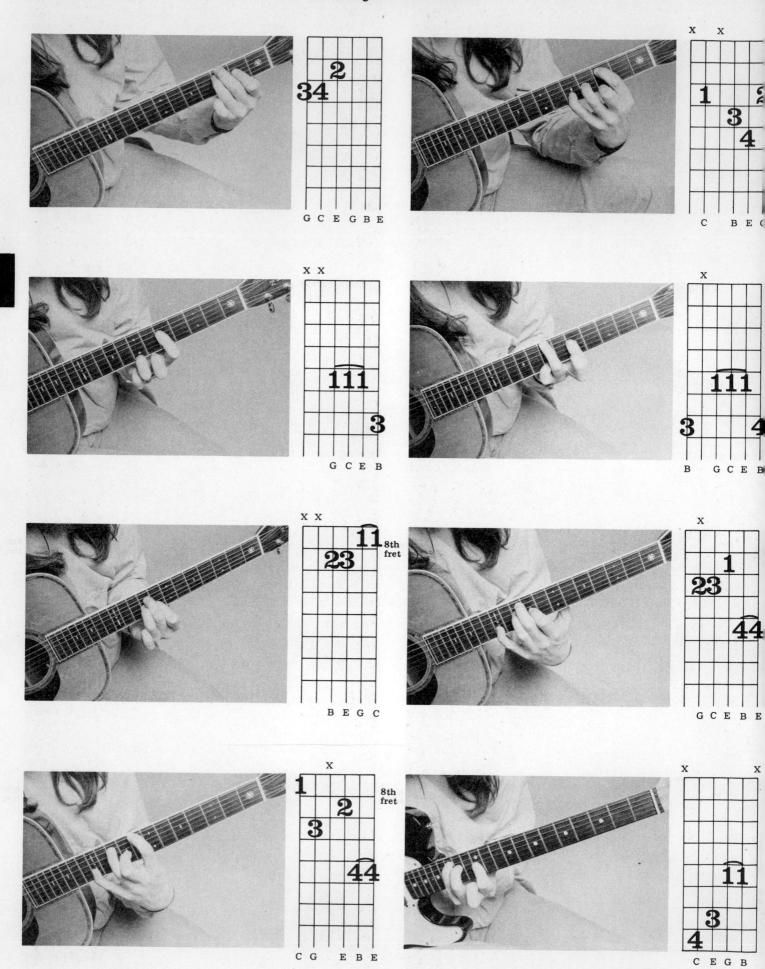

C Minor Seventh Flat Five

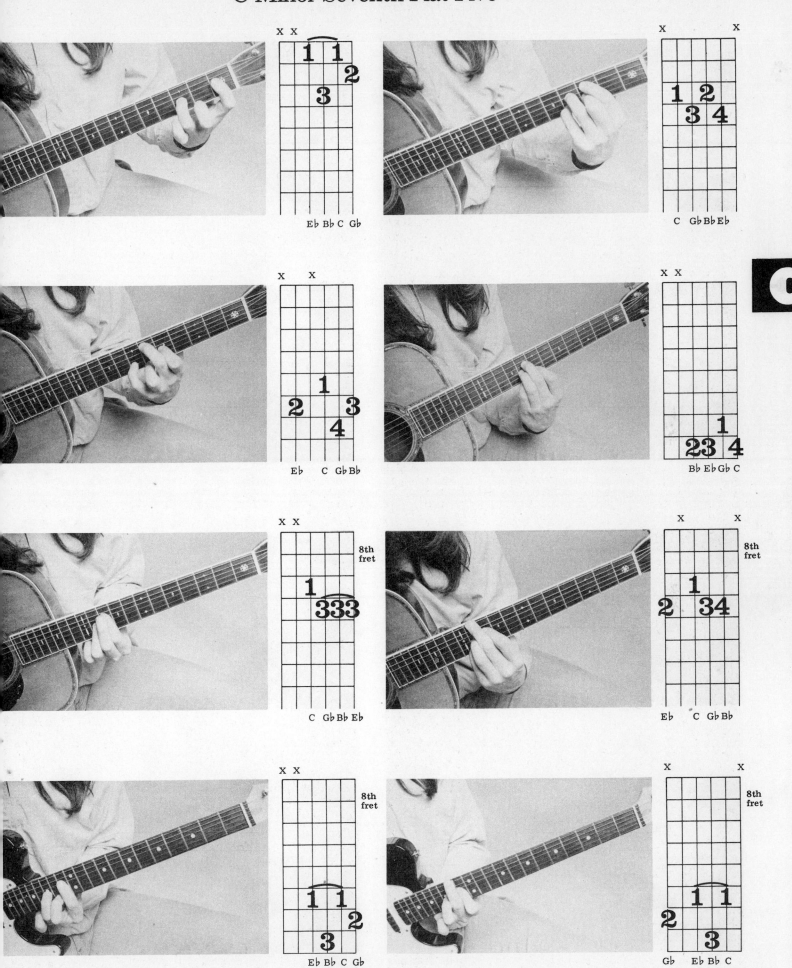

C Seventh Suspension Four

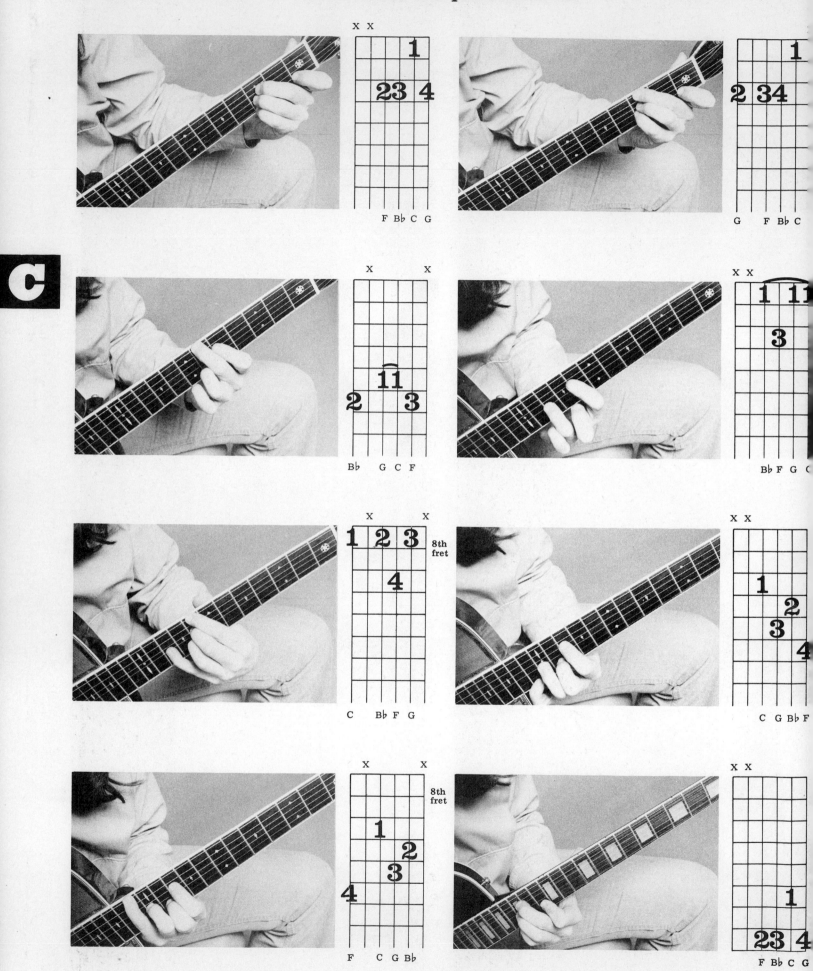

C Ninth

C Minor Ninth

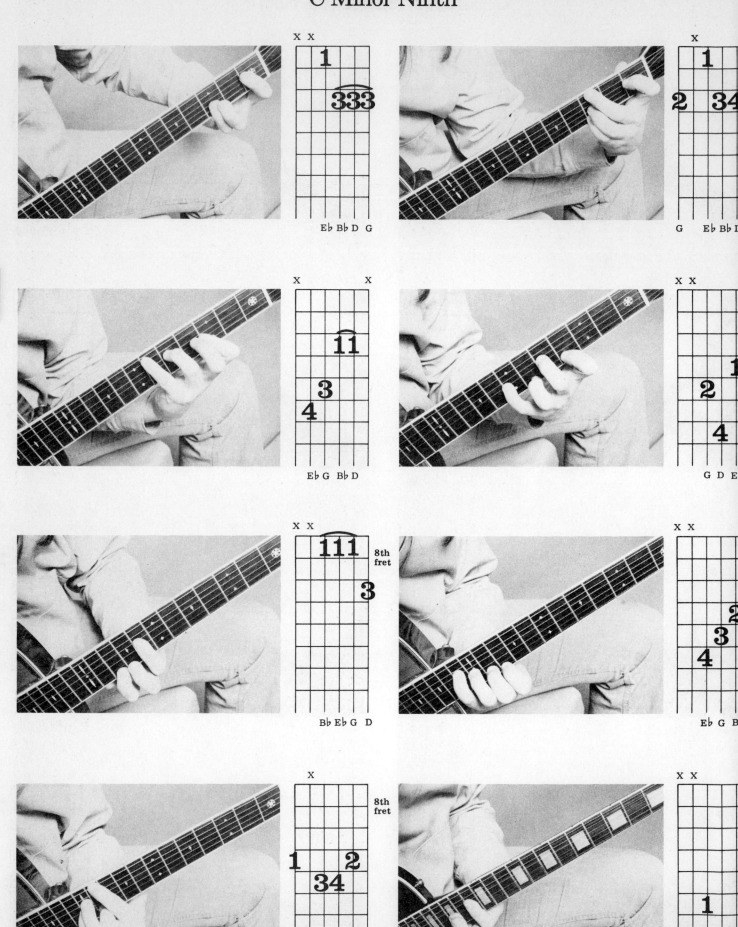

26

C Ninth Augmented Fifth

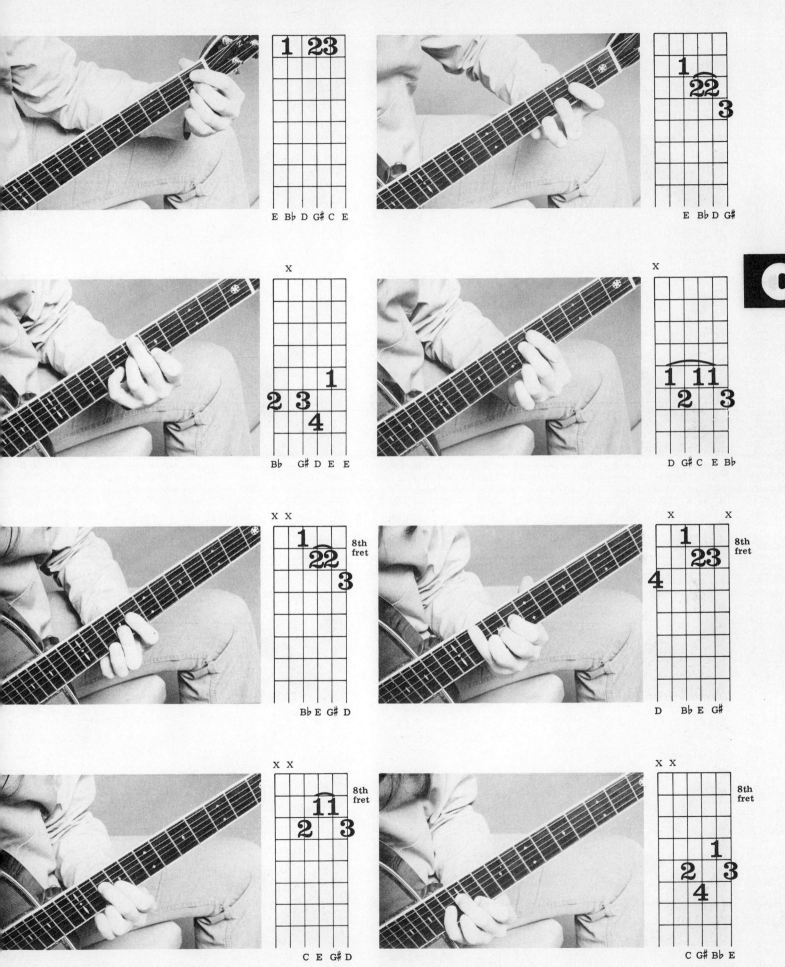

E Bb D G# C E

E Bb D G#

X

Bb G# D E E

X

D G# C E Bb

X X

8th fret

Bb E G# D

X X

8th fret

D Bb E G#

X X

8th fret

C E G# D

X X

8th fret

C G# Bb E

C Ninth Flat Five

C Major Ninth

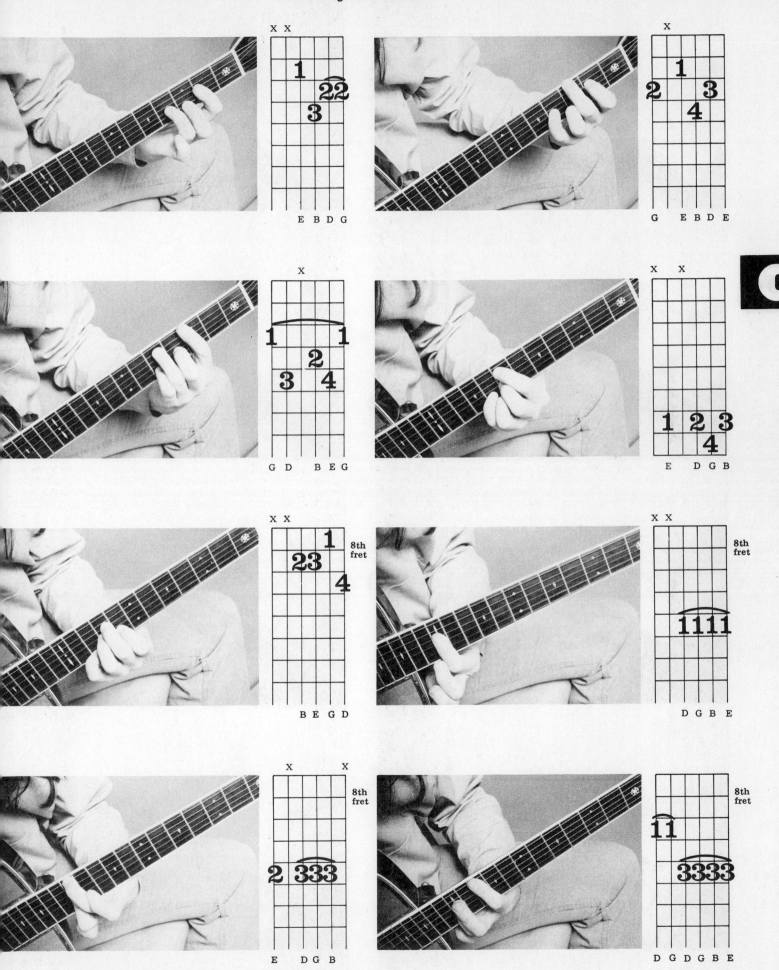

C Eleventh

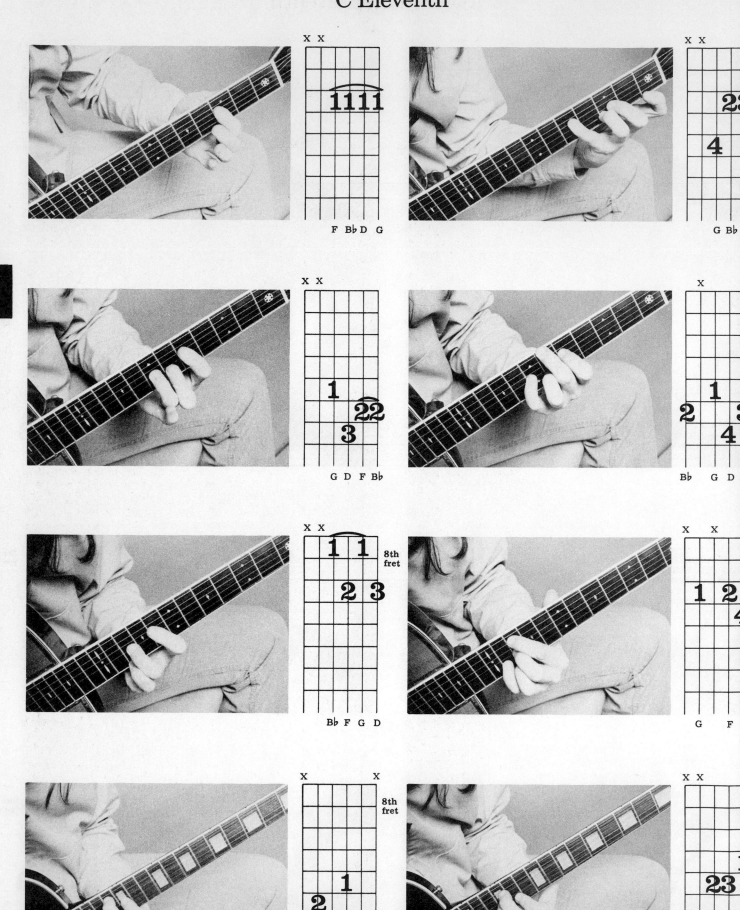

C Augmented Eleventh

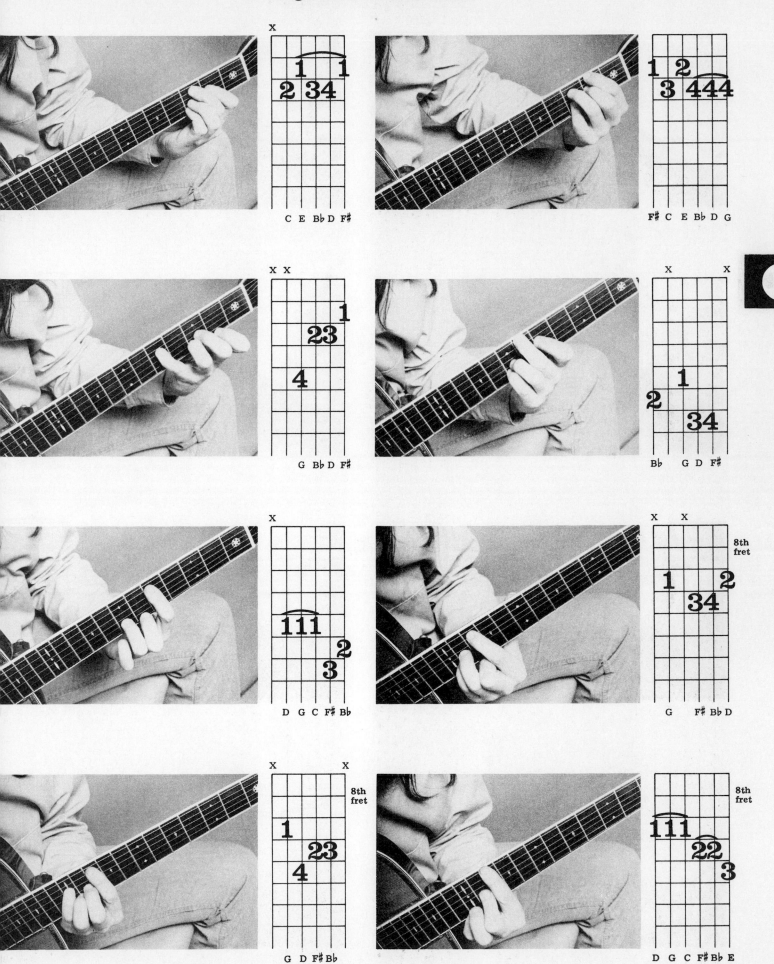

31

C Thirteenth

C Thirteenth Flat Nine

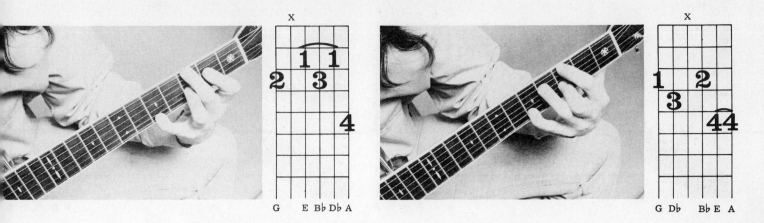

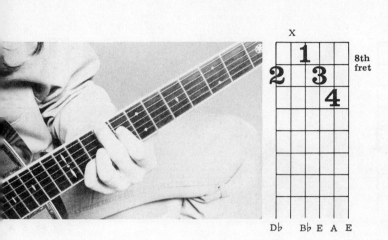

C Seven Six

C Nine Six

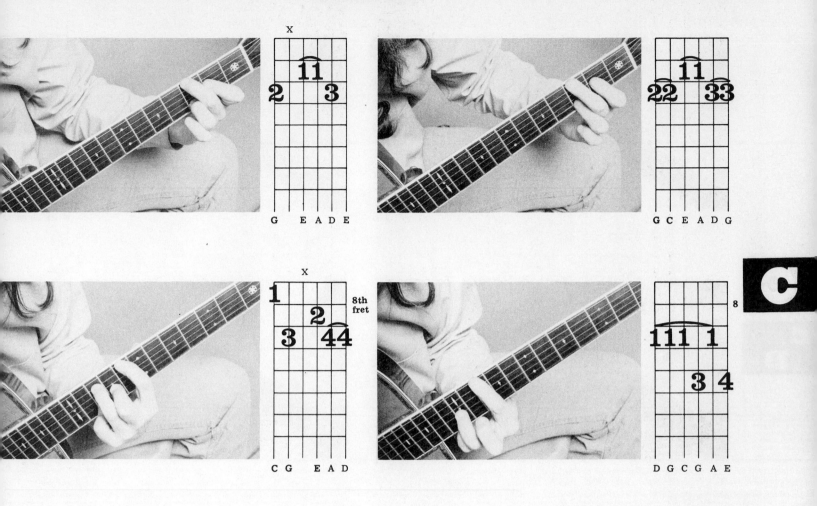

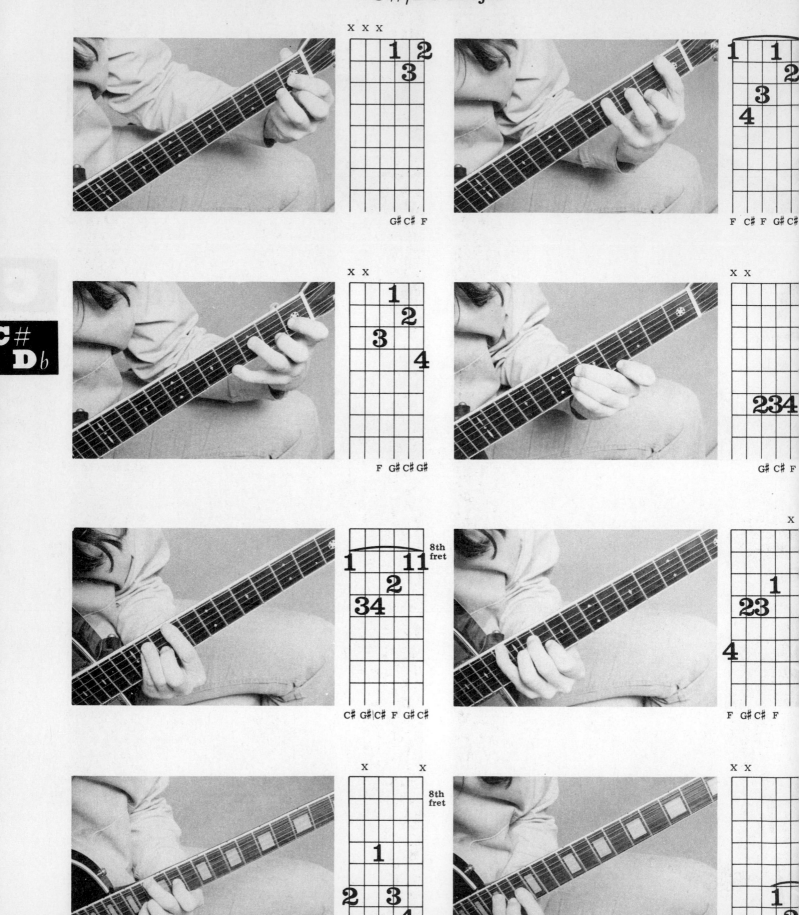

C#/Db Minor

37

C#/Db Major Sixth

C#/Db Minor Sixth

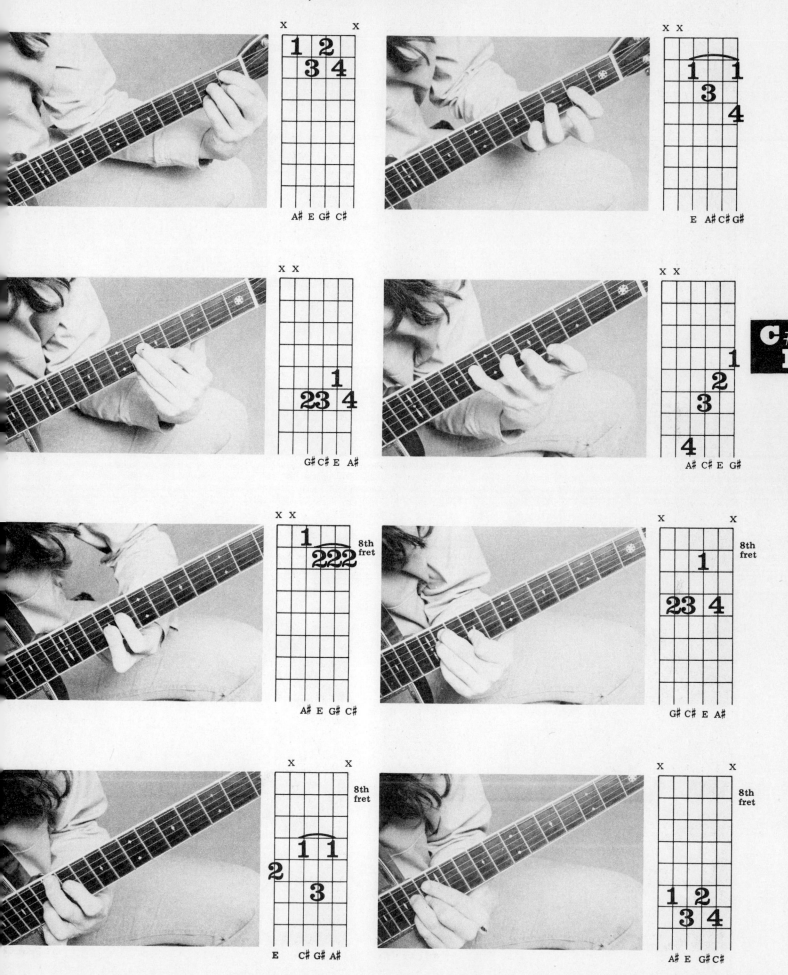

39

C#/D♭ Seventh

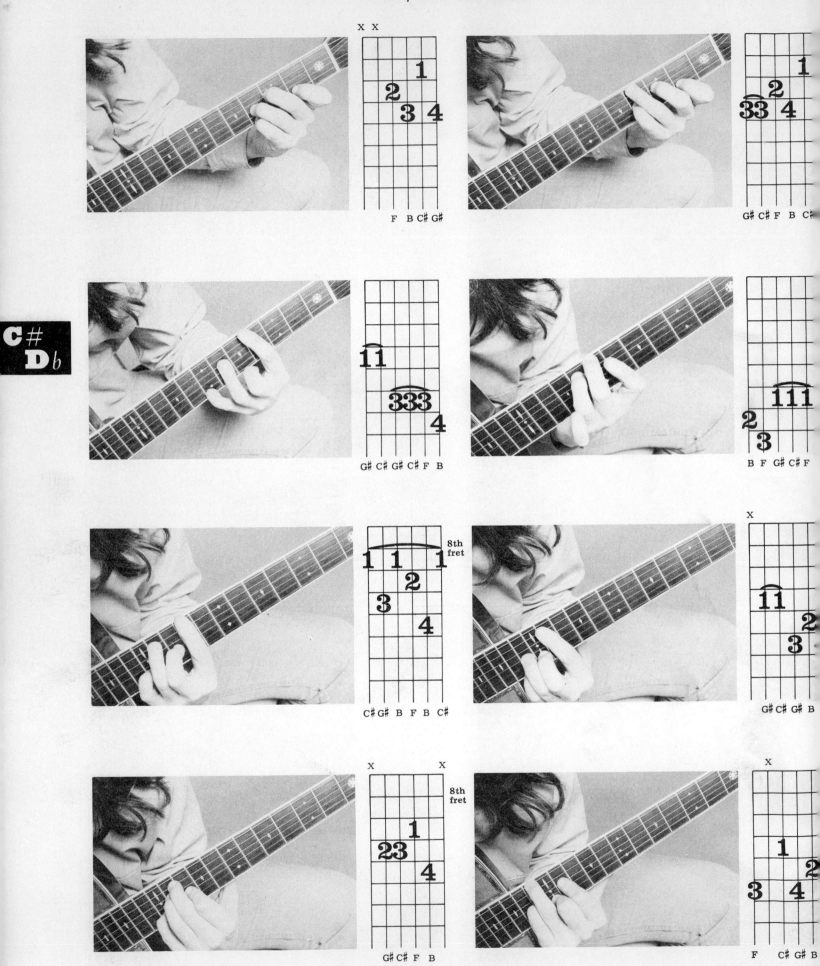

40

C#/Db Minor Seventh

C#/D♭ Diminished

C#/Db Augmented

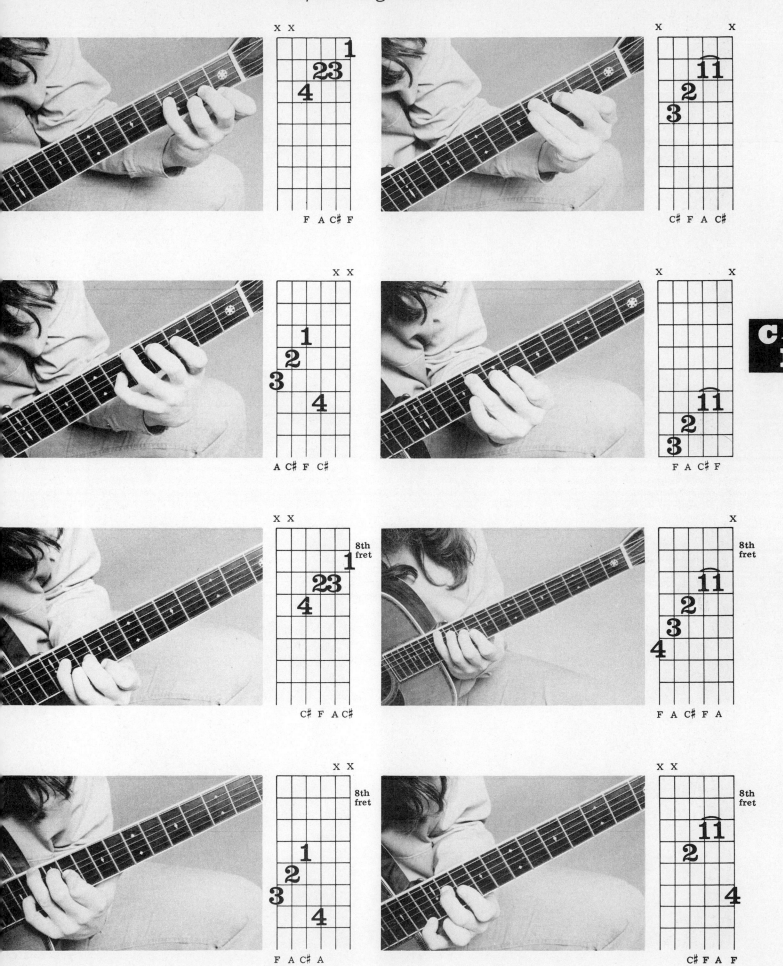

43

C#/Db Seventh Augmented Fifth

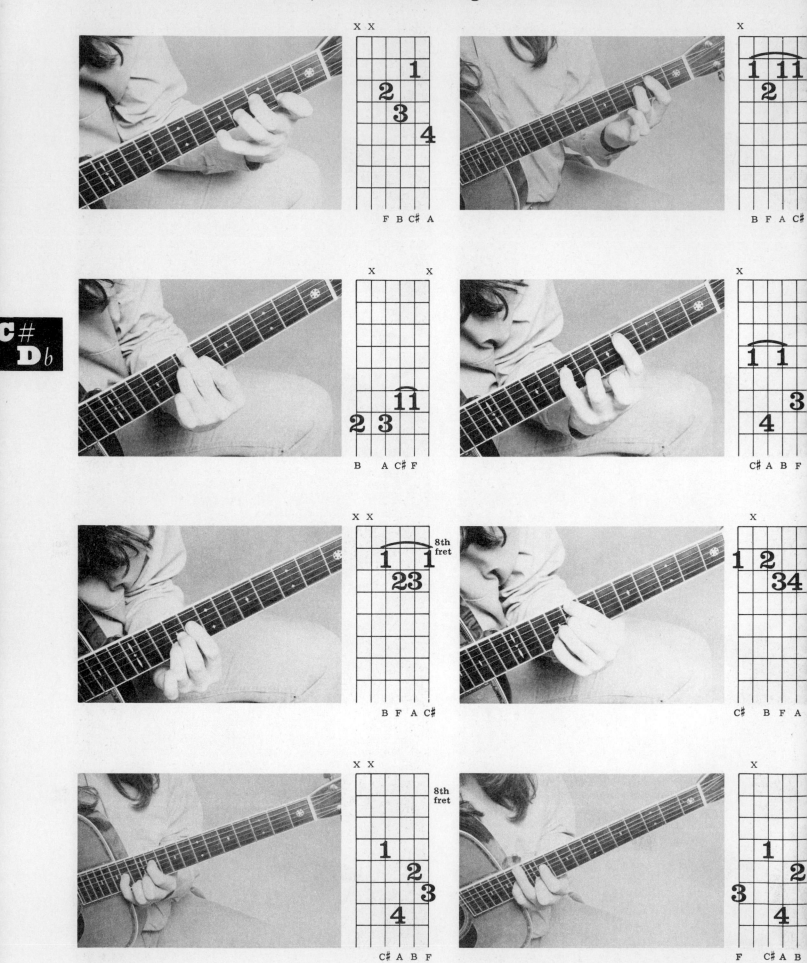

C#/Db Seventh Flat Five

45

C#/Db Seventh Flat Nine

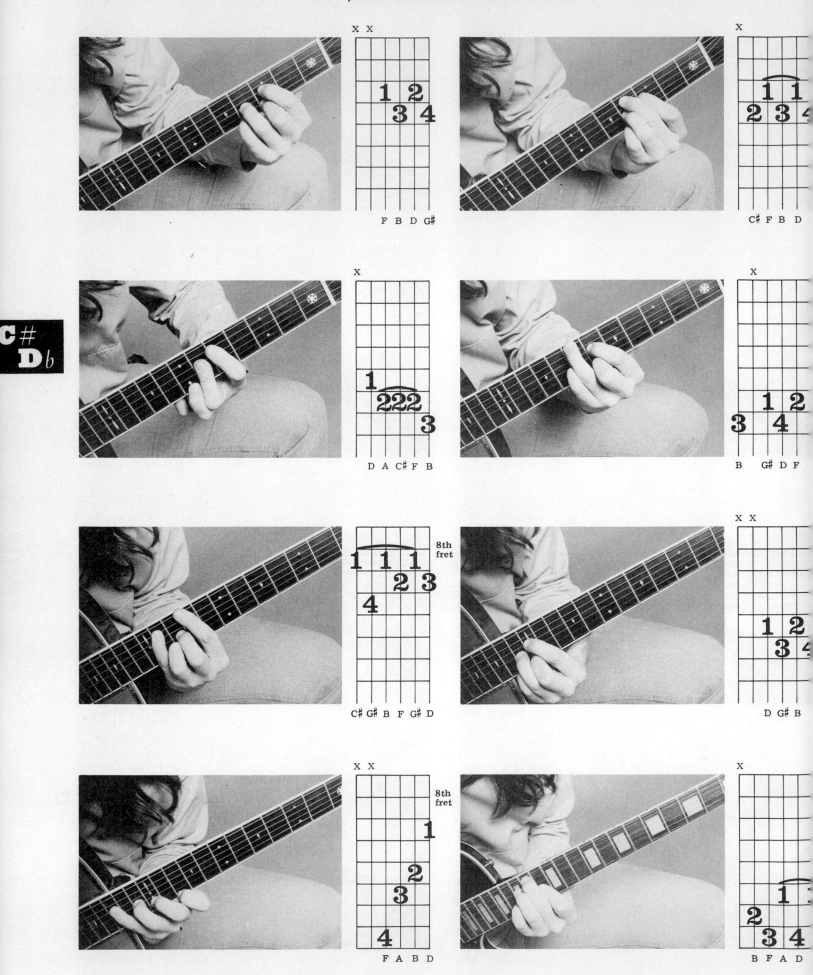

C#/Db Major Seventh

C#/Db Minor Seventh Flat Five

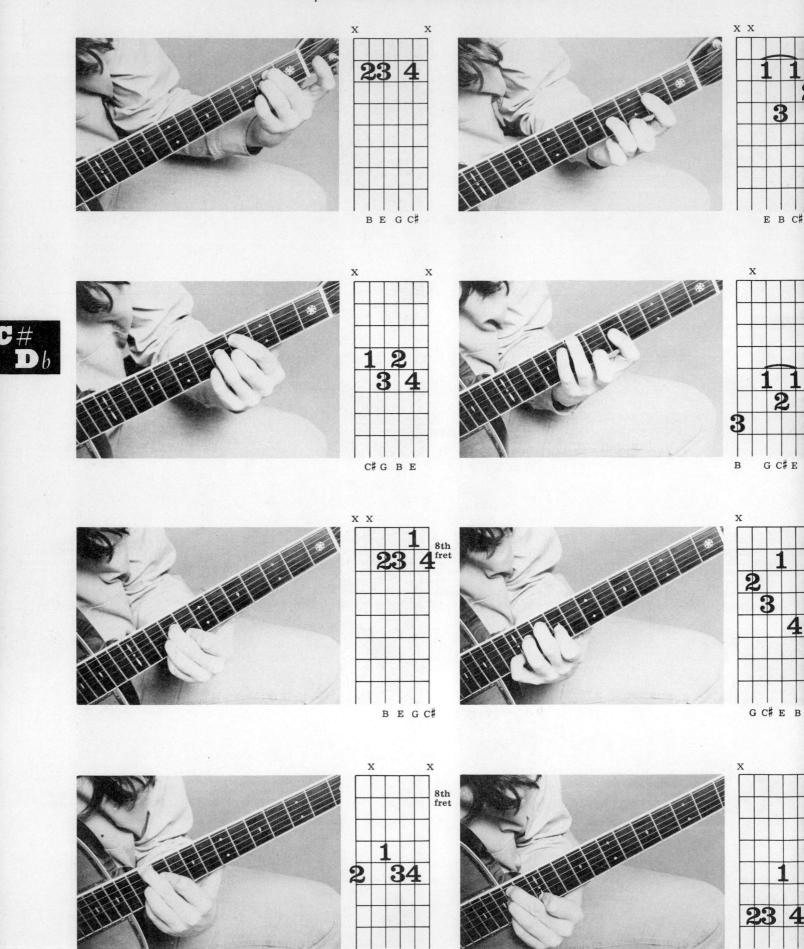

C#/Db Seventh Suspension Four

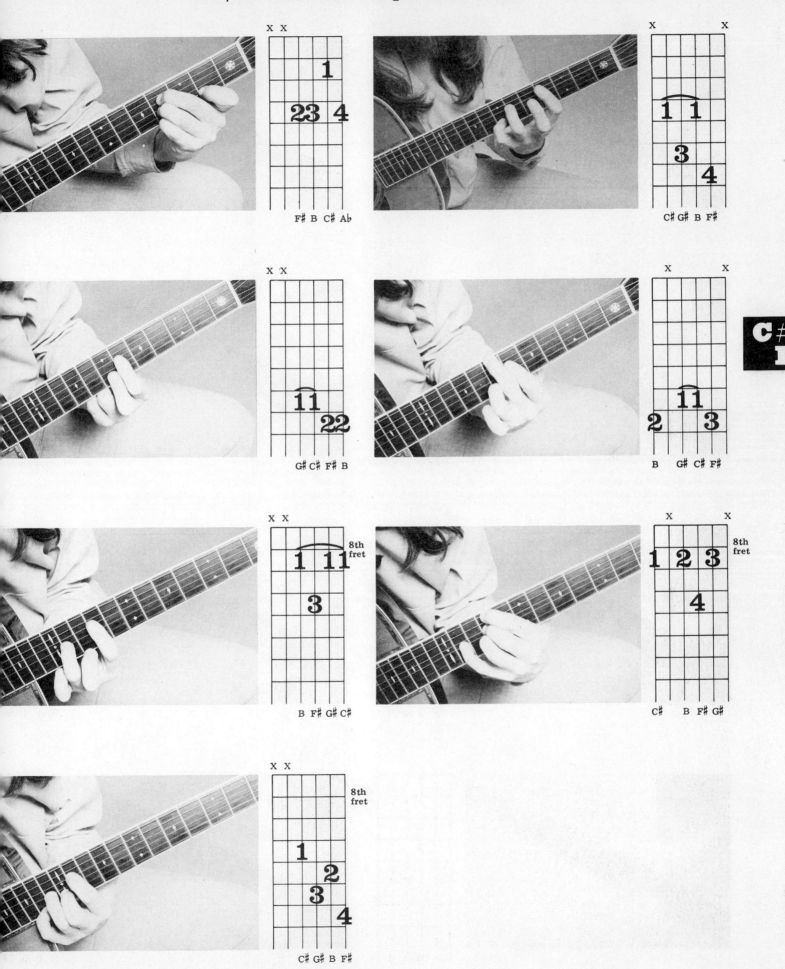

49

C#/Db Ninth

C#/Db Minor Ninth

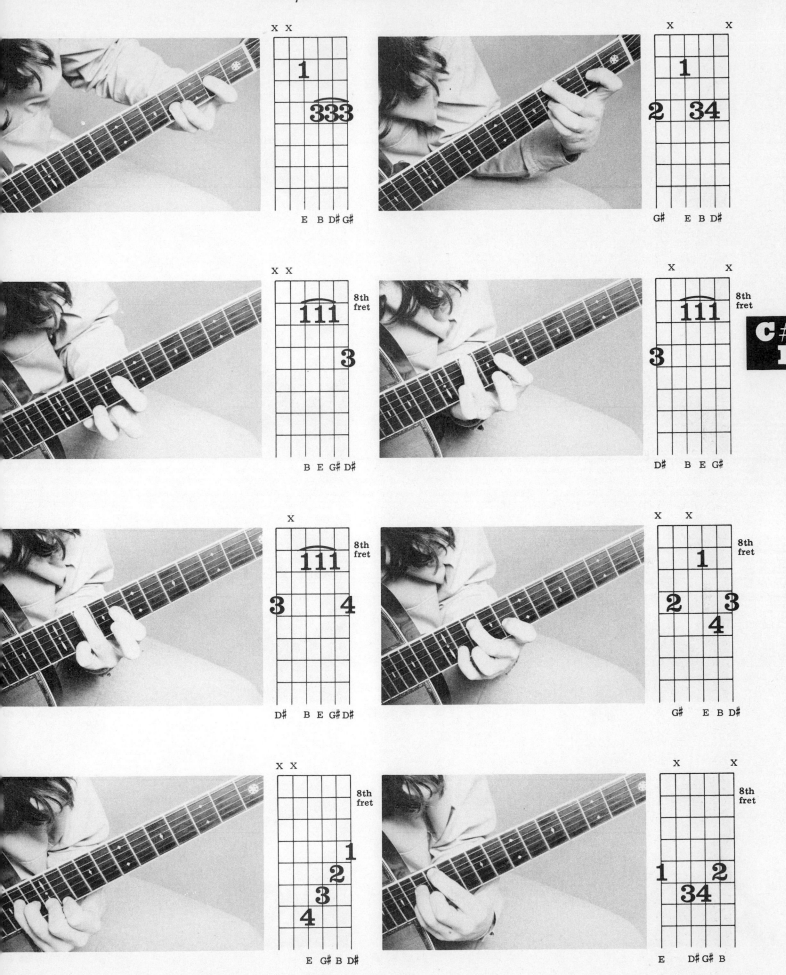

C#/Db Ninth Augmented Fifth

C#/Db Ninth Flat Five

C#/Db Major Ninth

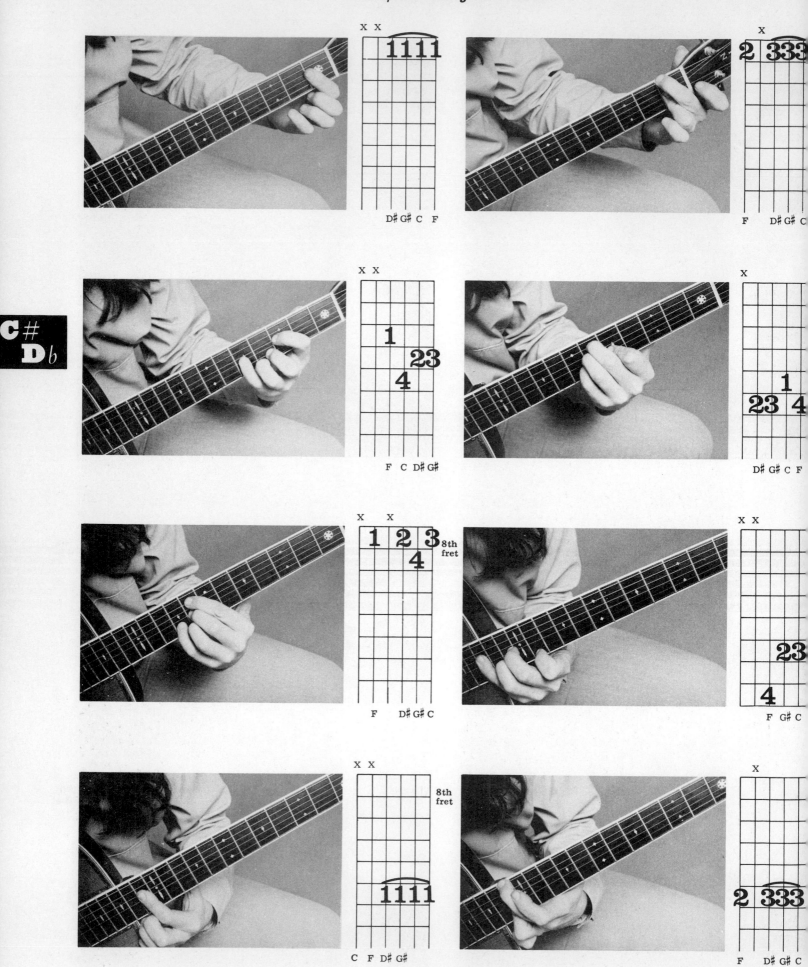

C#/Db Eleventh

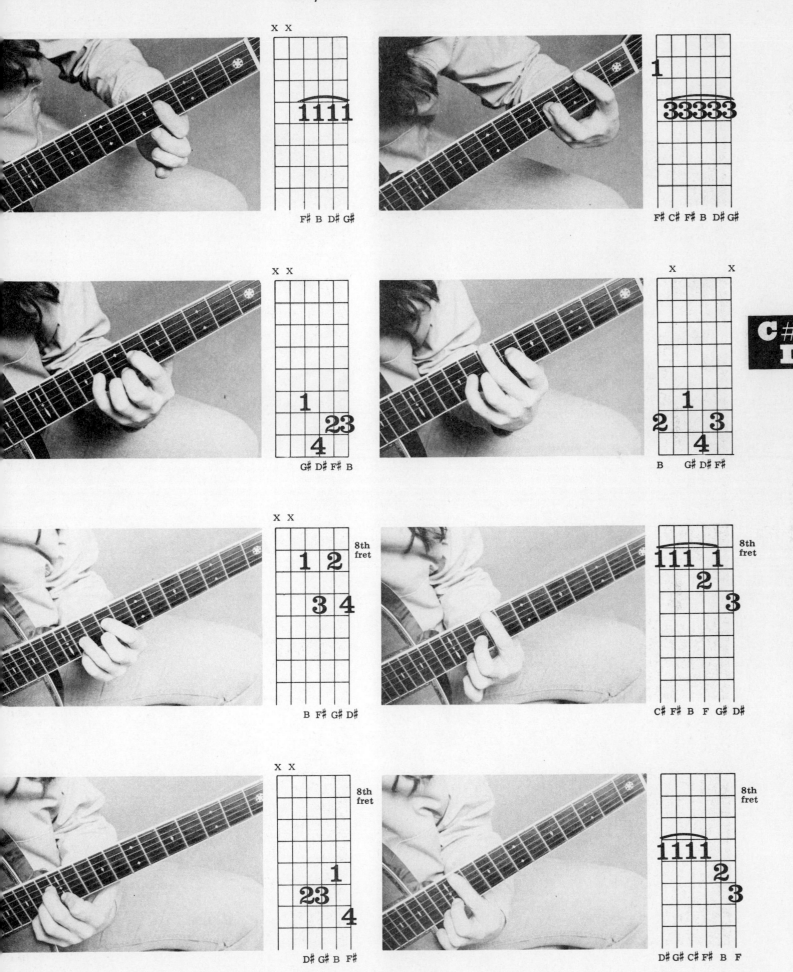

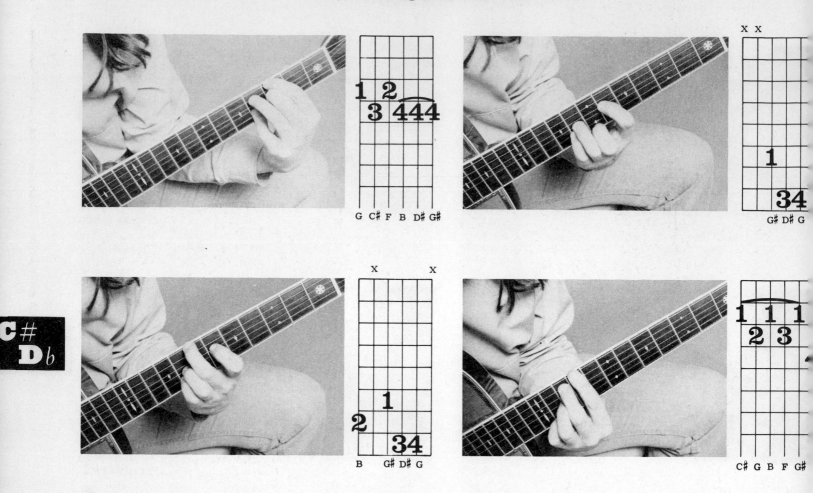

G C# F B D# G#

G# D# G

B G# D# G

C# G B F G#

C#/Db Thirteenth

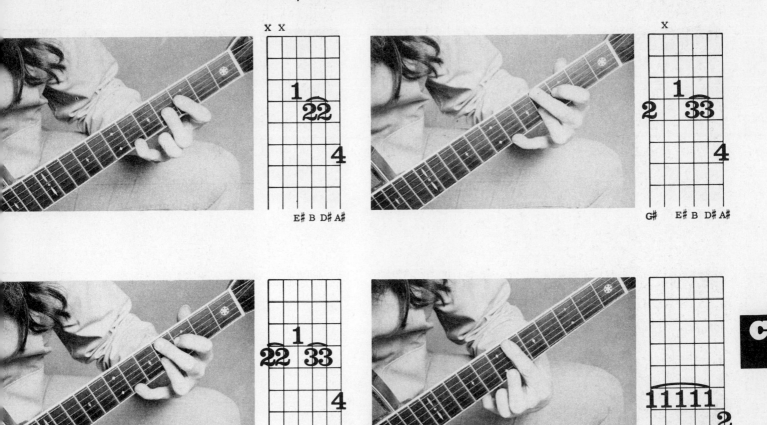

C#/Db Thirteenth Flat Nine

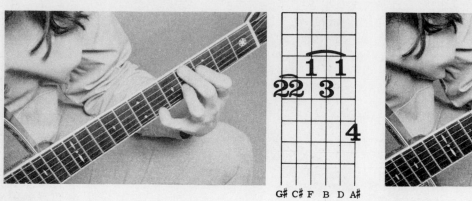

C#/Db Seven Six

x   x

| 1 | | 2 |
| 34 |

B E# A# C#

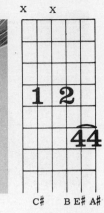

x   x

| 1 | 2 |
| 44 |

C#   B E# A#

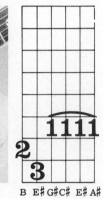

| 1111 |
| 2 | 3 |

B E# G#C# E# A#

59

C#/Db Nine Six

x   x

11

2   3

G# F A# D#

11

22 3

G# C# F A# I

111111

A# D# G# C# F A#

60

D Major

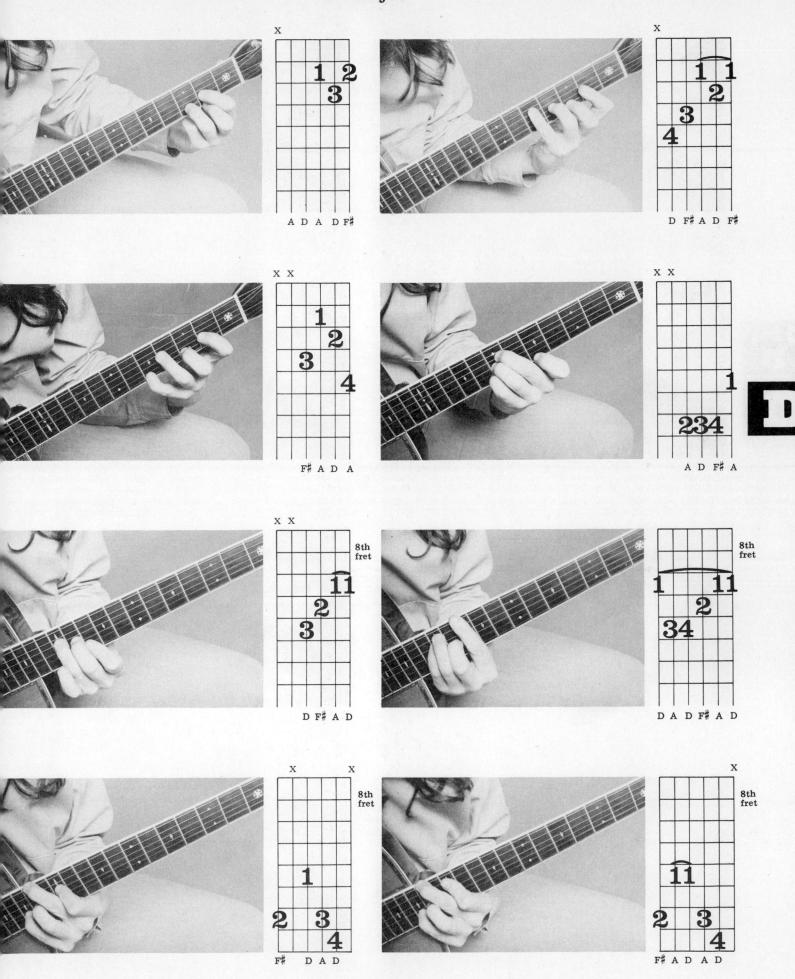

D Minor

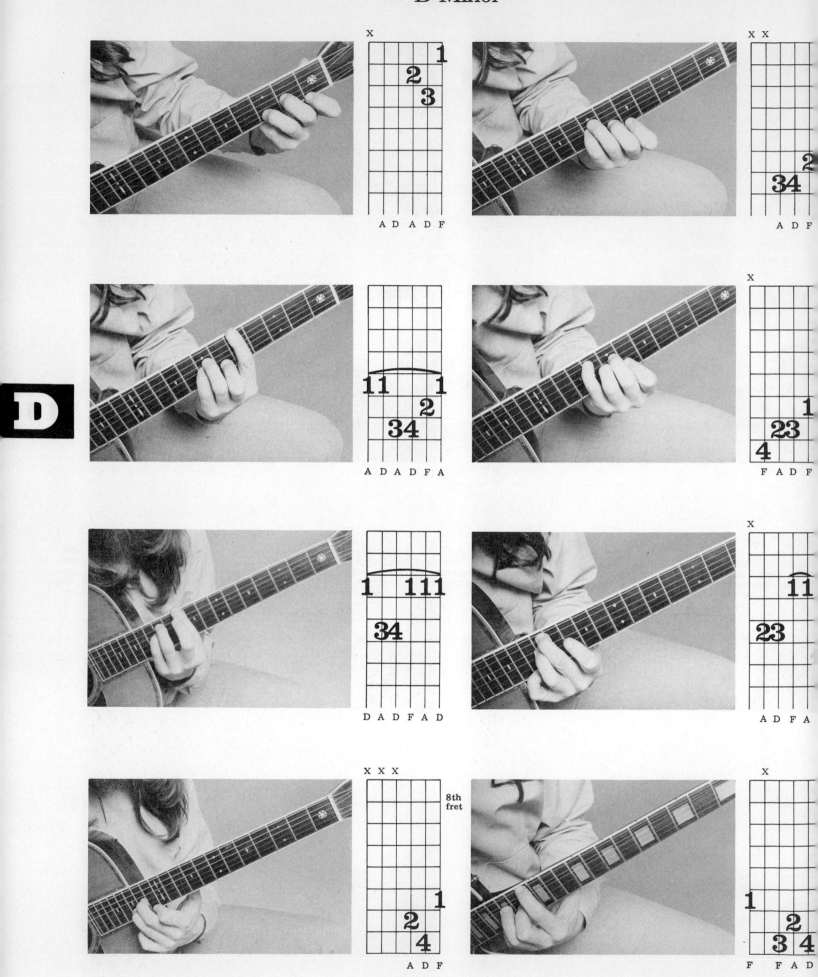

D Major Sixth

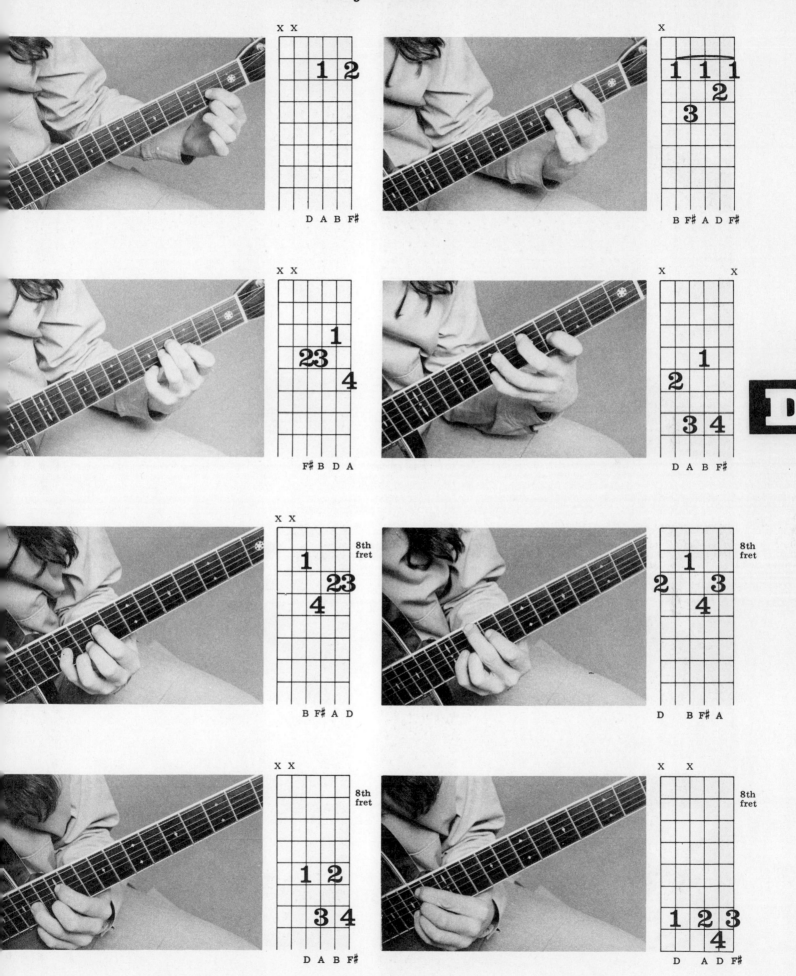

D Minor Sixth

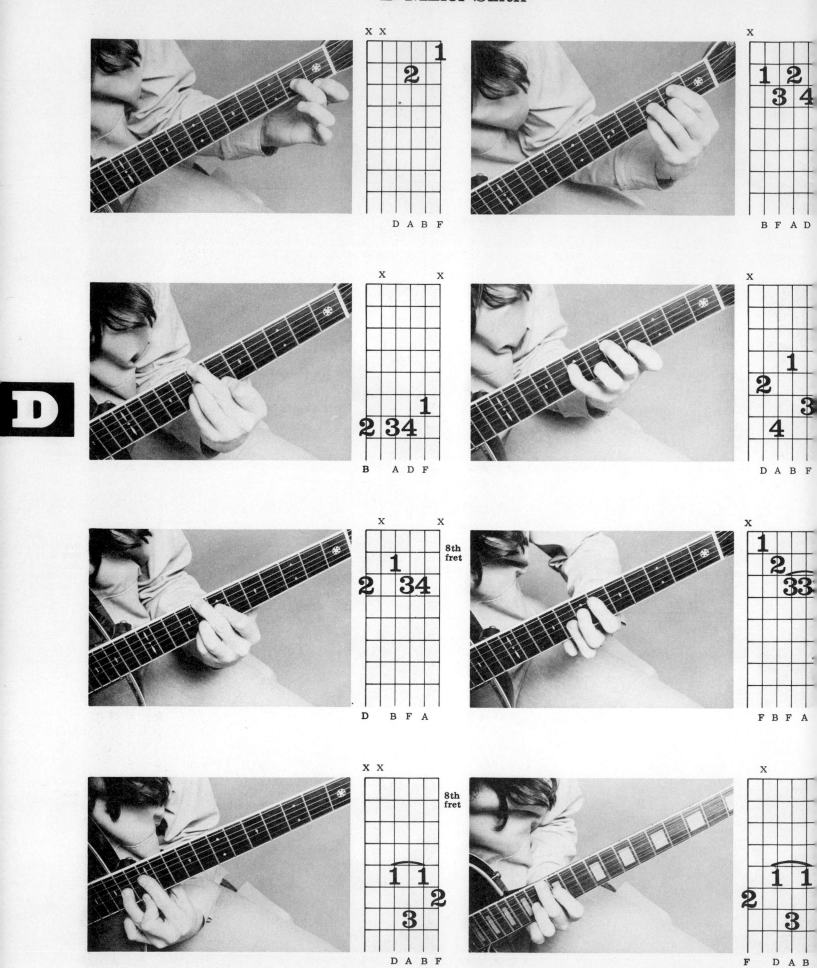

D Seventh

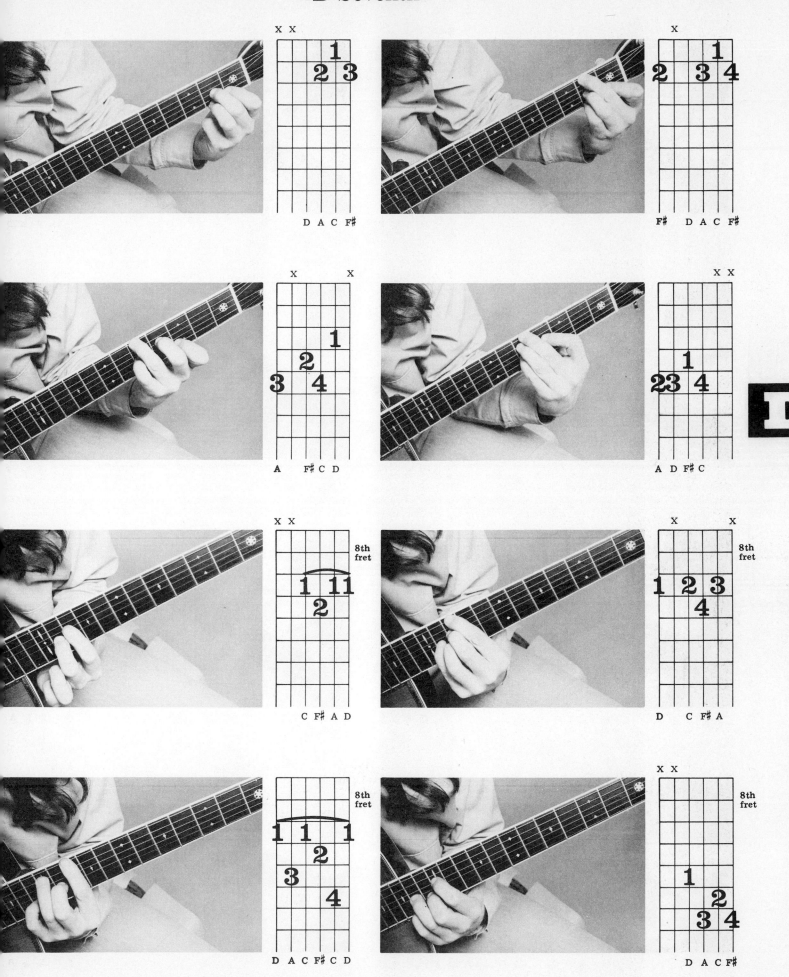

65

D Minor Seventh

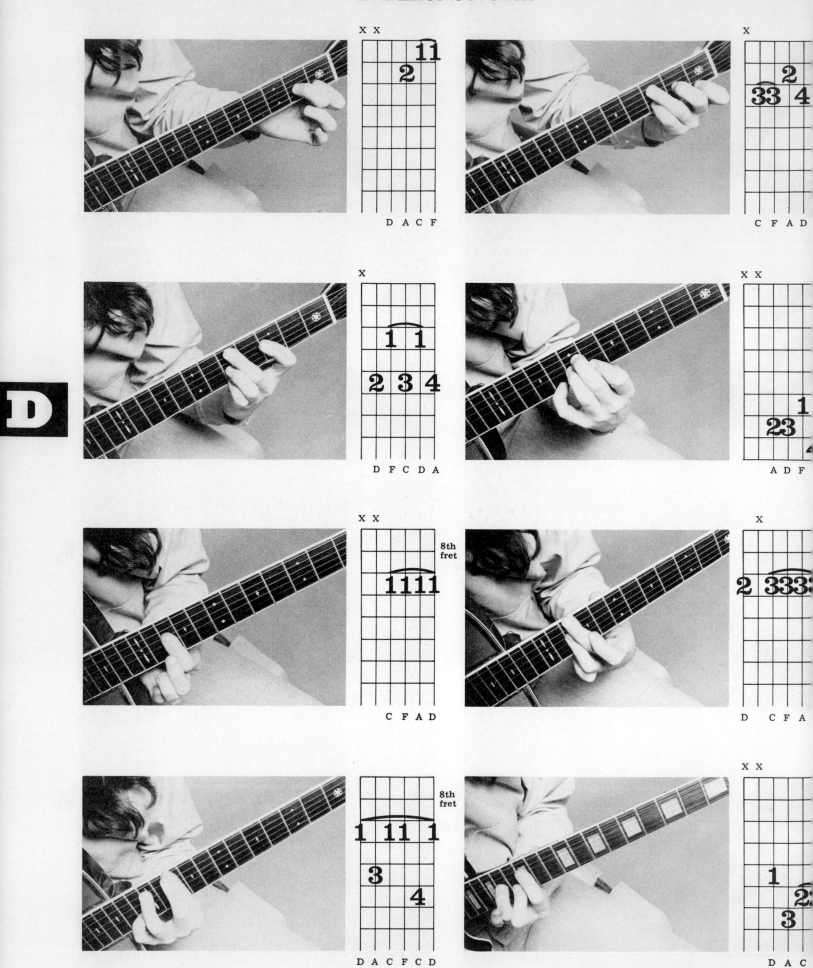

66

D Diminished

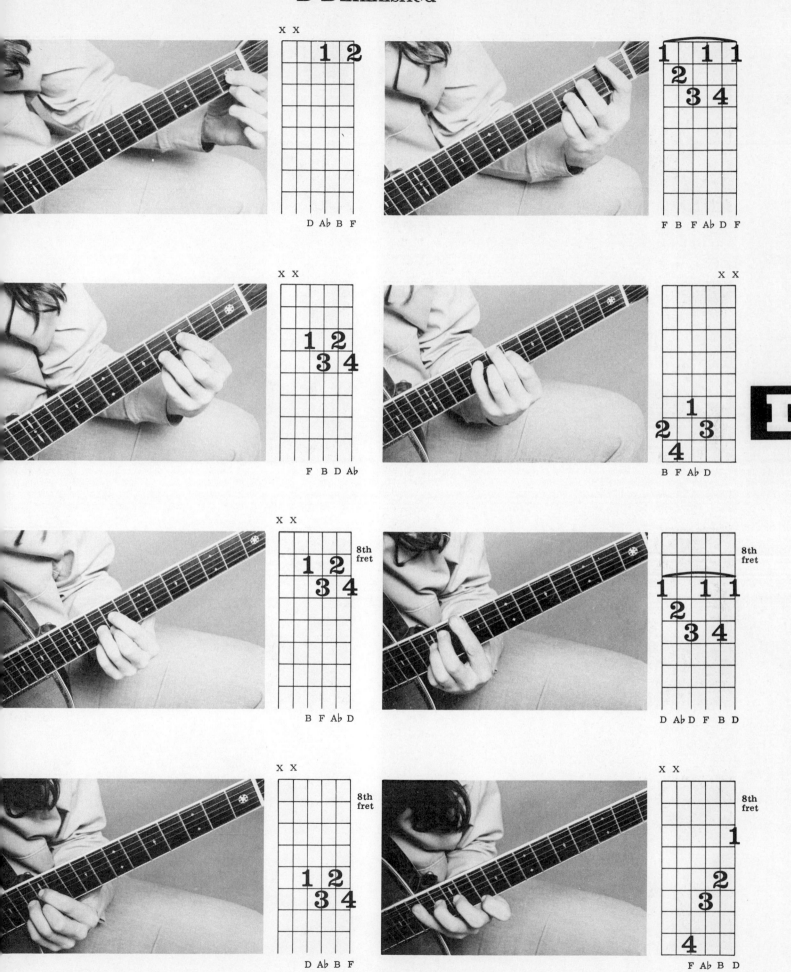

67

D Augmented

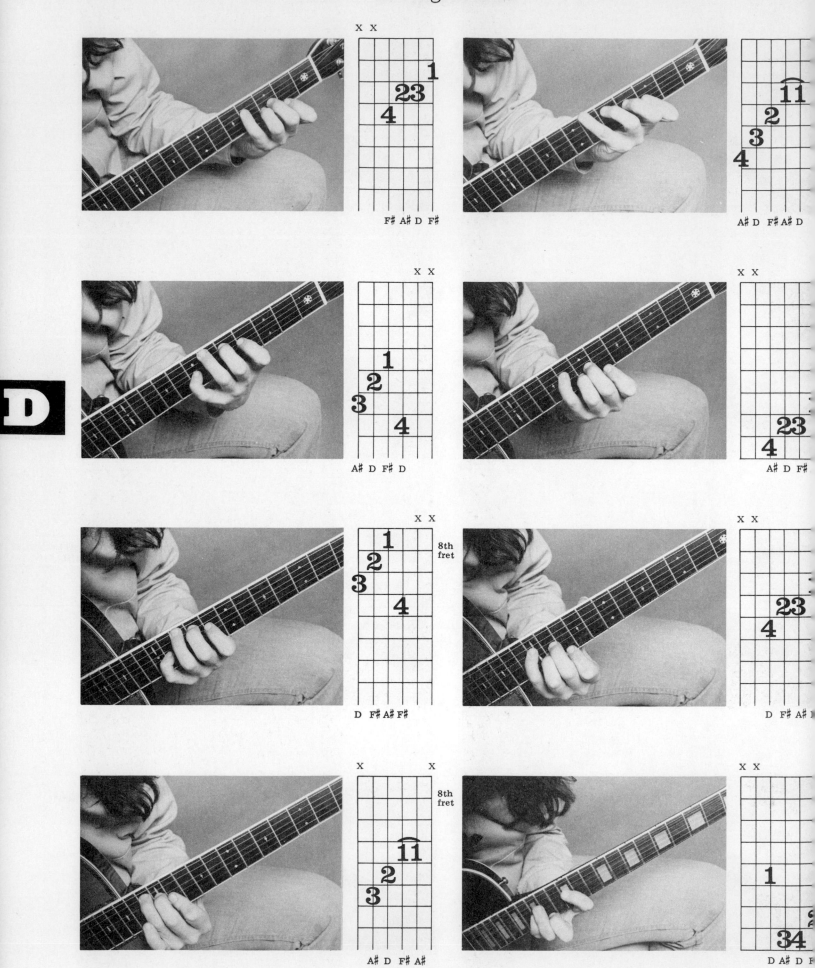

F# A# D F#

A# D F# A# D

A# D F# D

A# D F#

D F# A# F#

8th
fret

D F# A#

A# D F# A#

8th
fret

D A# D

68

D Seventh Augmented Fifth

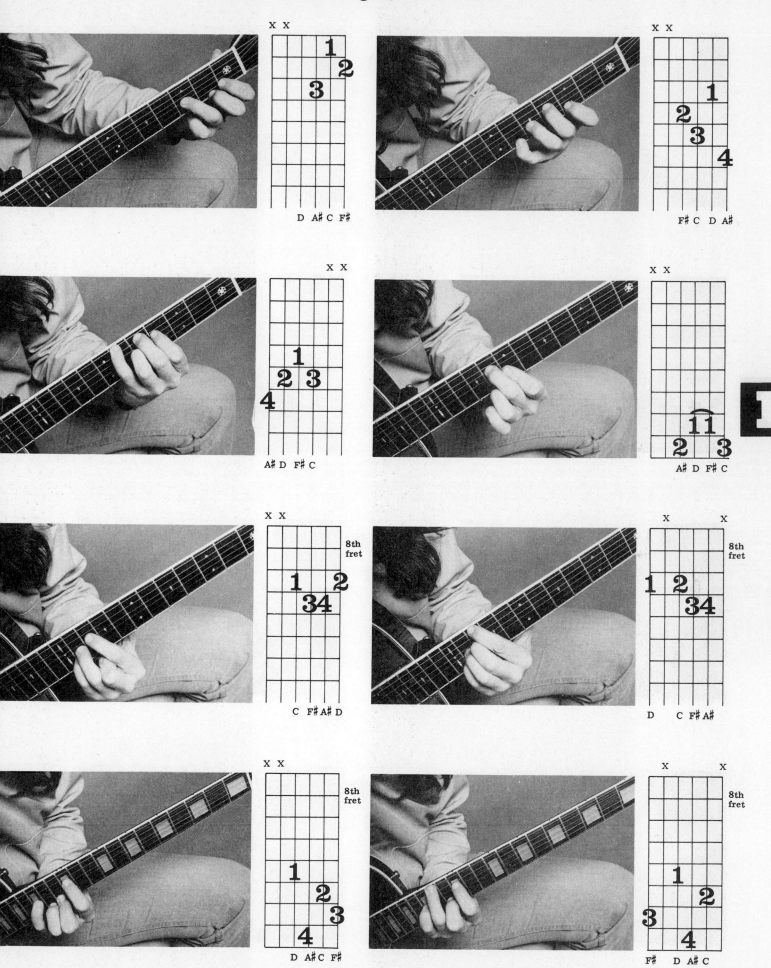

69

D Seventh Flat Five

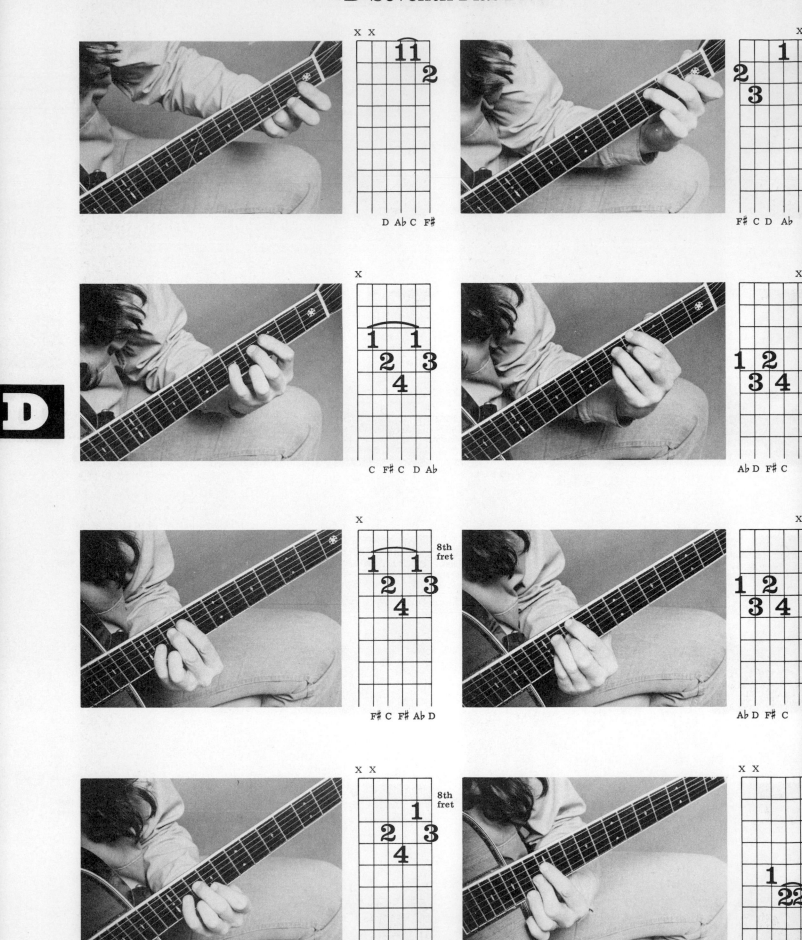

70

D Seventh Flat Nine

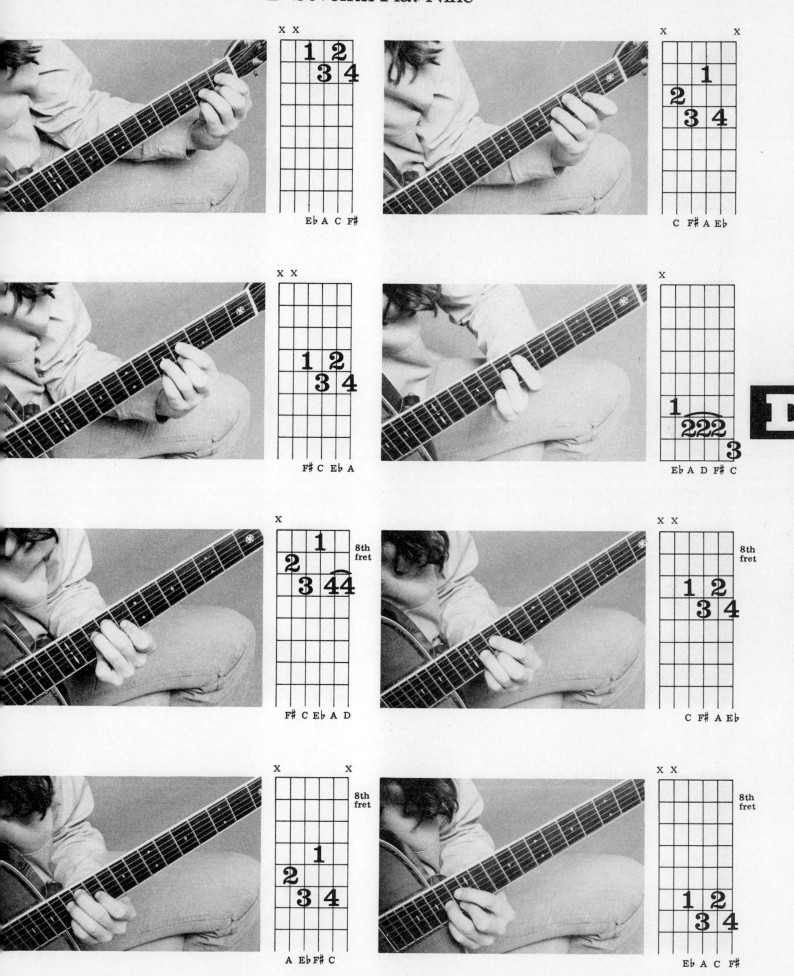

71

D Major Seventh

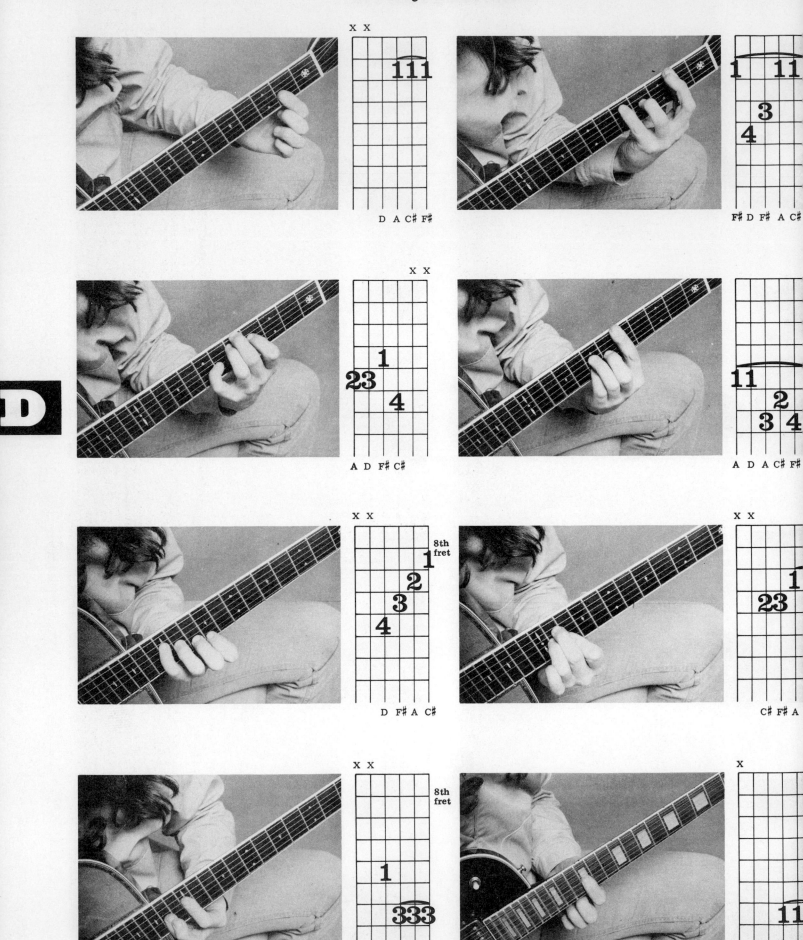

D Minor Seventh Flat Five

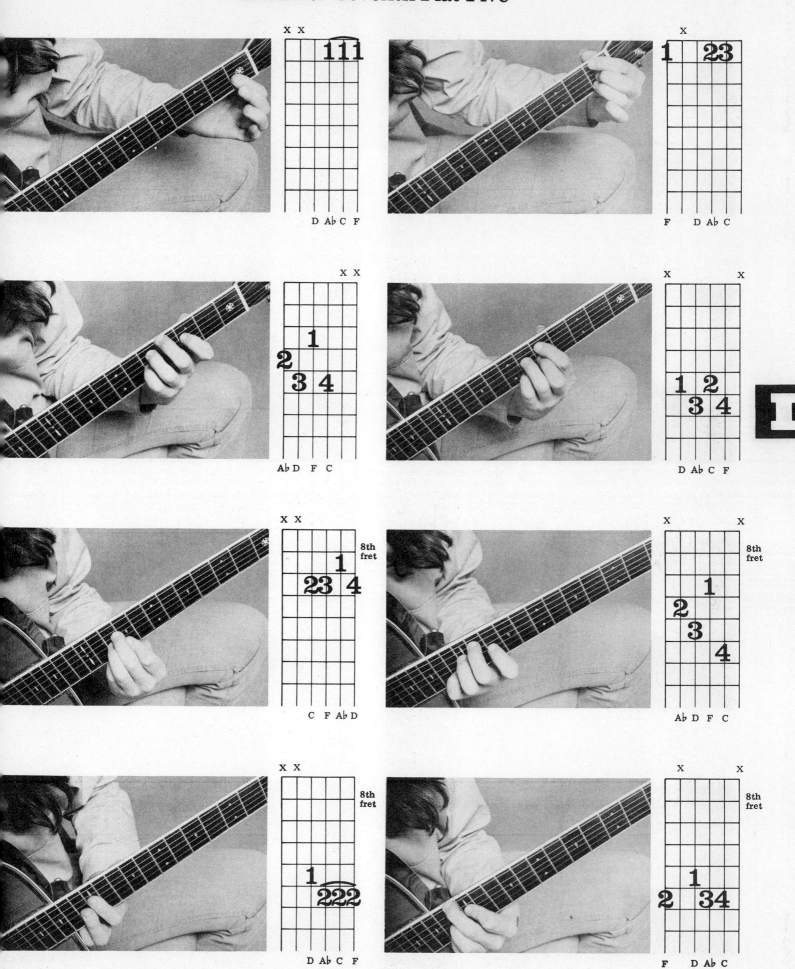

73

D Seventh Suspension Four

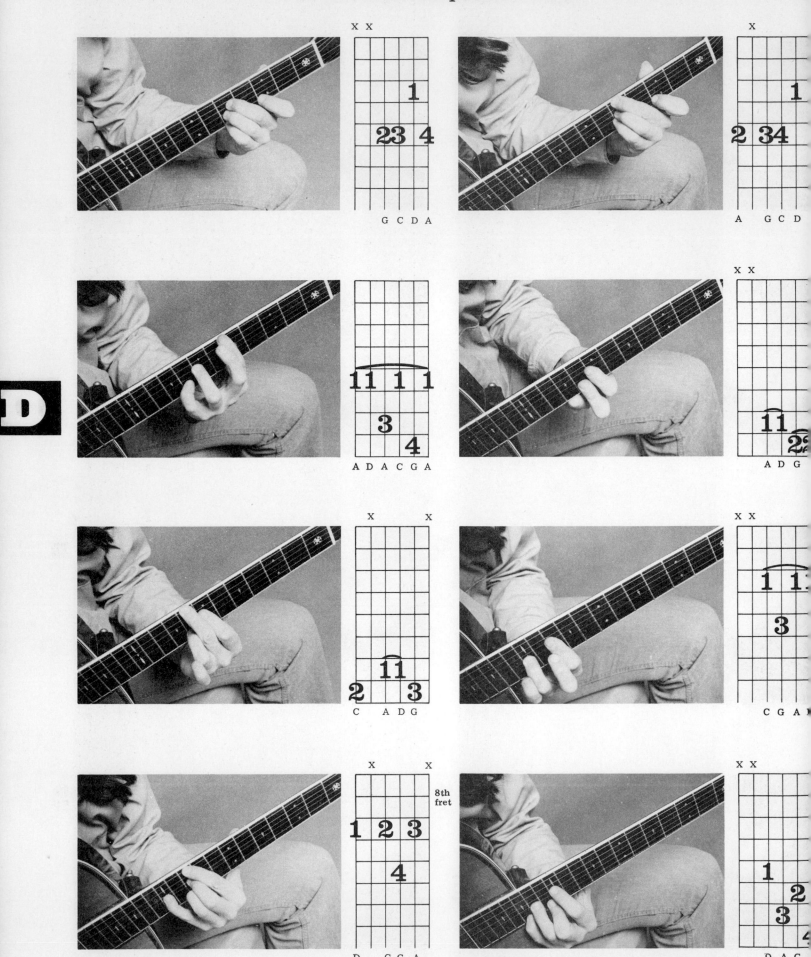

74

D Ninth

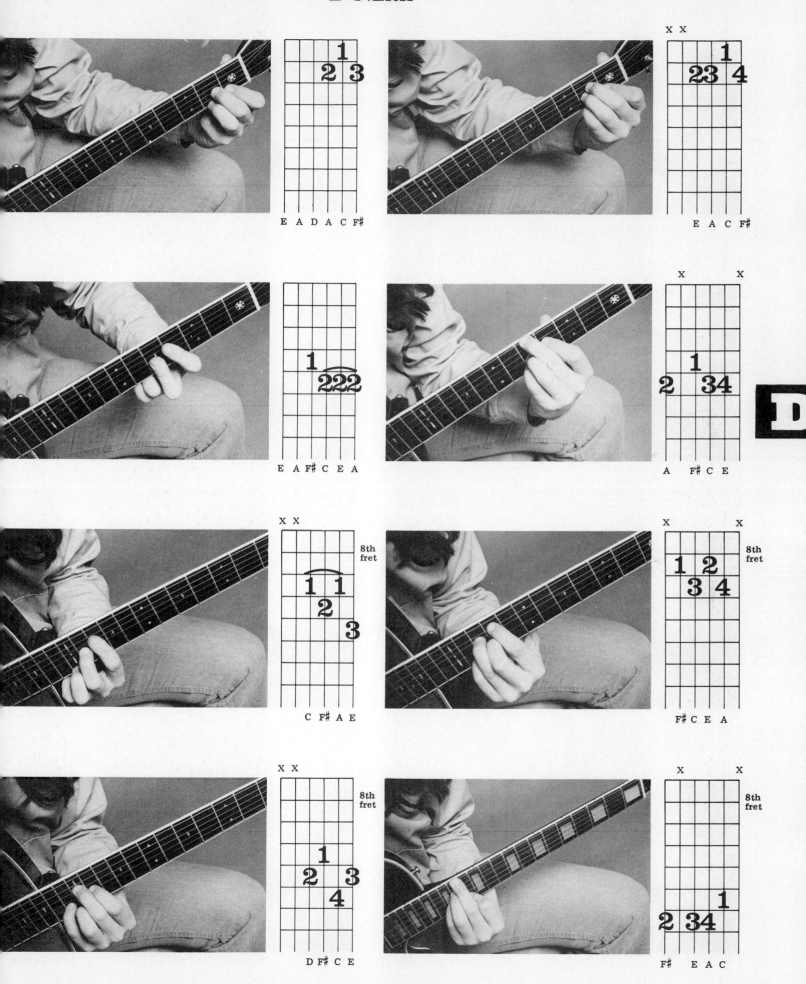

D Minor Ninth

D Ninth Augmented Fifth

D Ninth Flat Five

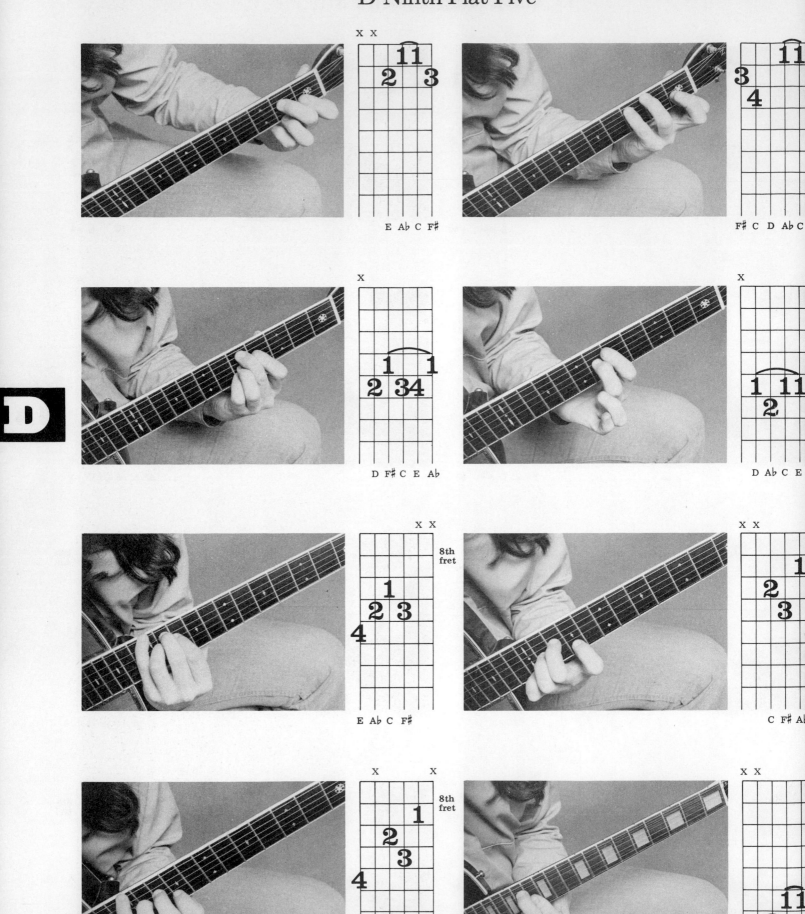

D Major Ninth

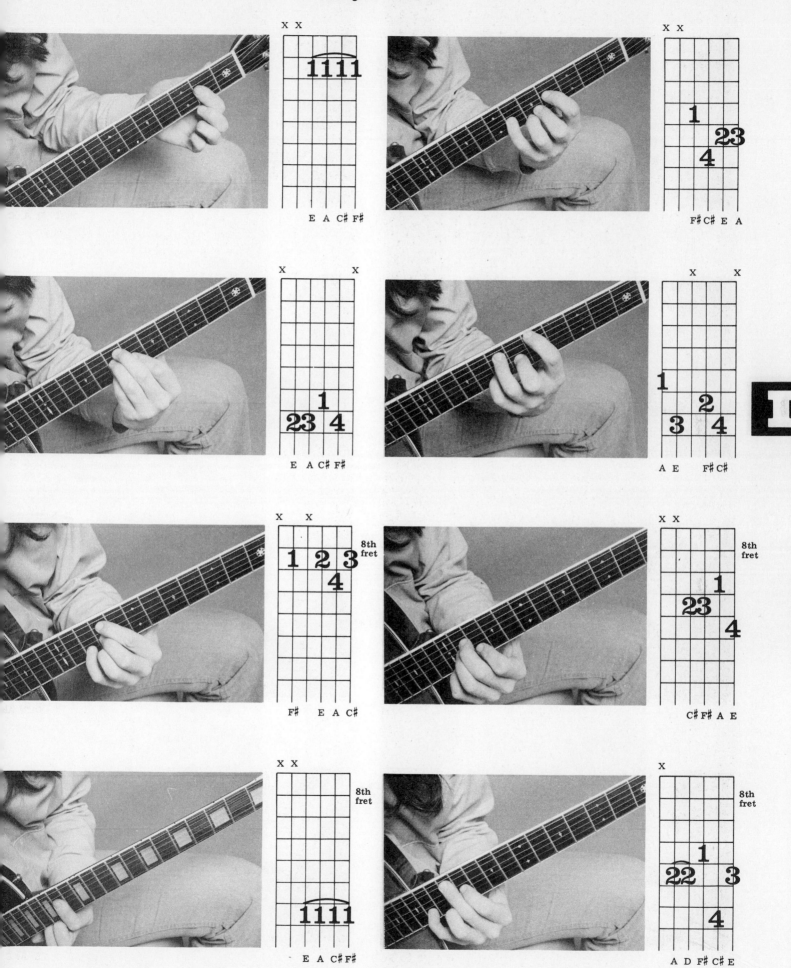

D Eleventh

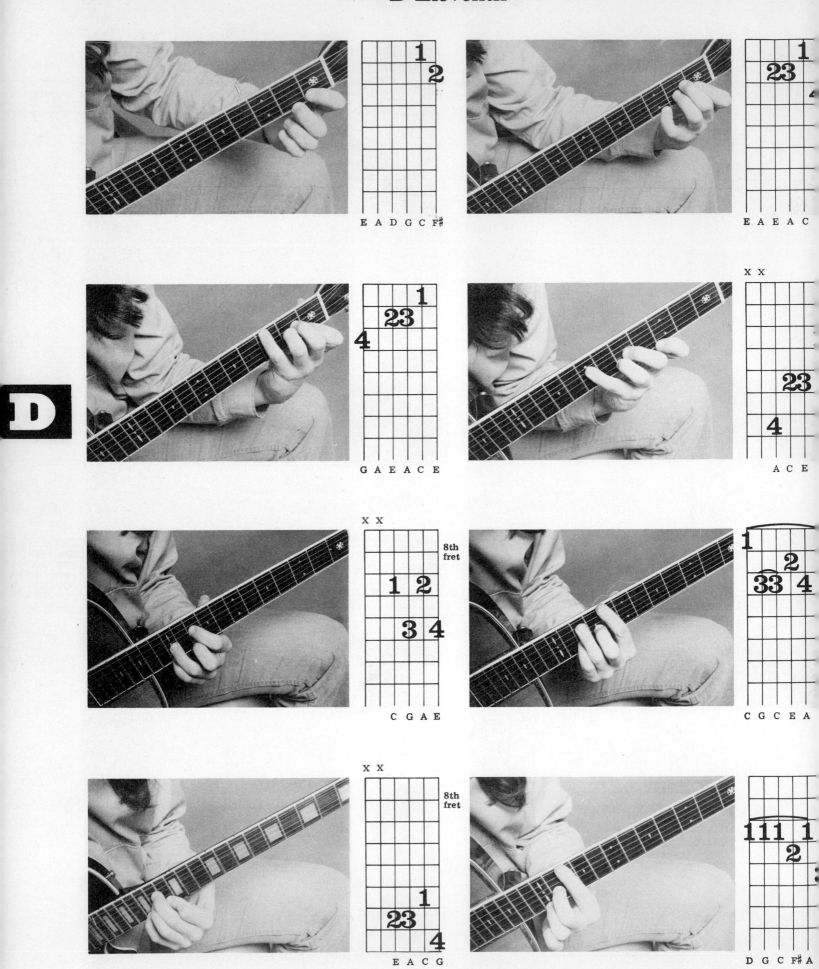

80

D Augmented Eleventh

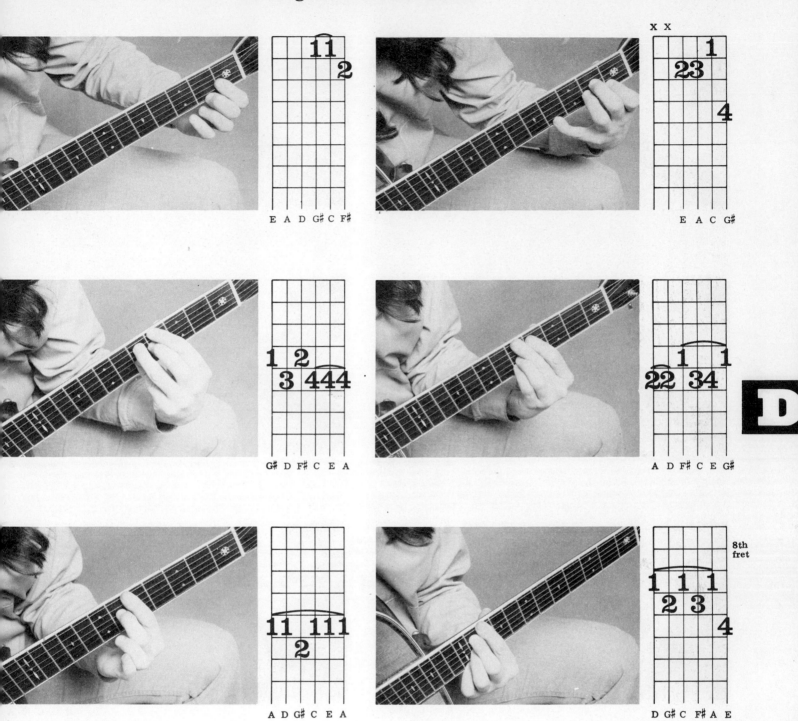

E A D G# C F#

E A C G#

G# D F# C E A

A D F# C E G#

A D G# C E A

D G# C F# A E

8th fret

D

81

D Thirteenth

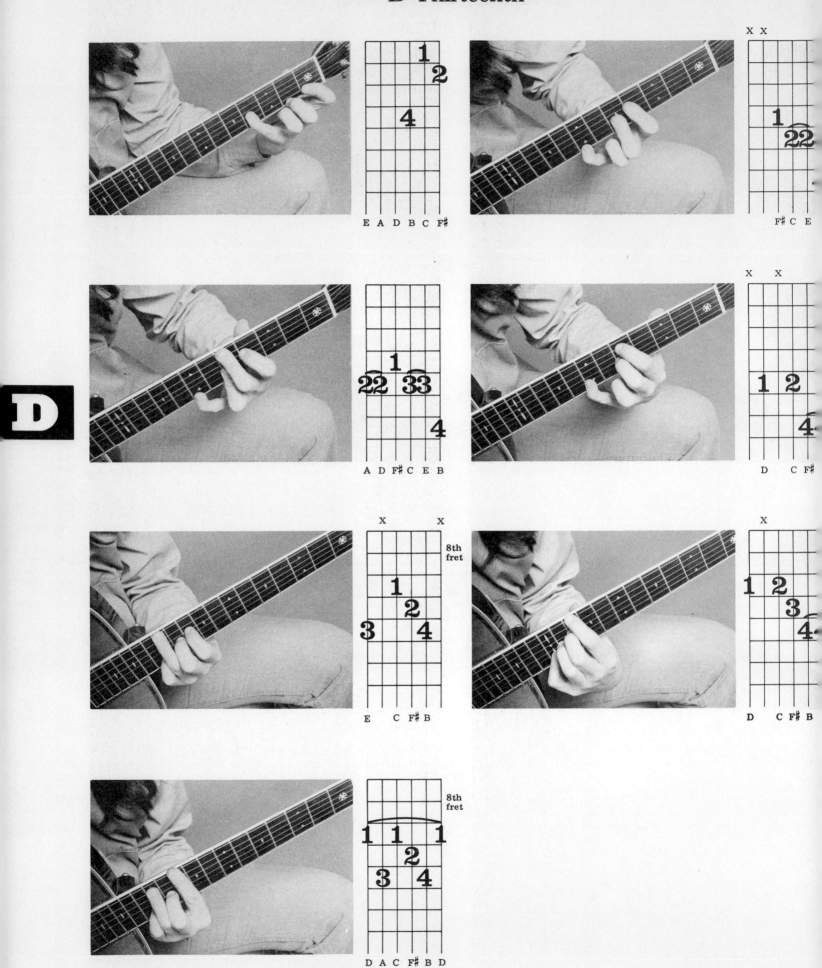

82

D Thirteenth Flat Nine

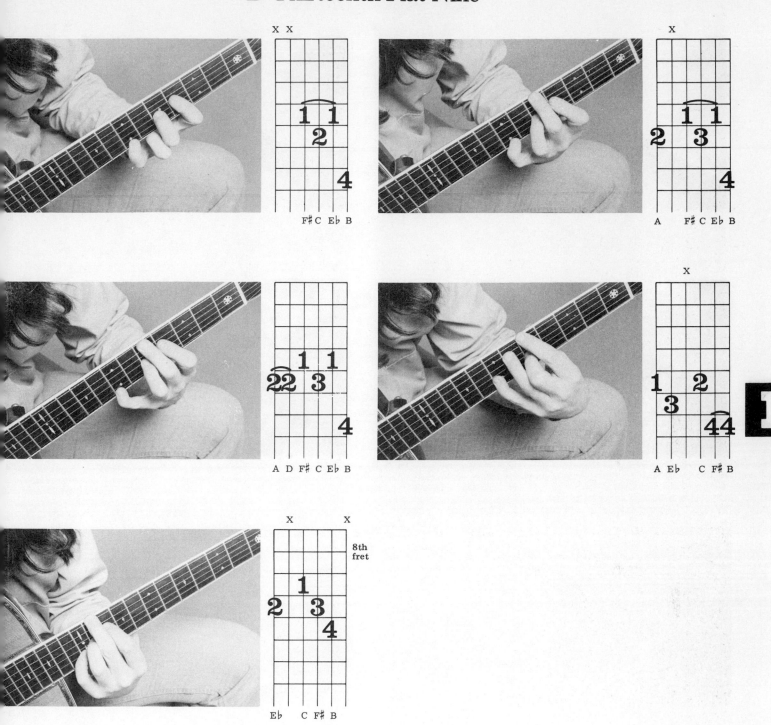

D Seven Six

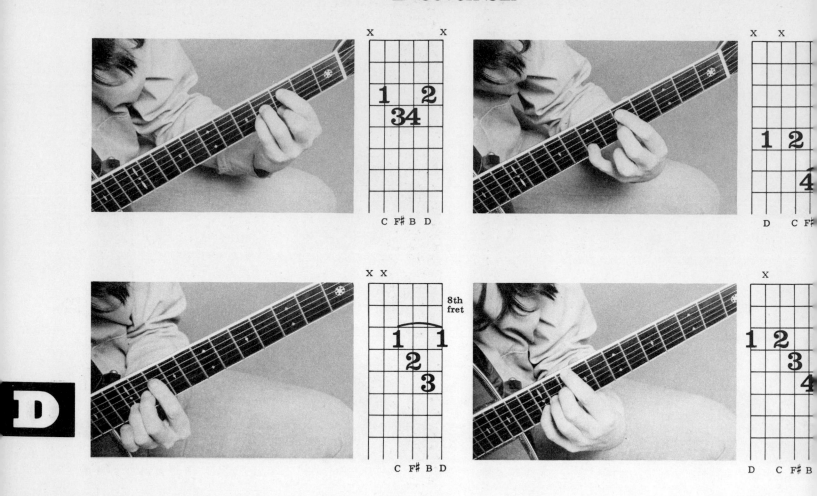

D Nine Six

D#/Eb Major

D#/Eb Minor

87

D#/Eb Major Sixth

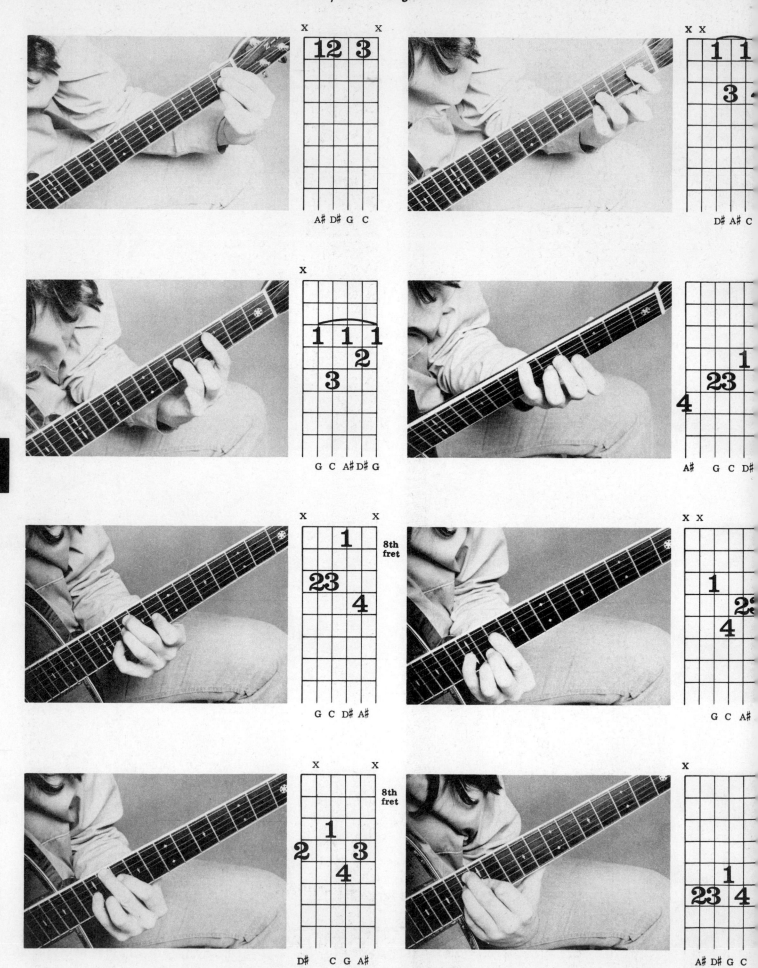

88

D#/E♭ Minor Sixth

D#/Eb Seventh

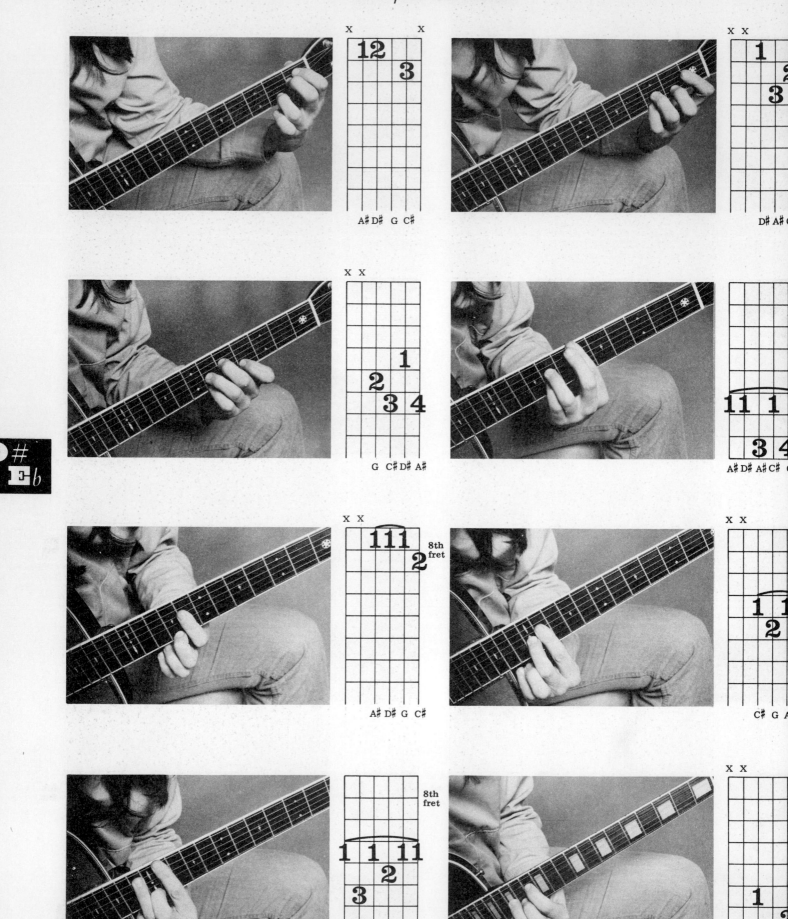

D#/E♭ Minor Seventh

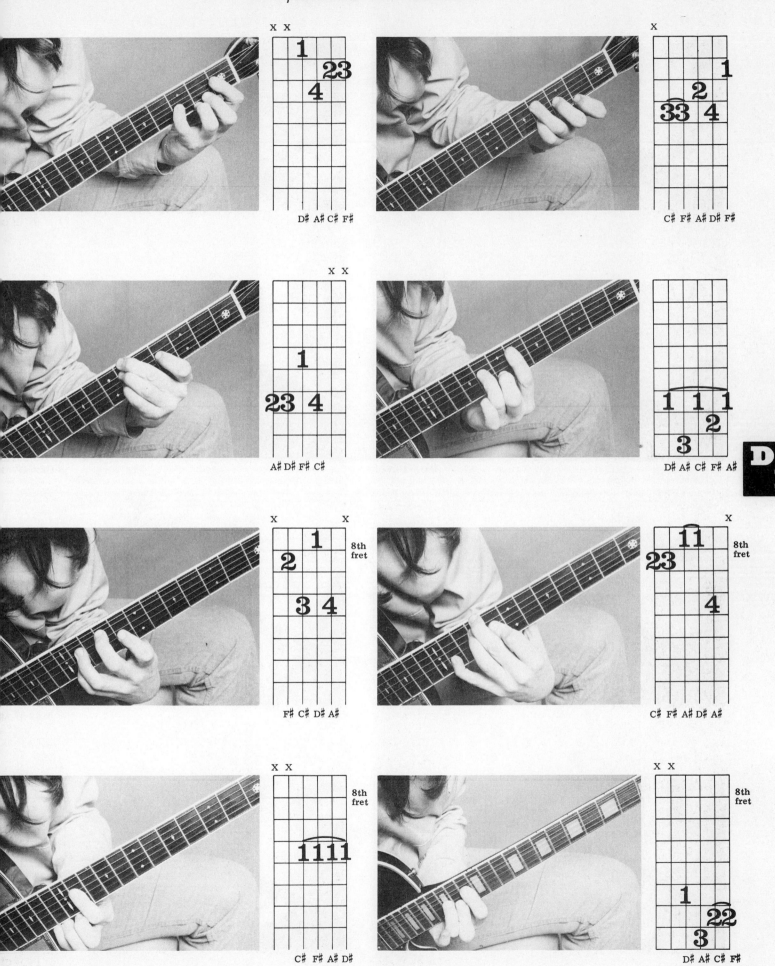

D# A# C# F#

C# F# A# D# F#

A# D# F# C#

D# A# C# F# A#

F# C# D# A#

C# F# A# D# A#

C# F# A# D#

D# A# C# F#

91

D#/E♭ Diminished

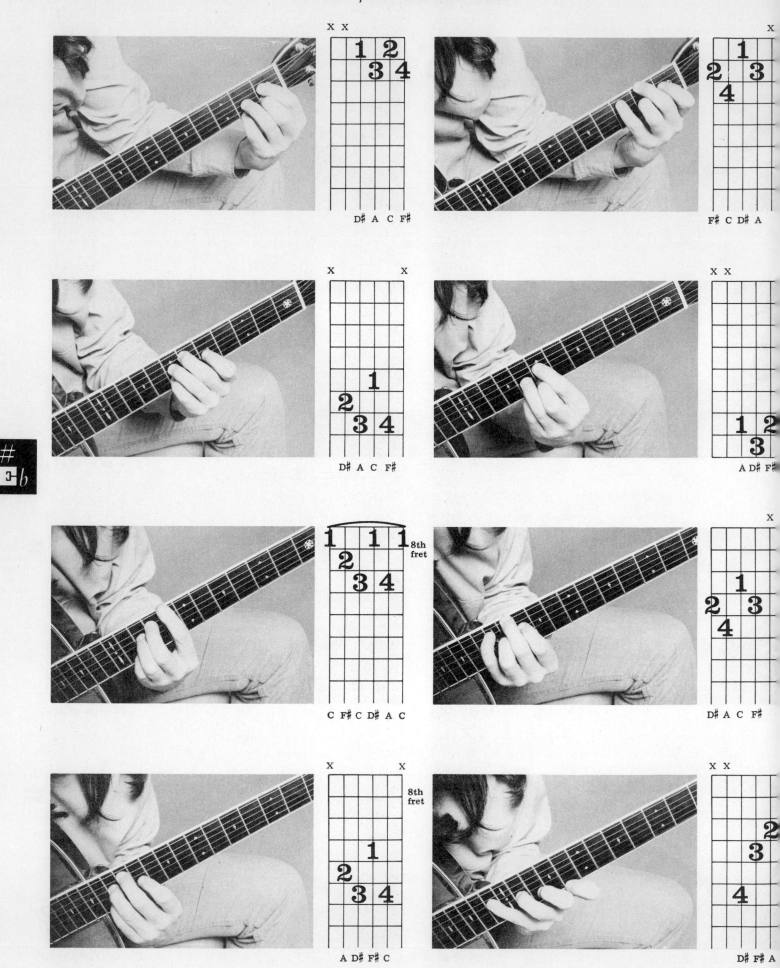

D#/E♭ Augmented

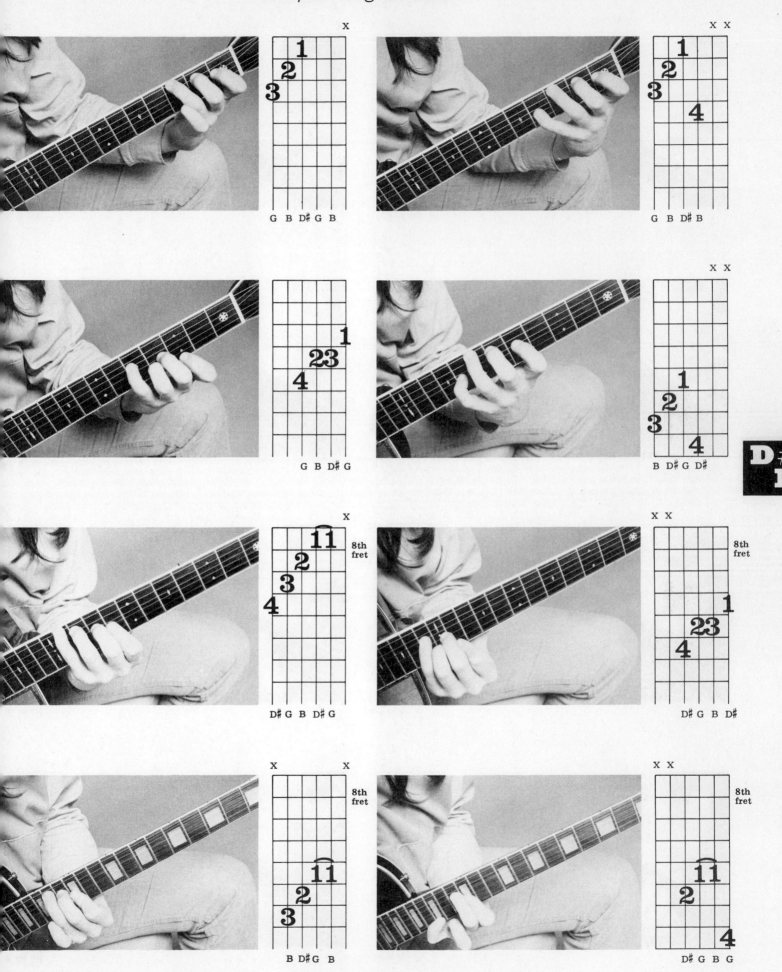

93

D#/Eb Seventh Augmented Fifth

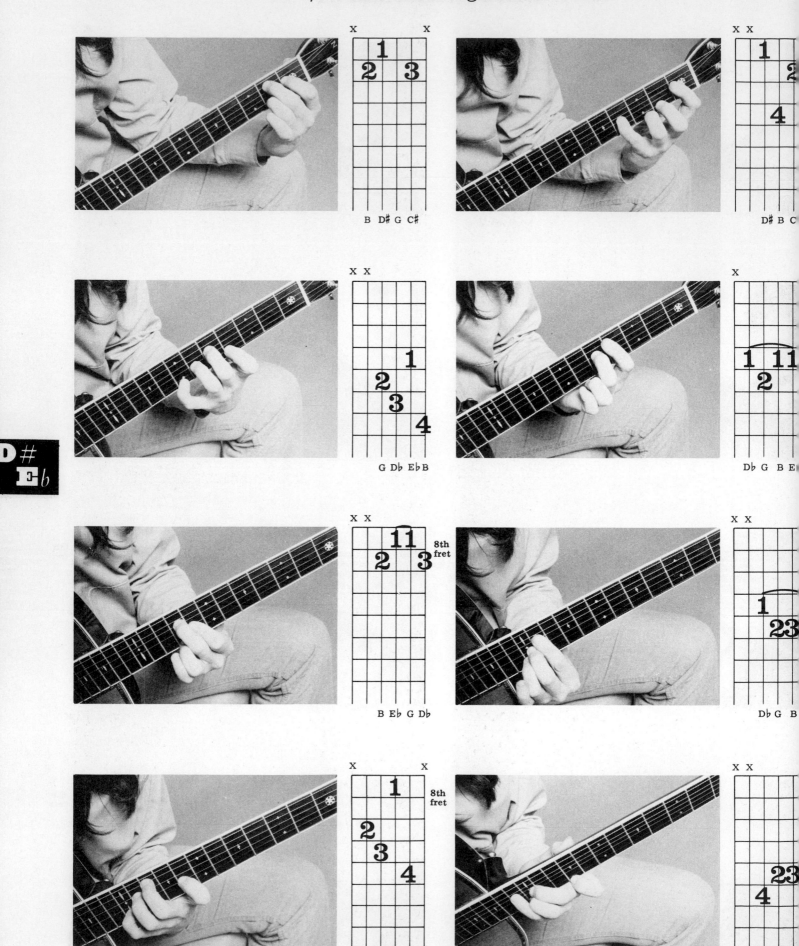

94

D#/Eb Seventh Flat Five

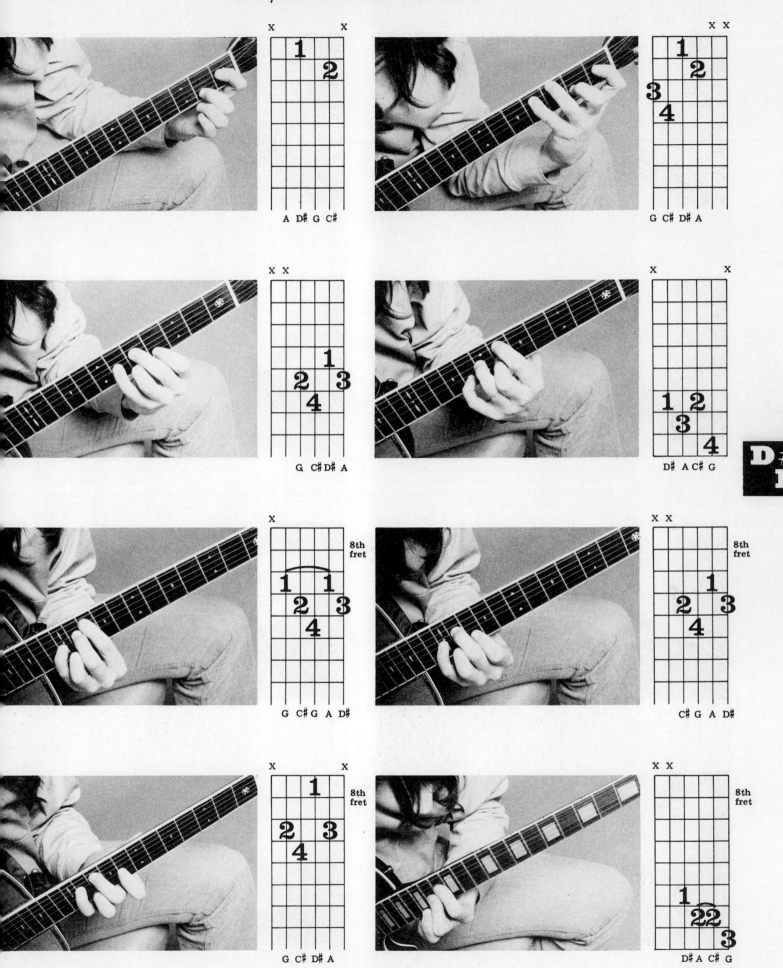

95

D#/Eb Seventh Flat Nine

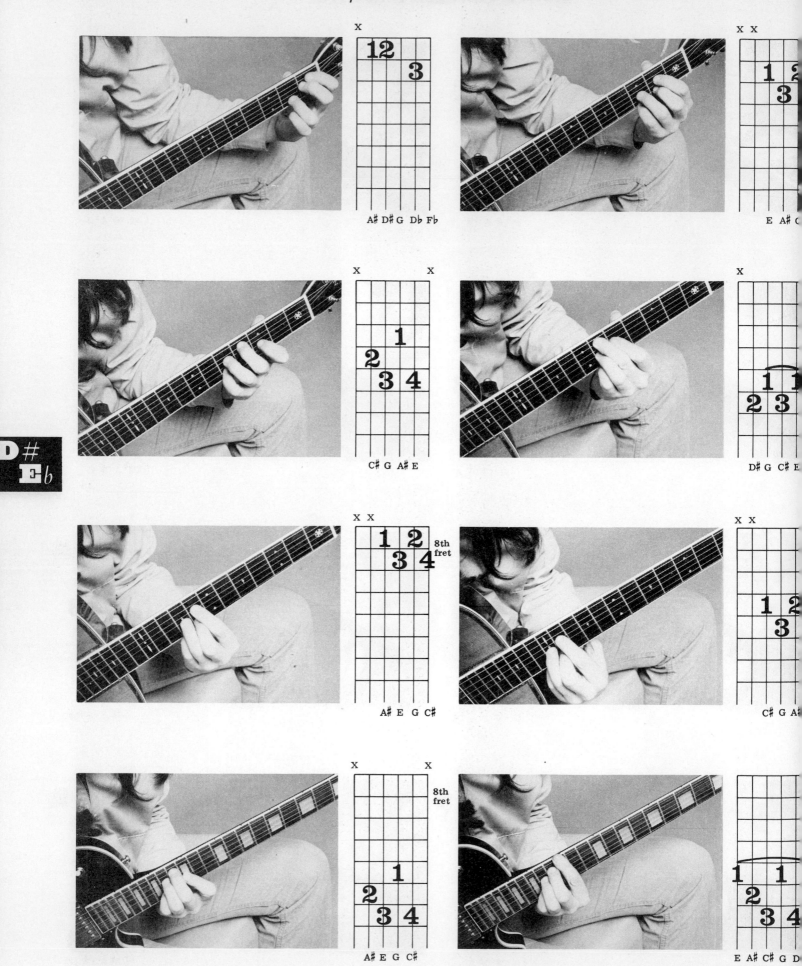

D#/E♭ Major Seventh

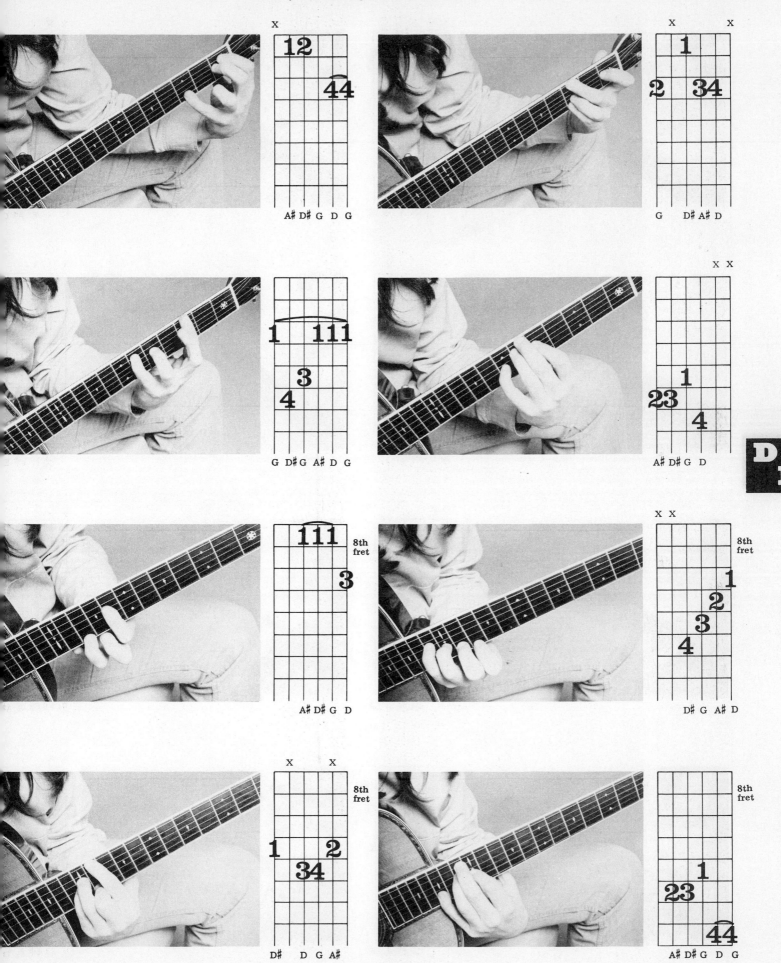

97

D#/Eb Minor Seventh Flat Five

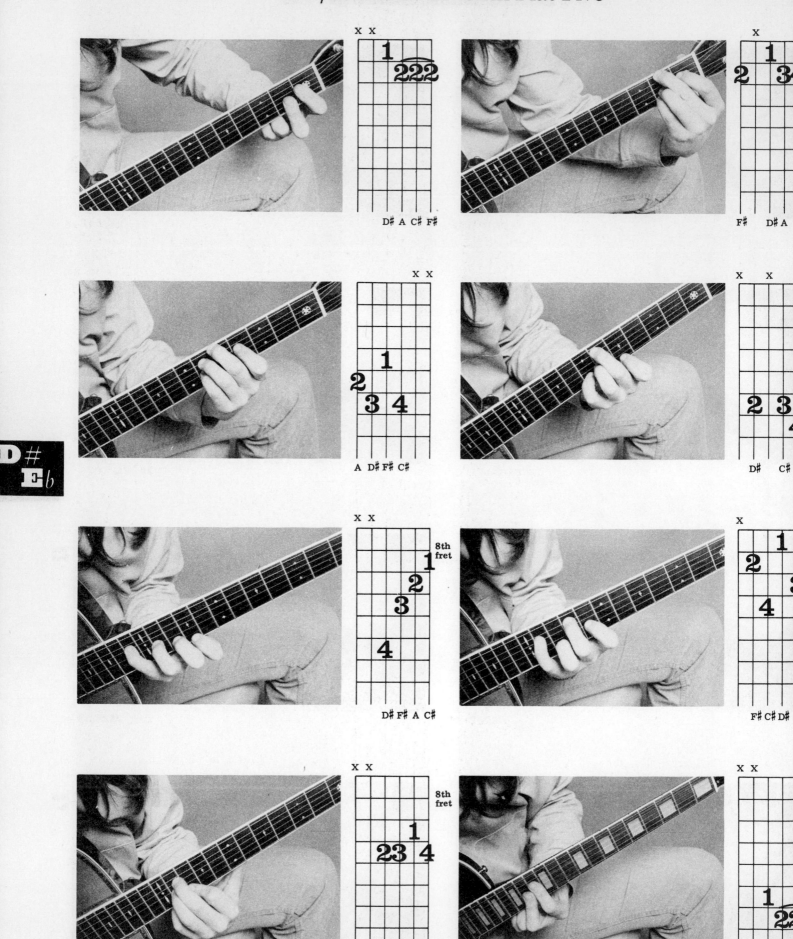

98

D#/Eb Seventh Suspension Four

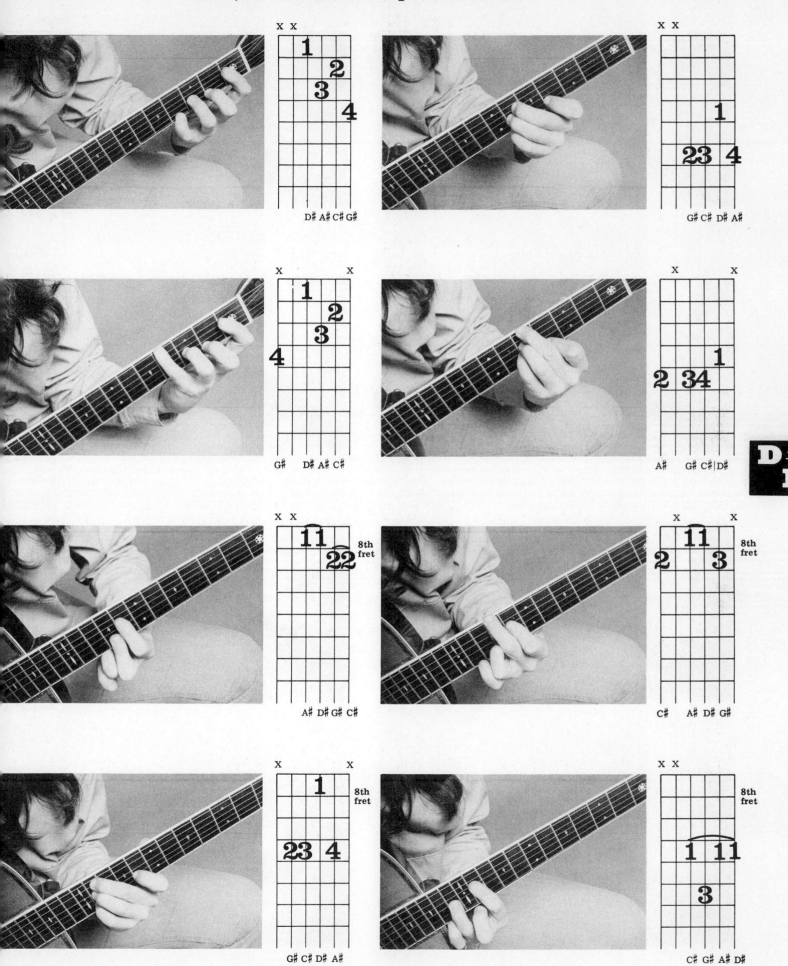

99

D#/Eb Ninth

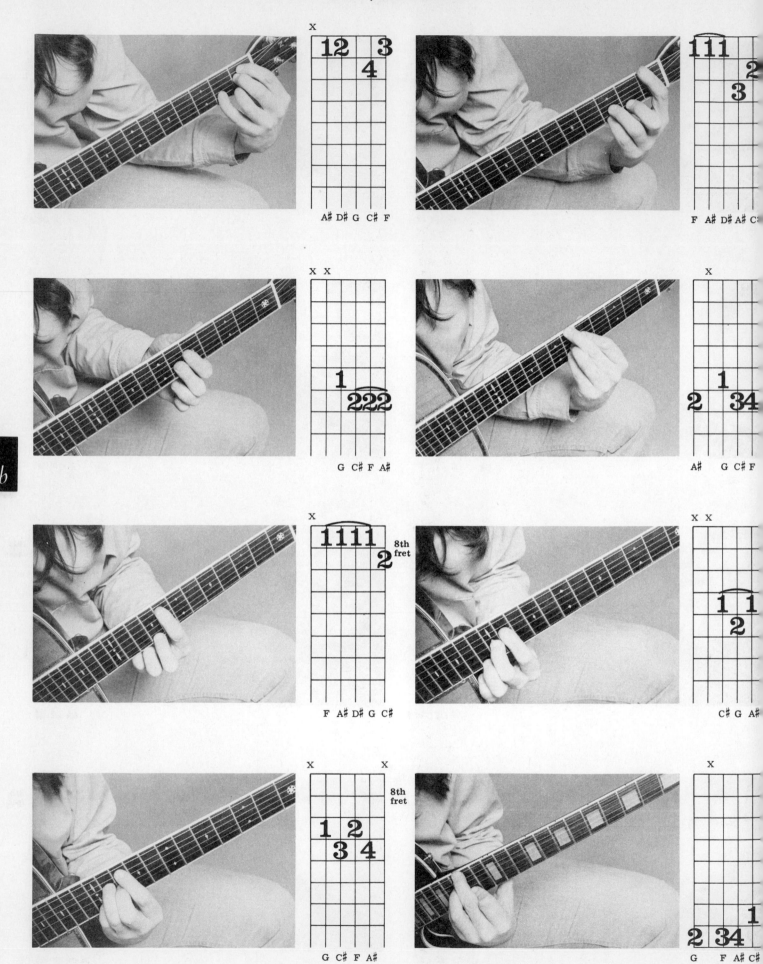

100

D#/Eb Minor Ninth

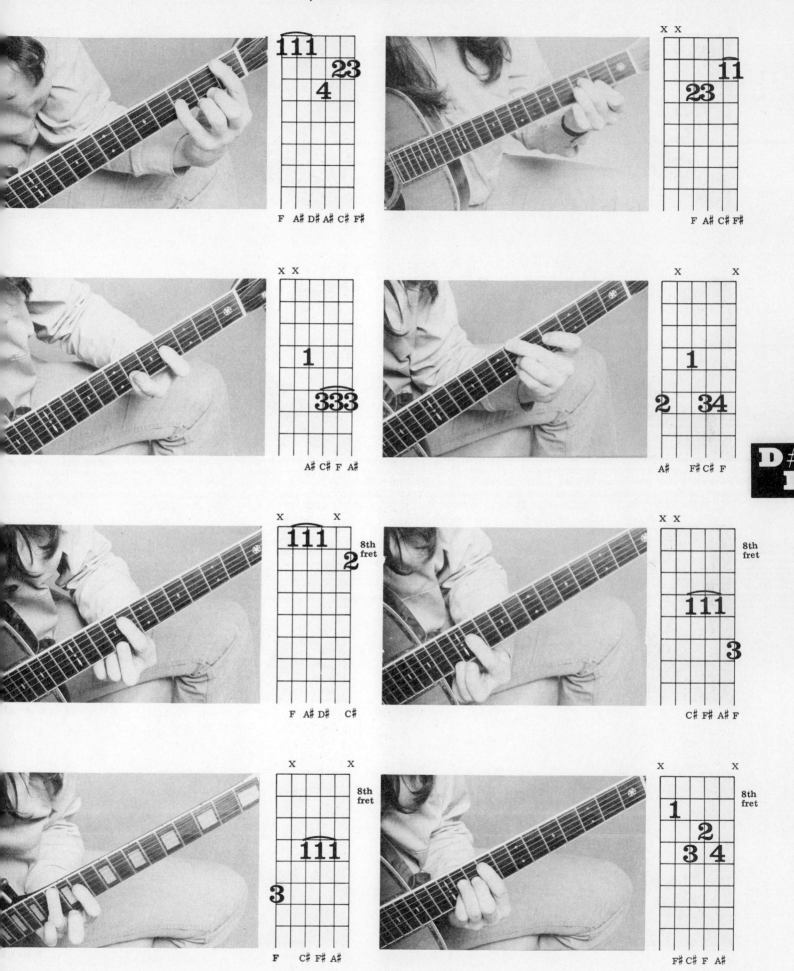

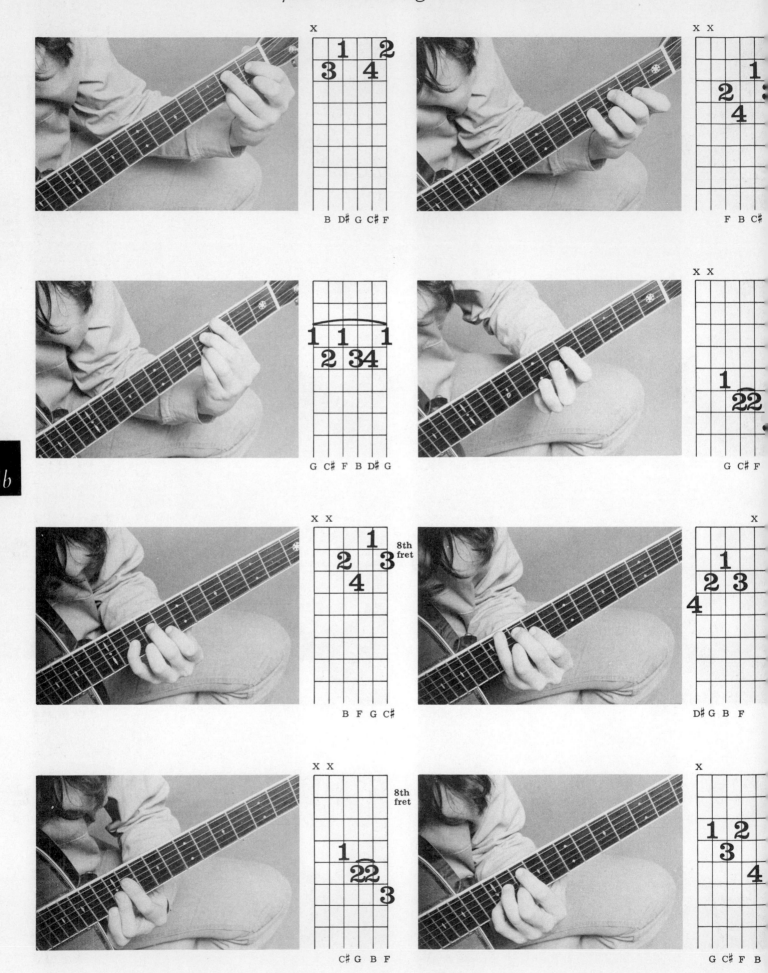

D#/E♭ Ninth Flat Five

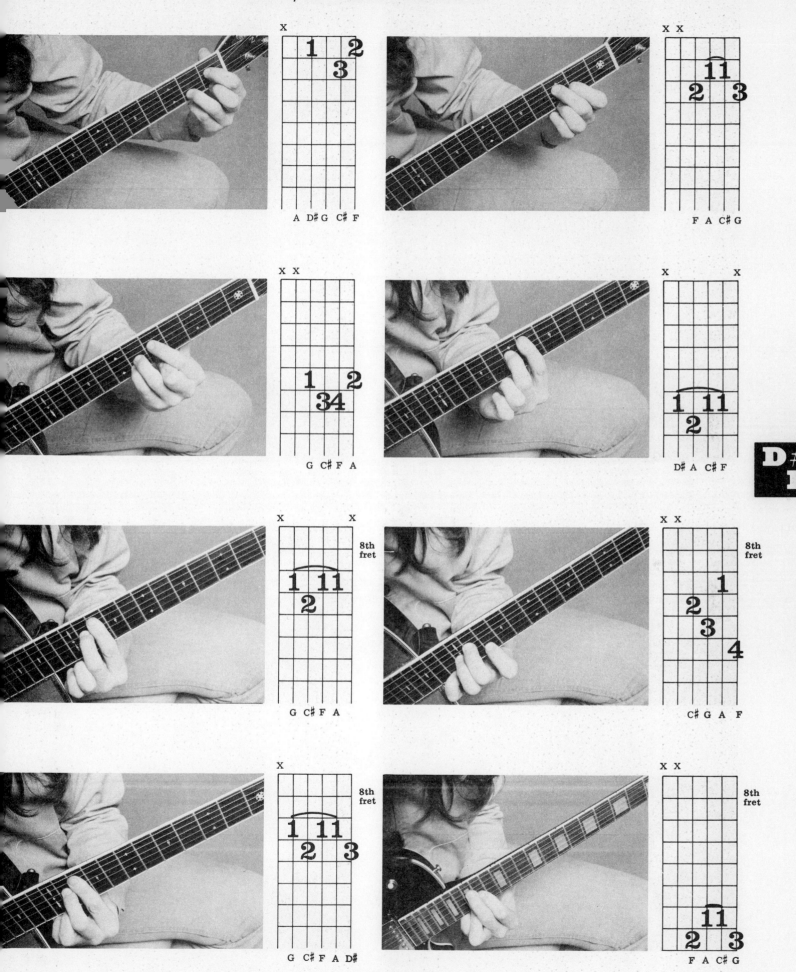

103

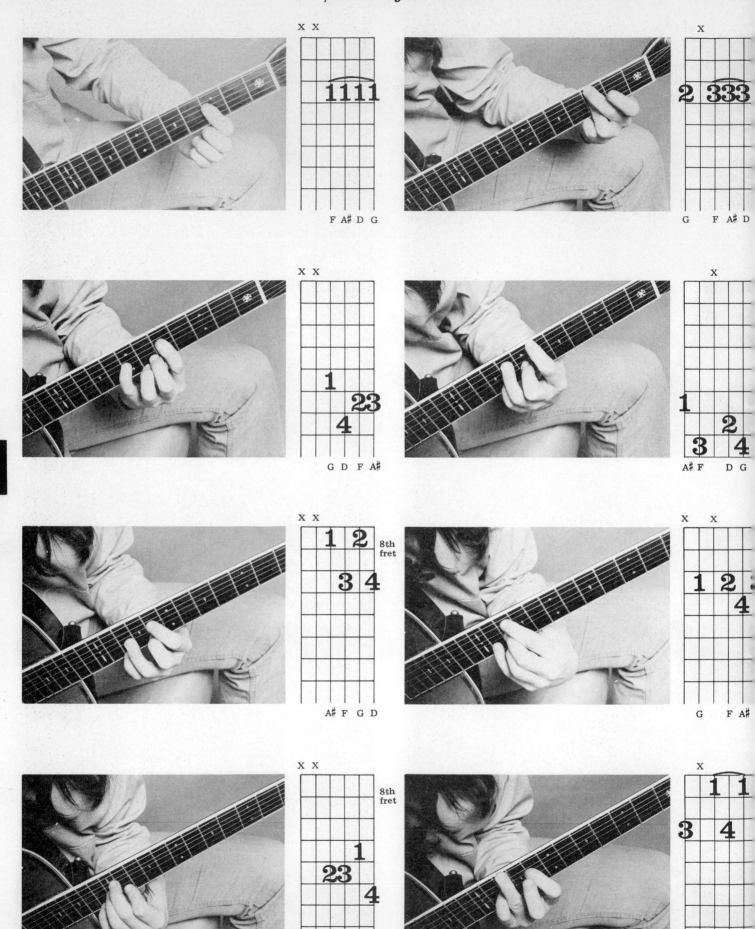

D#/Eb Eleventh

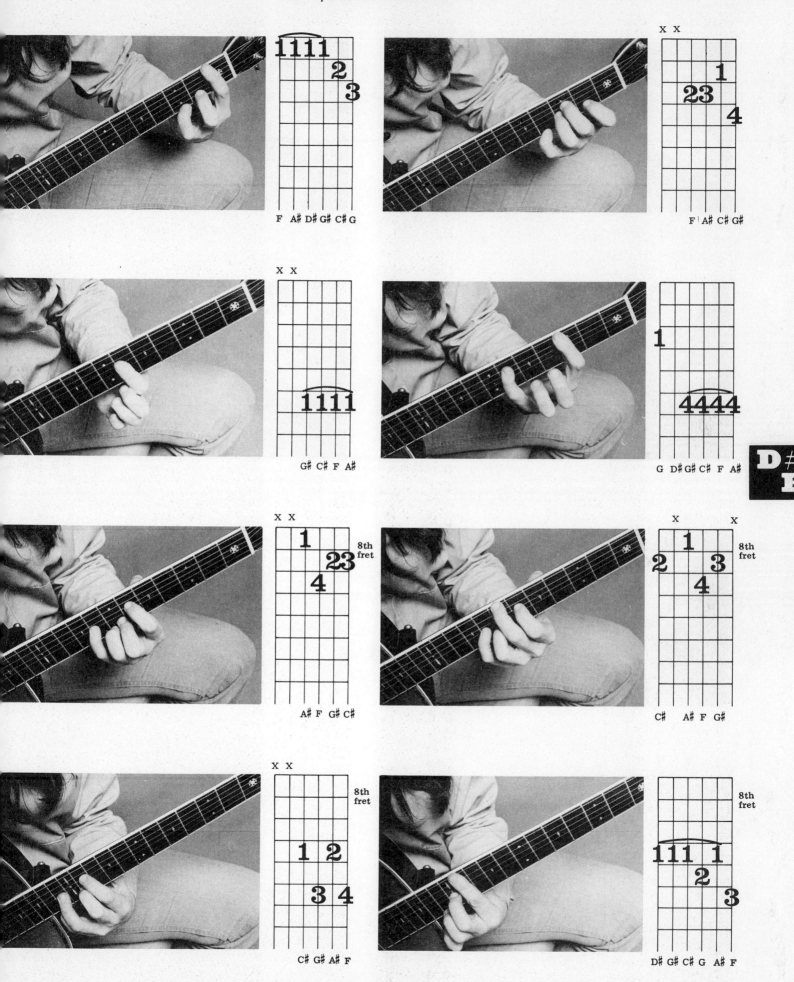

105

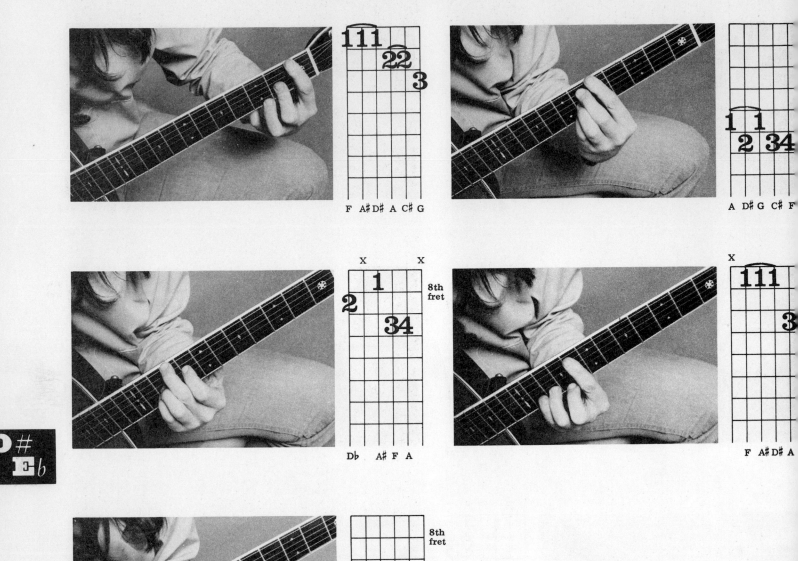

F A# D# A C# G

A D# G C# F

X X

8th
fret

Db A# F A

X

F A# D# A

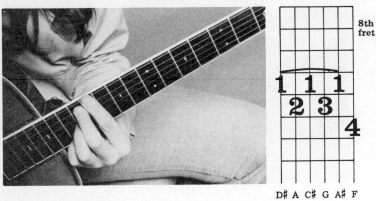

8th
fret

D# A C# G A# F

D#/E♭ Thirteenth

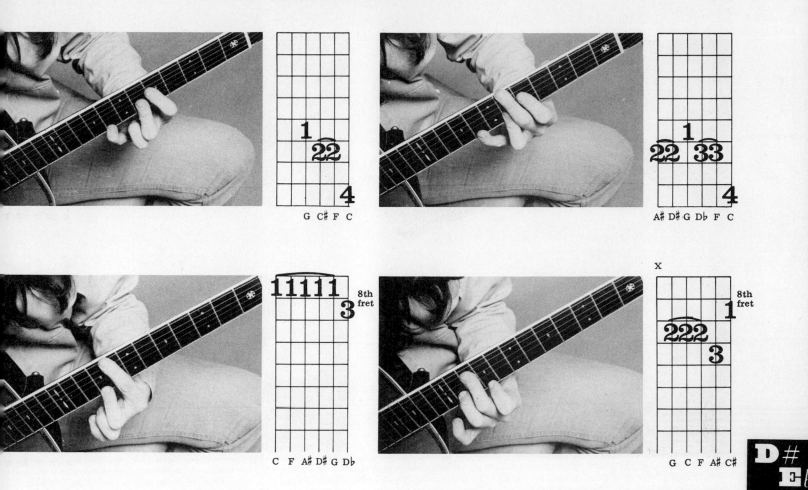

G C# F C

A# D# G D♭ F C

C F A# D# G D♭ — 8th fret

X — 8th fret

G C F A# C#

D#/E♭

107

D#/Eb Thirteenth Flat Nine

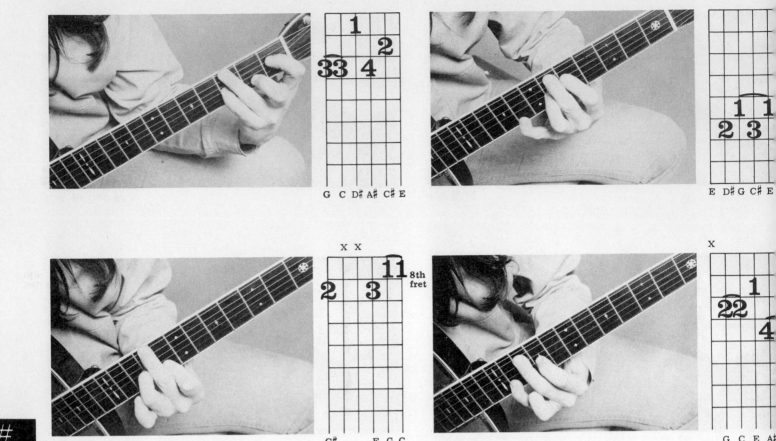

D#/Eb Seven Six

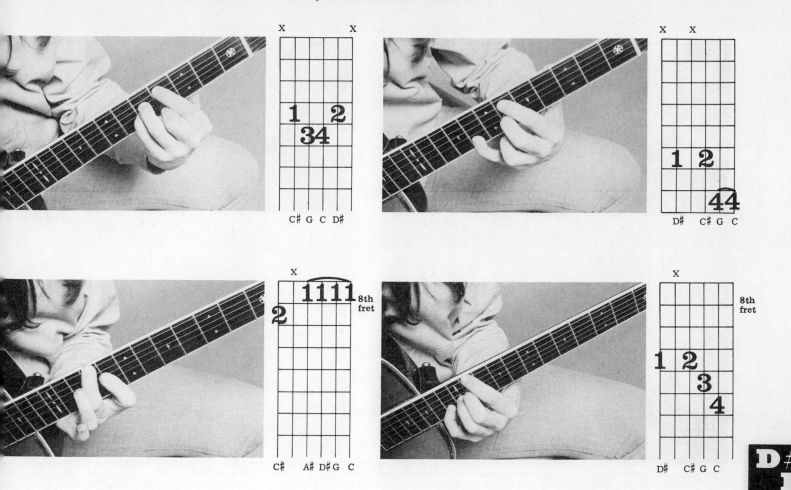

D#/E♭ Nine Six

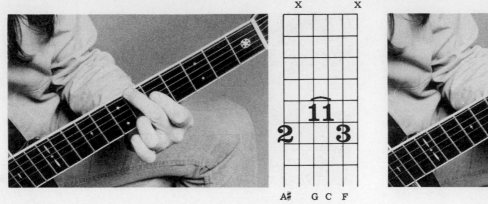

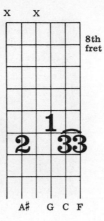

E Major

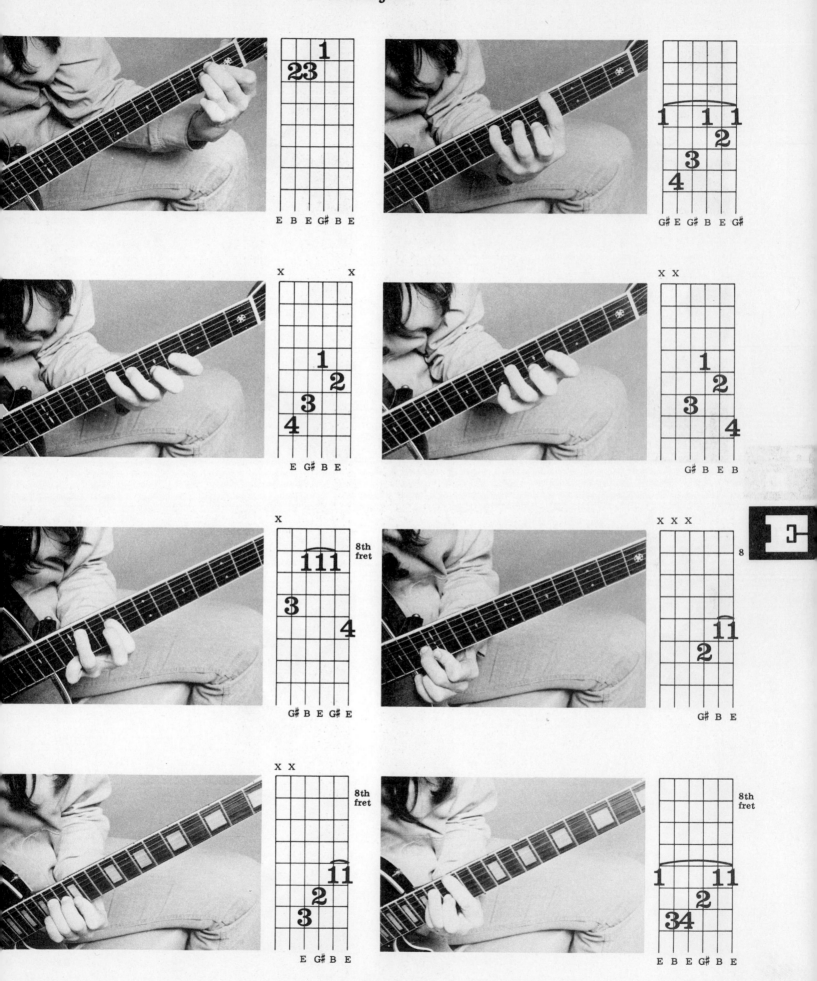

111

E Minor

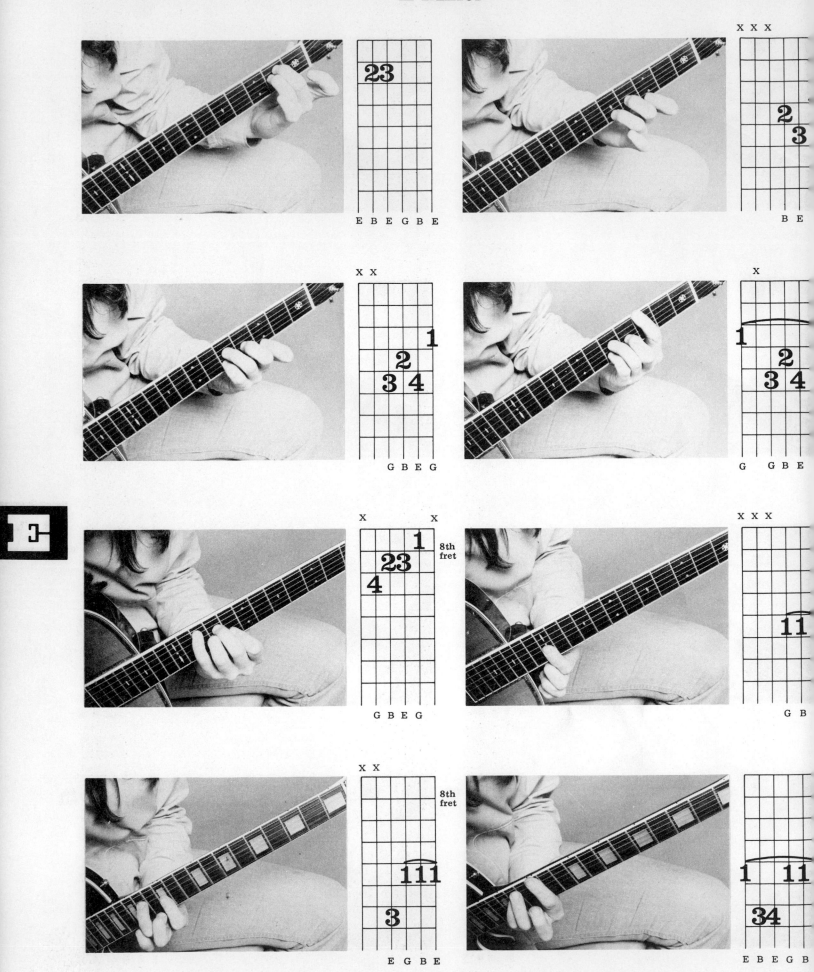

E Major Sixth

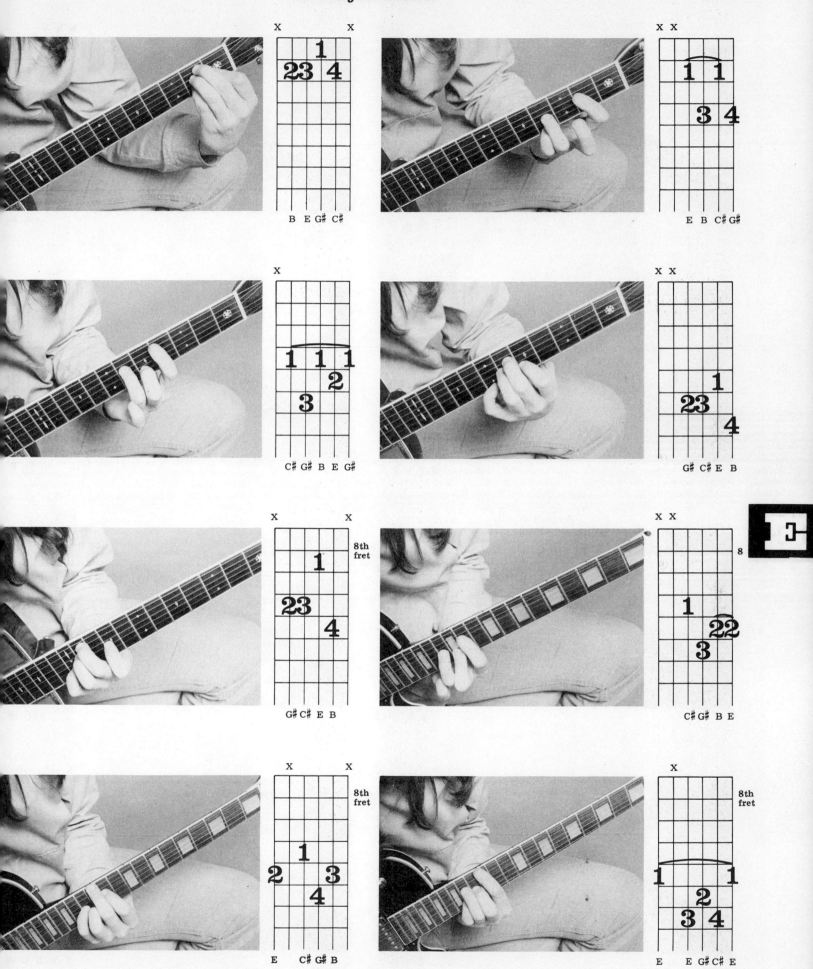

113

E Minor Sixth

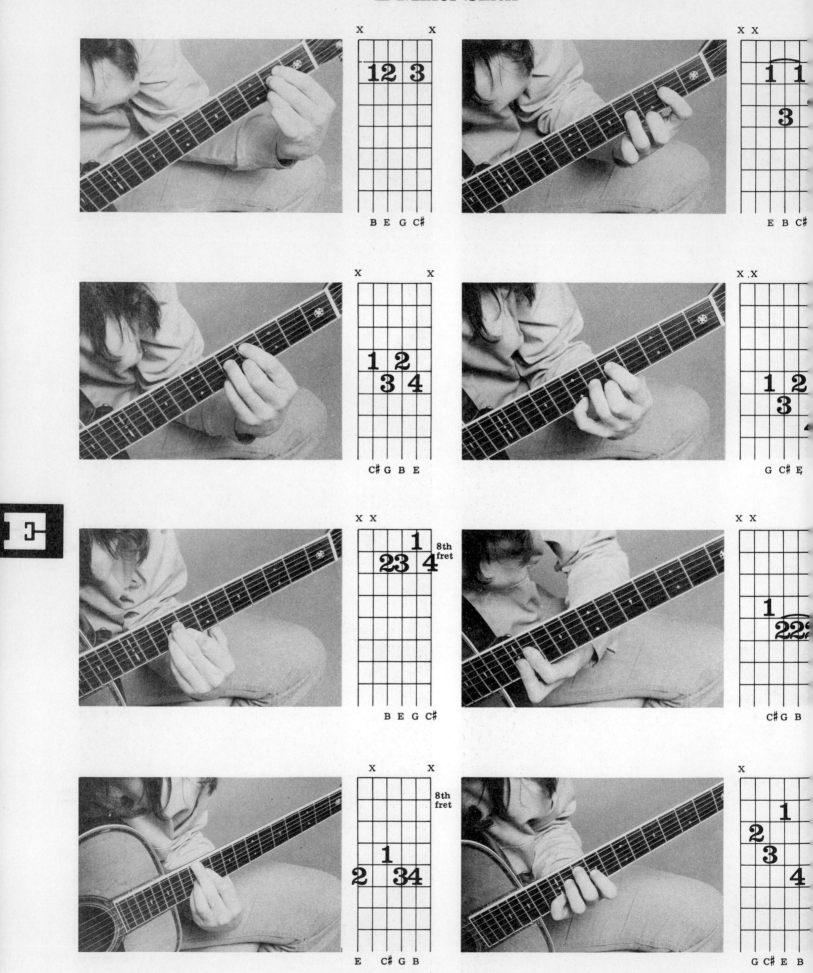

114

E Seventh

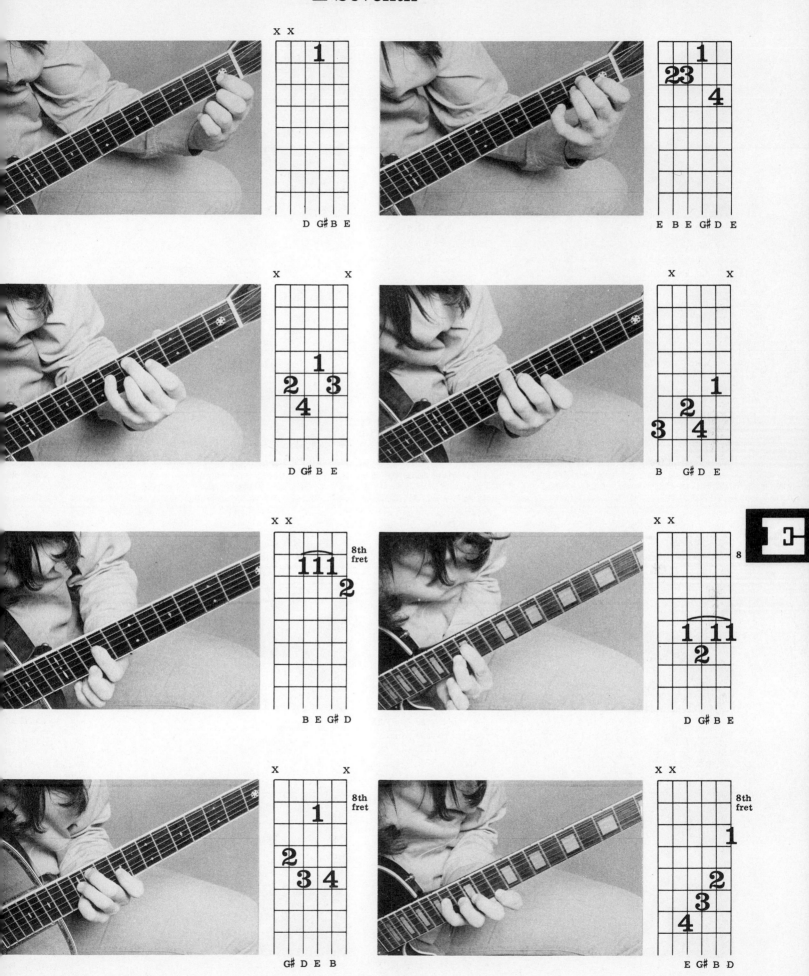

115

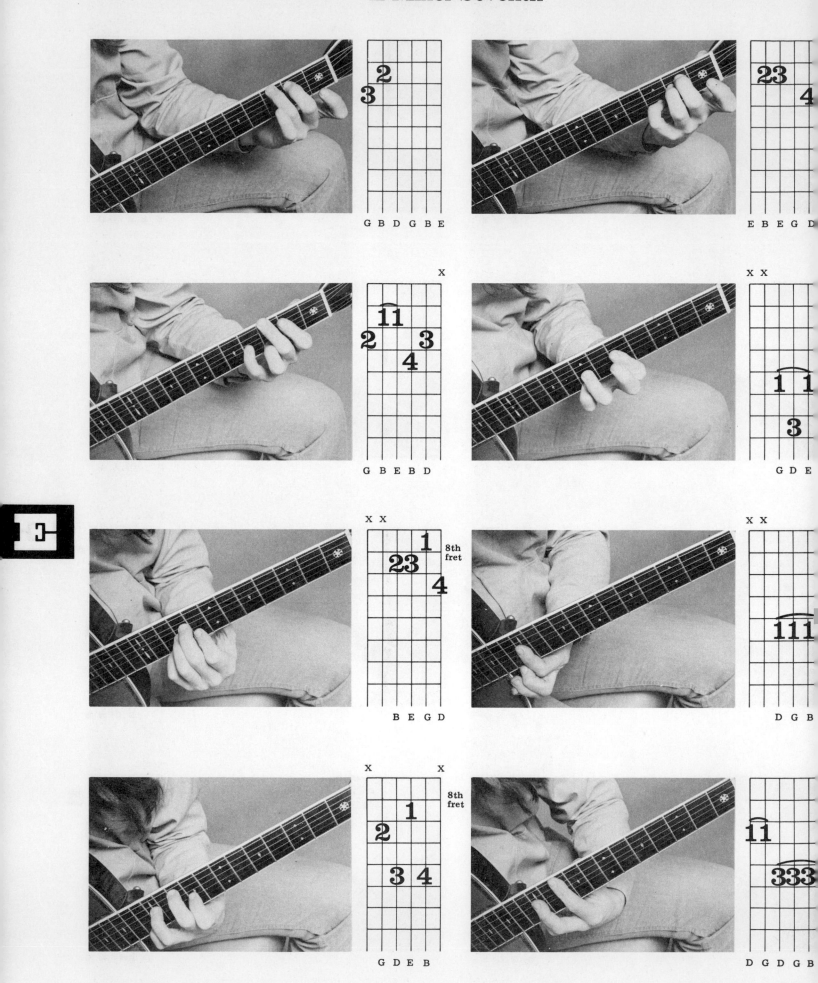

E Diminished

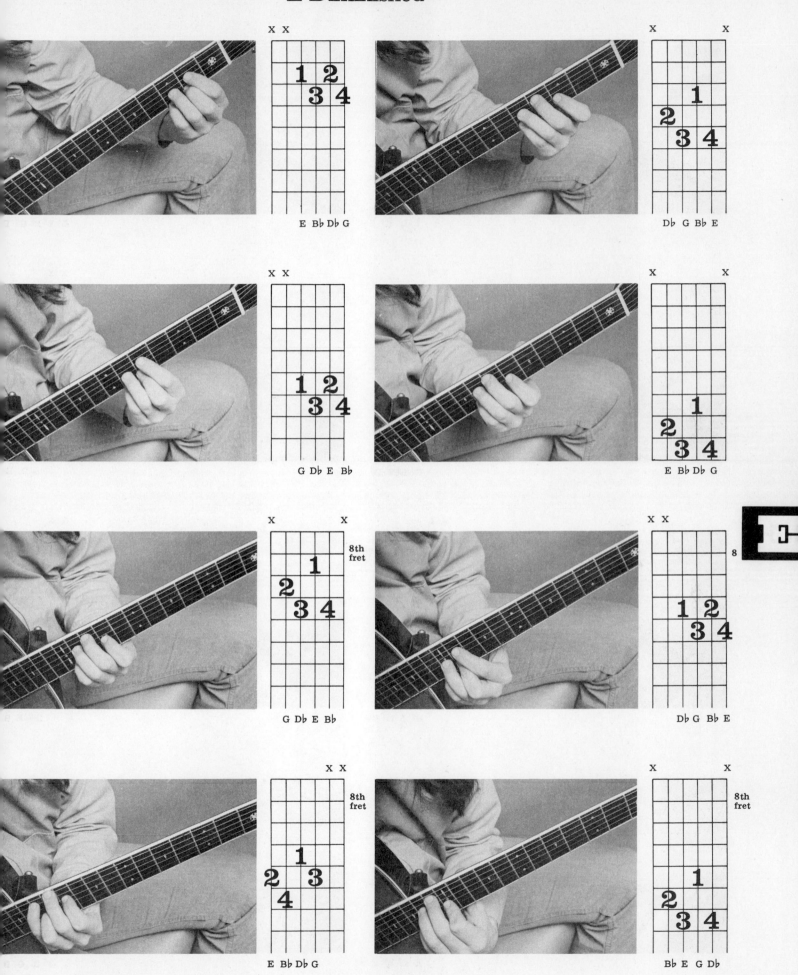

117

E Augmented

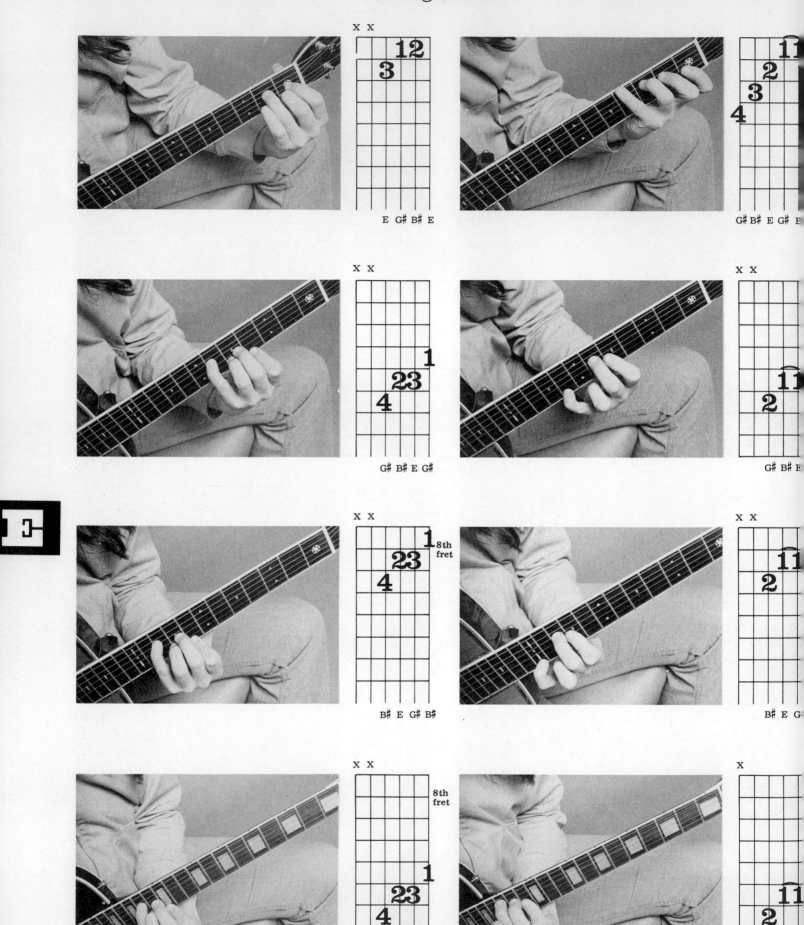

118

E Seventh Augmented Fifth

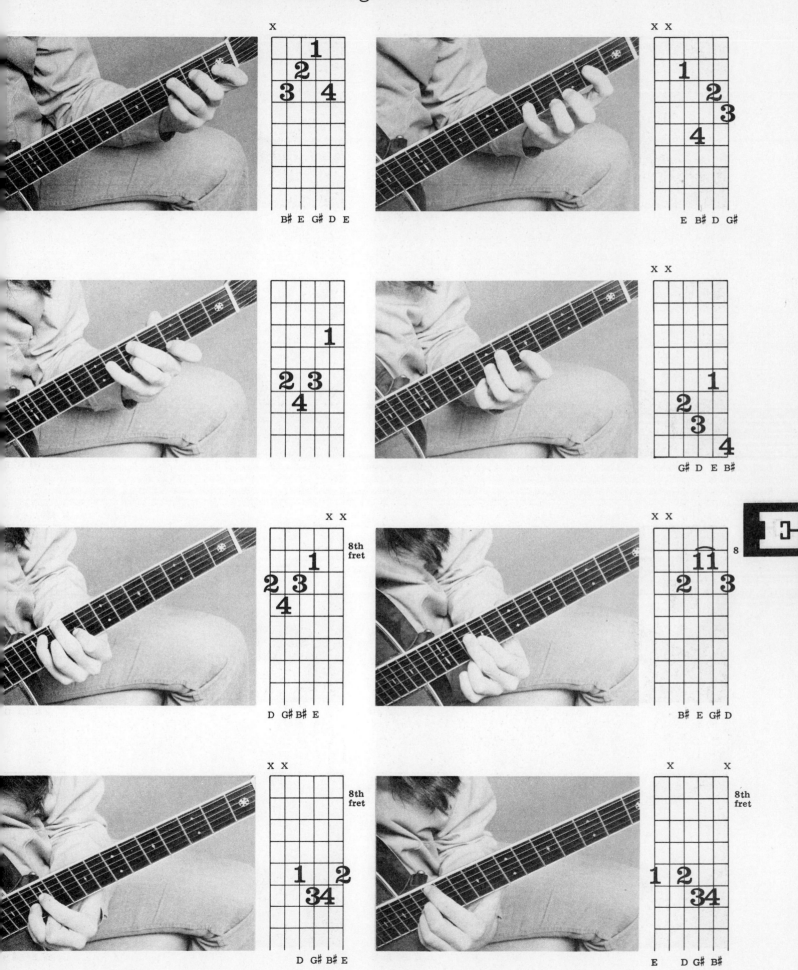

119

E Seventh Flat Five

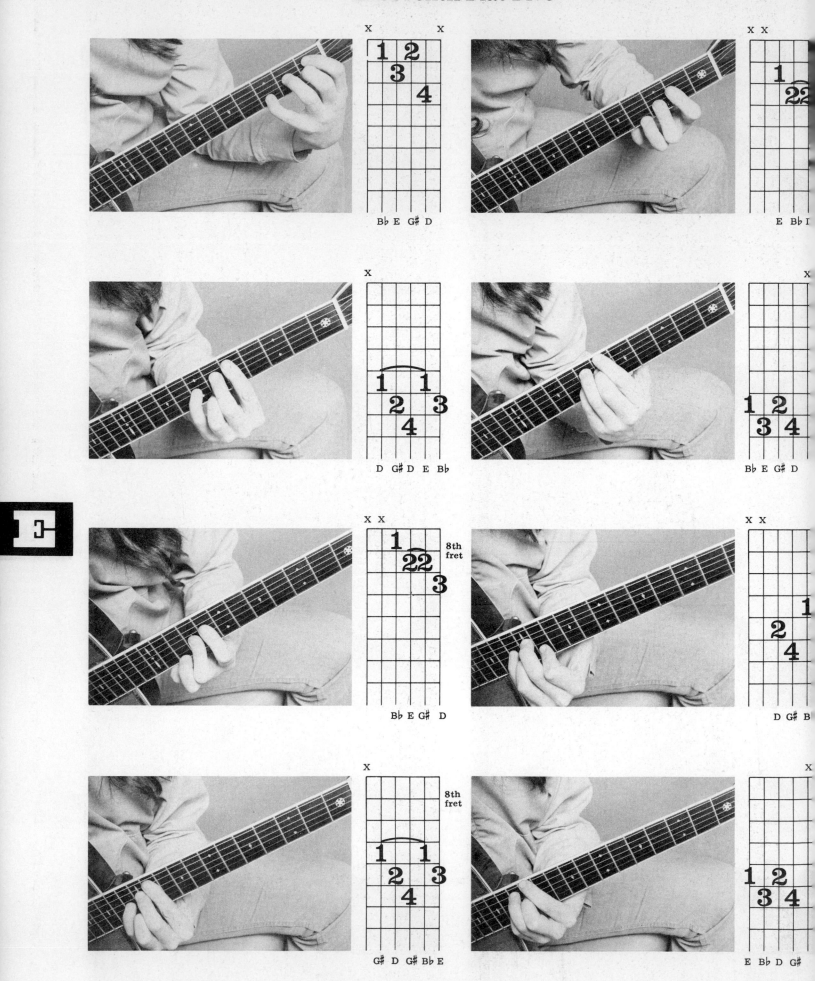

120

E Seventh Flat Nine

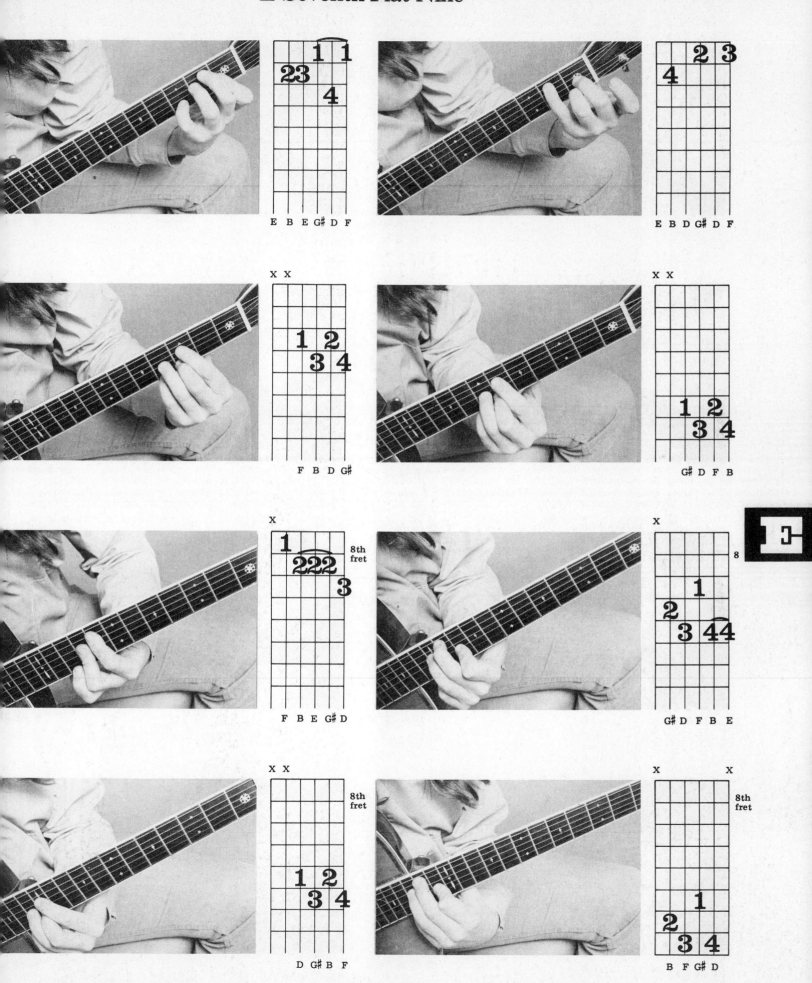

121

E Major Seventh

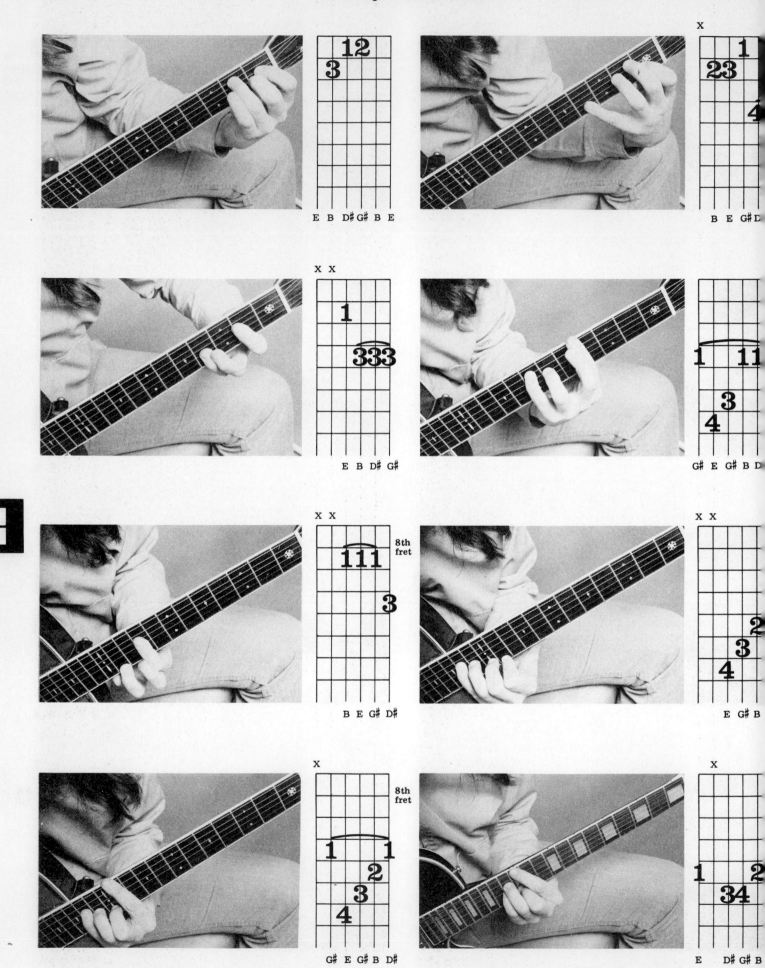

122

E Minor Seventh Flat Five

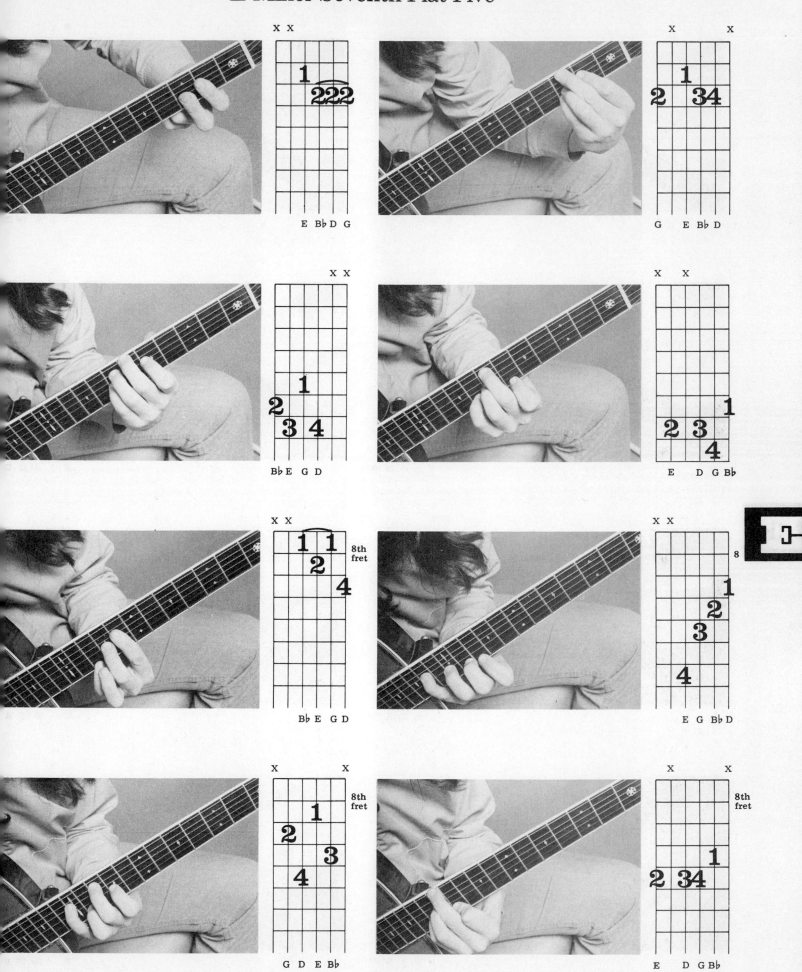

E Seventh Suspension Four

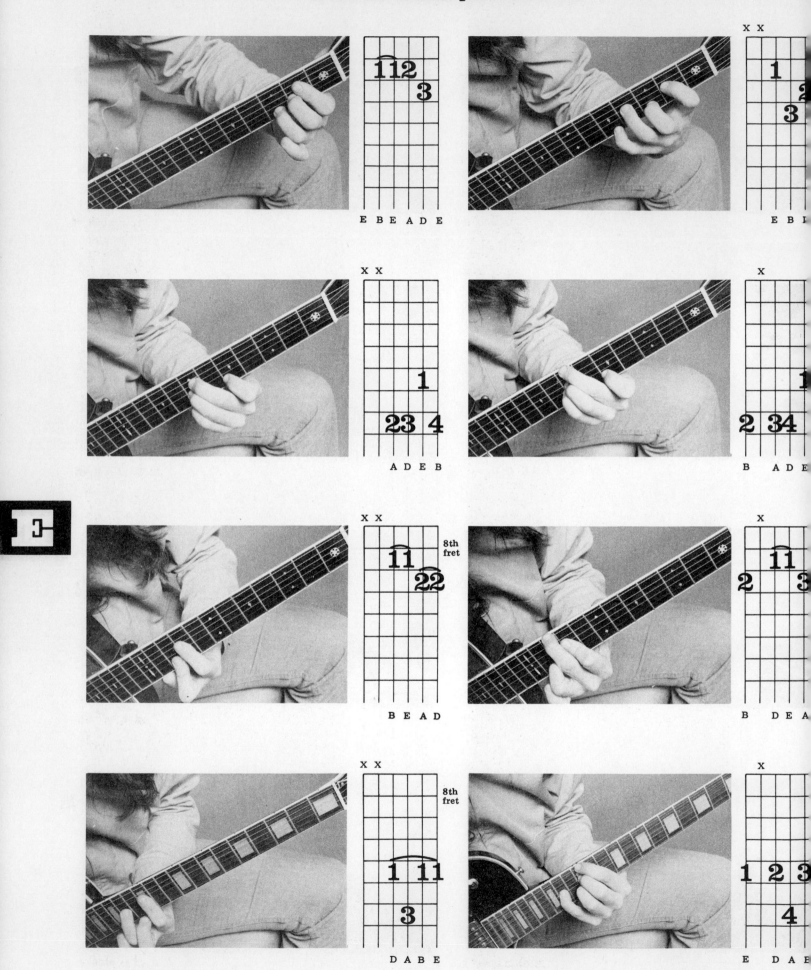

124

E Ninth

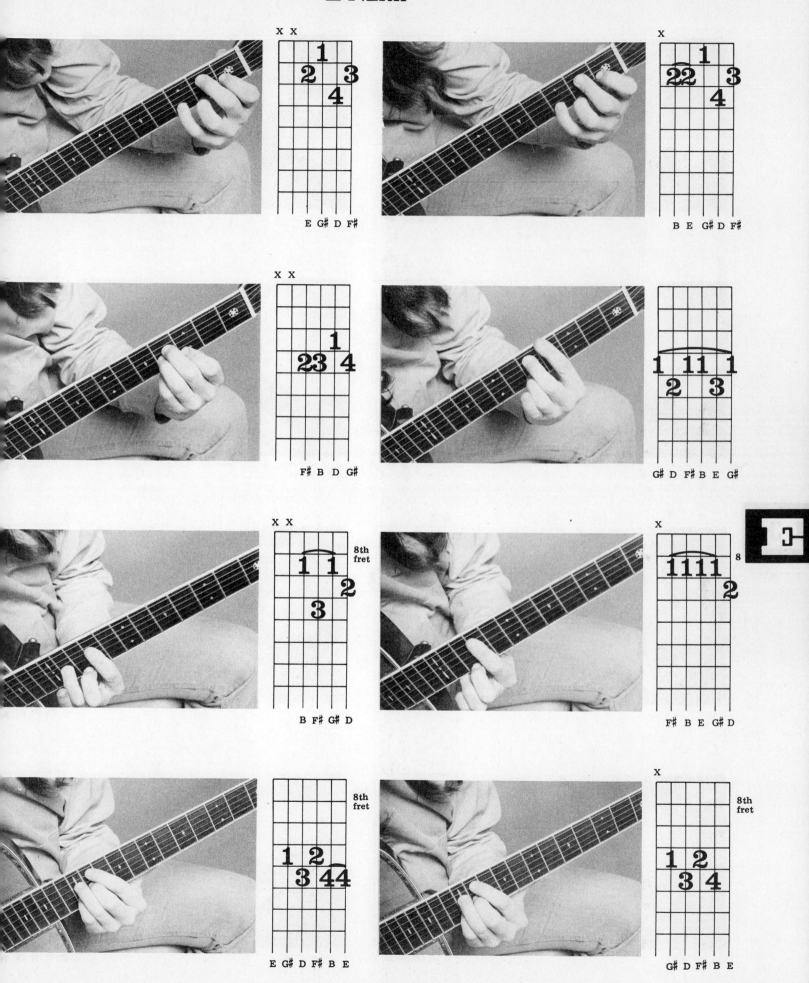

E Minor Ninth

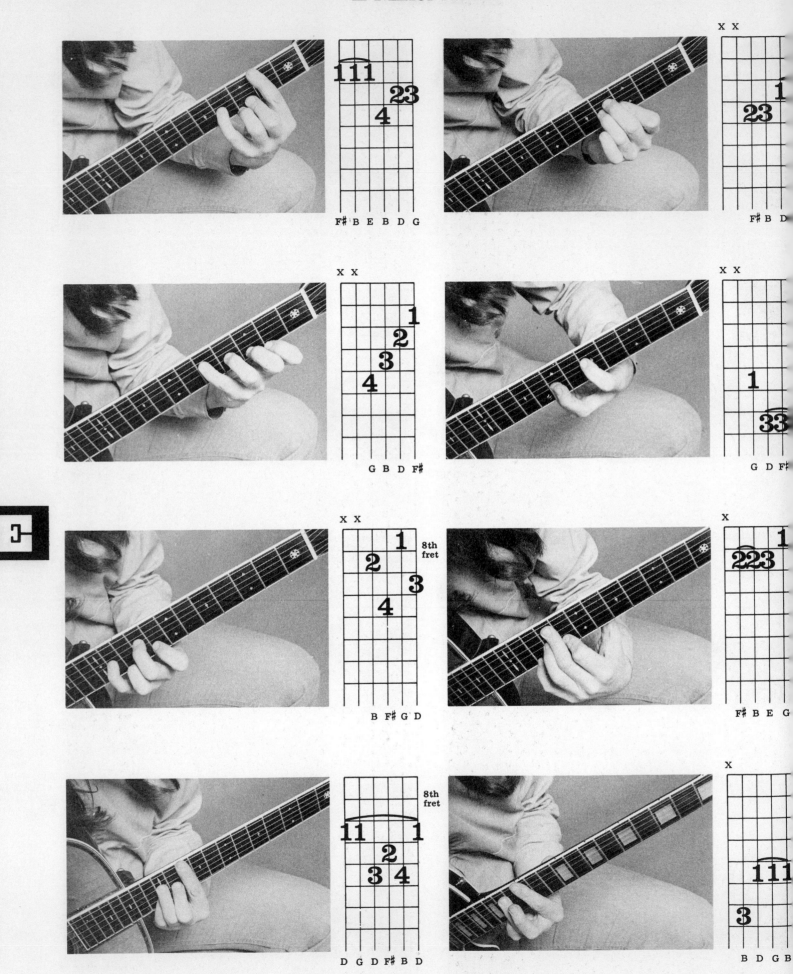

126

E Ninth Augmented Fifth

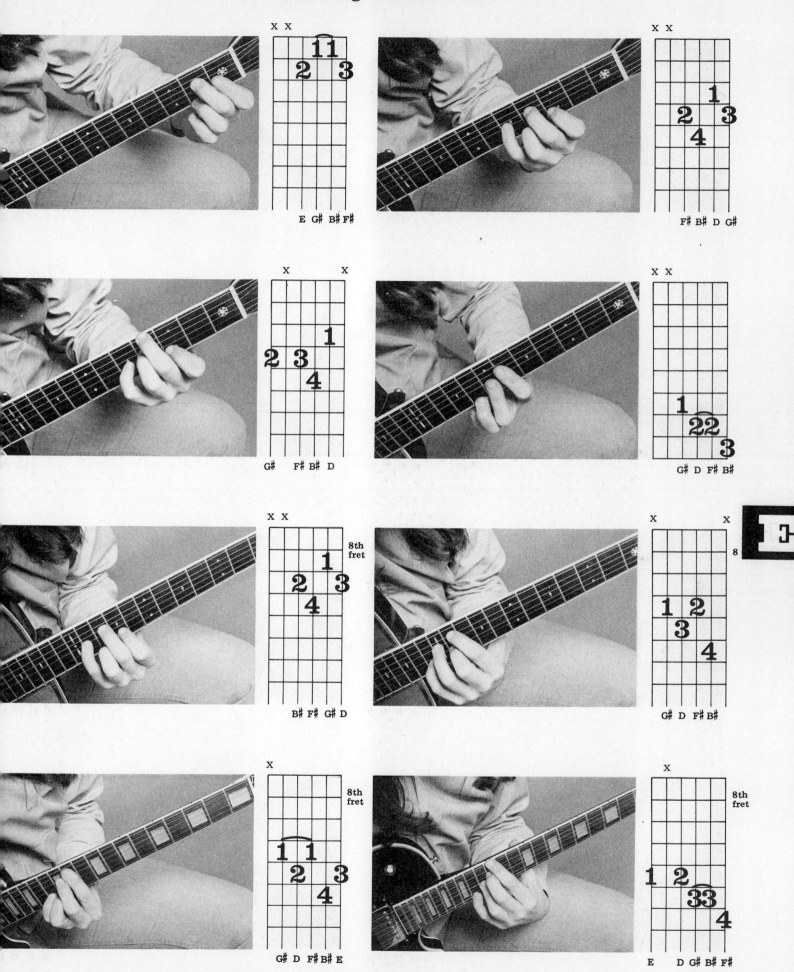

127

E Ninth Flat Five

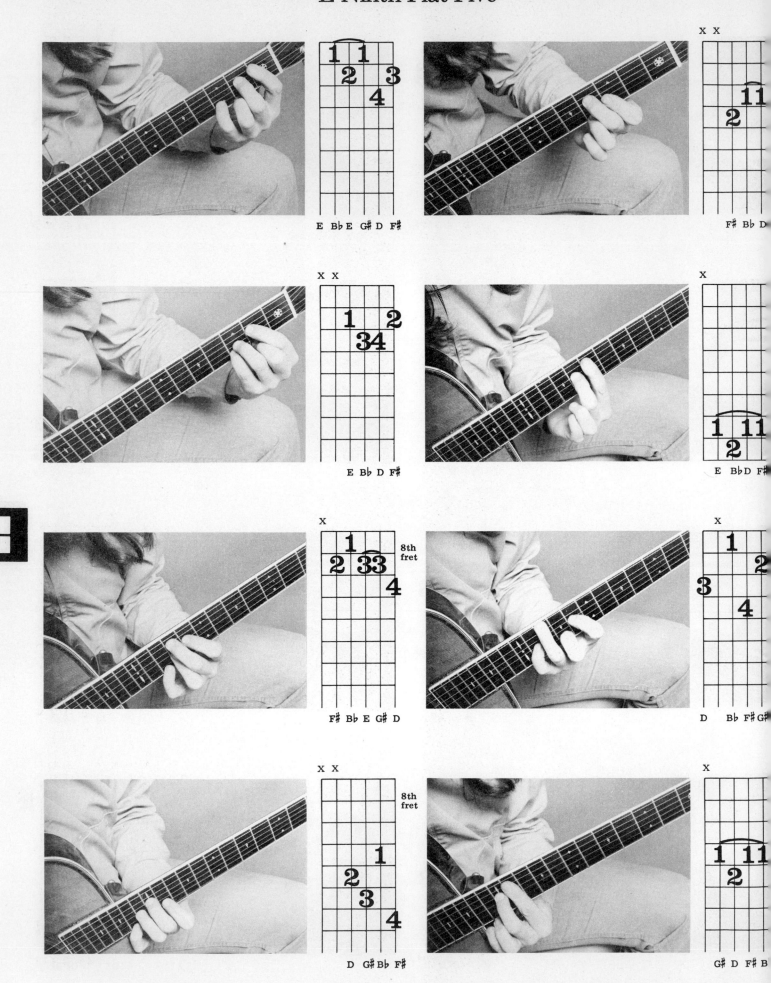

E Major Ninth

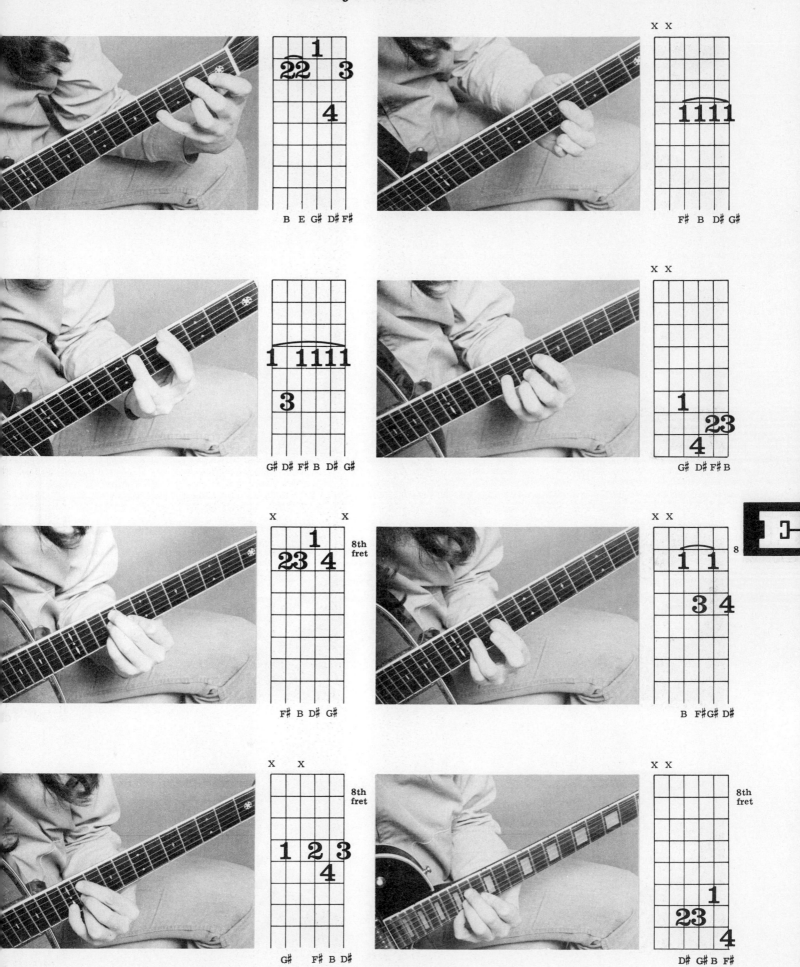

129

E Eleventh

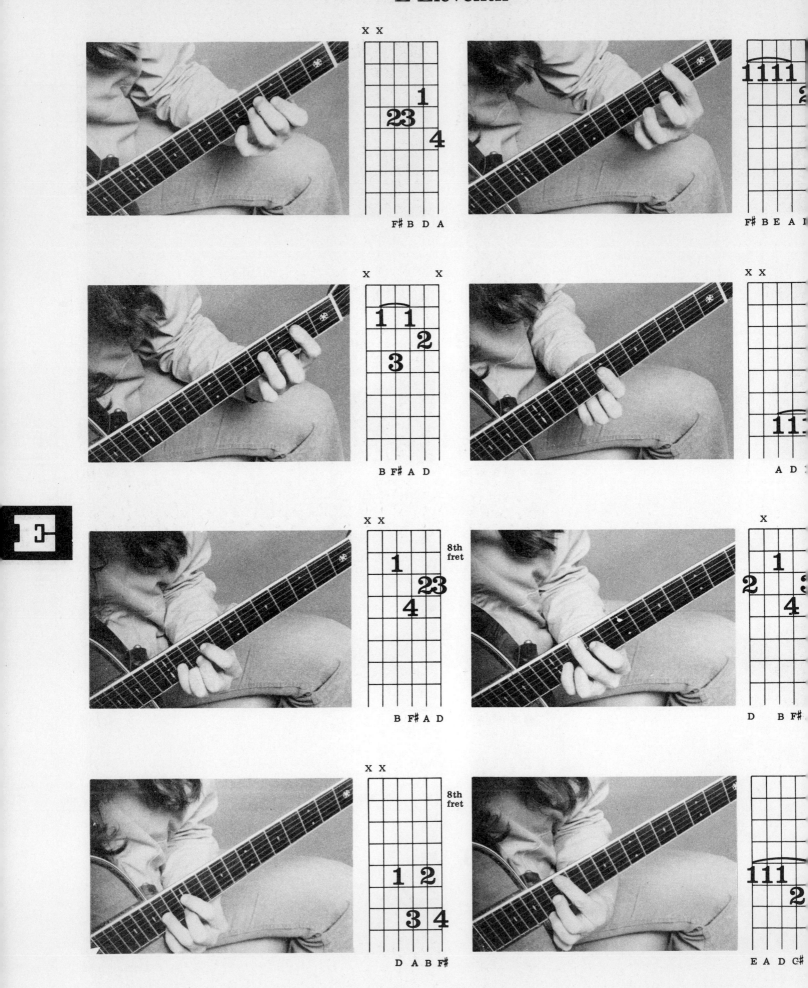

130

E Augmented Eleventh

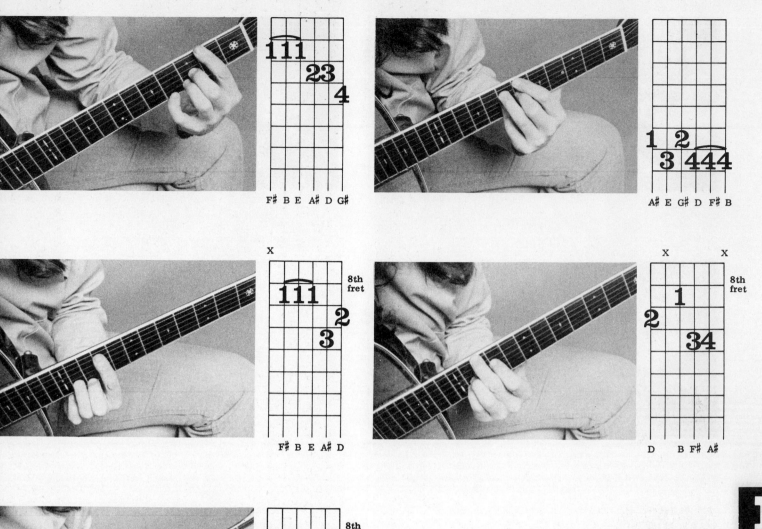

F# B E A# D G#

A# E G# D F# B

X
8th fret
F# B E A# D

X   X
8th fret
D   B F# A#

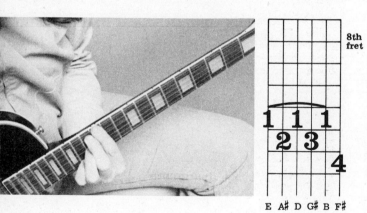

8th fret
E A# D G# B F#

131

E Thirteenth

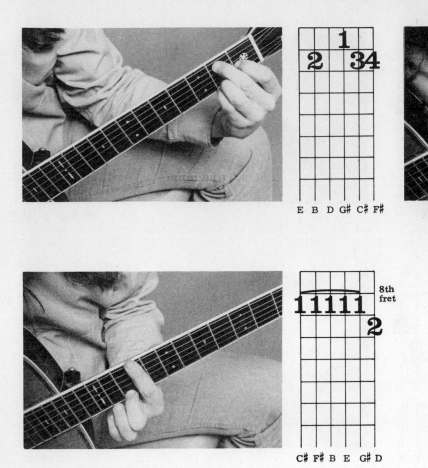

E B D G# C# F#

D B F# G#

8th
fret

C# F# B E G# D

E Thirteenth Flat Nine

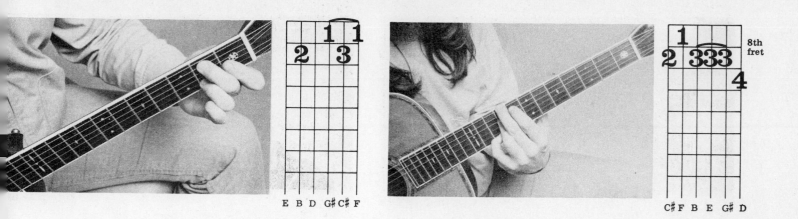

E B D G# C# F

C# F B E G# D

8th fret

E Seven Six

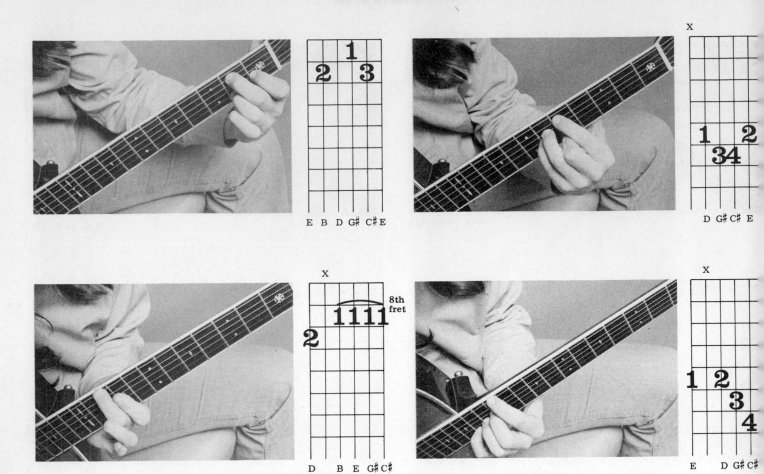

E Nine Six

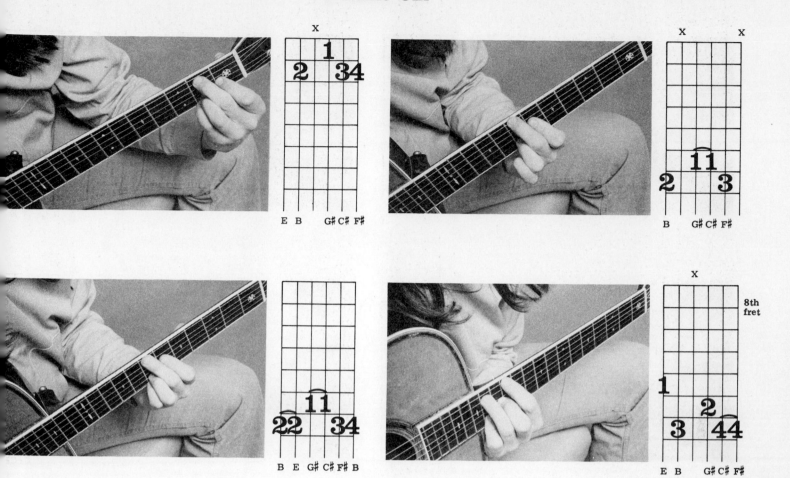

F Major

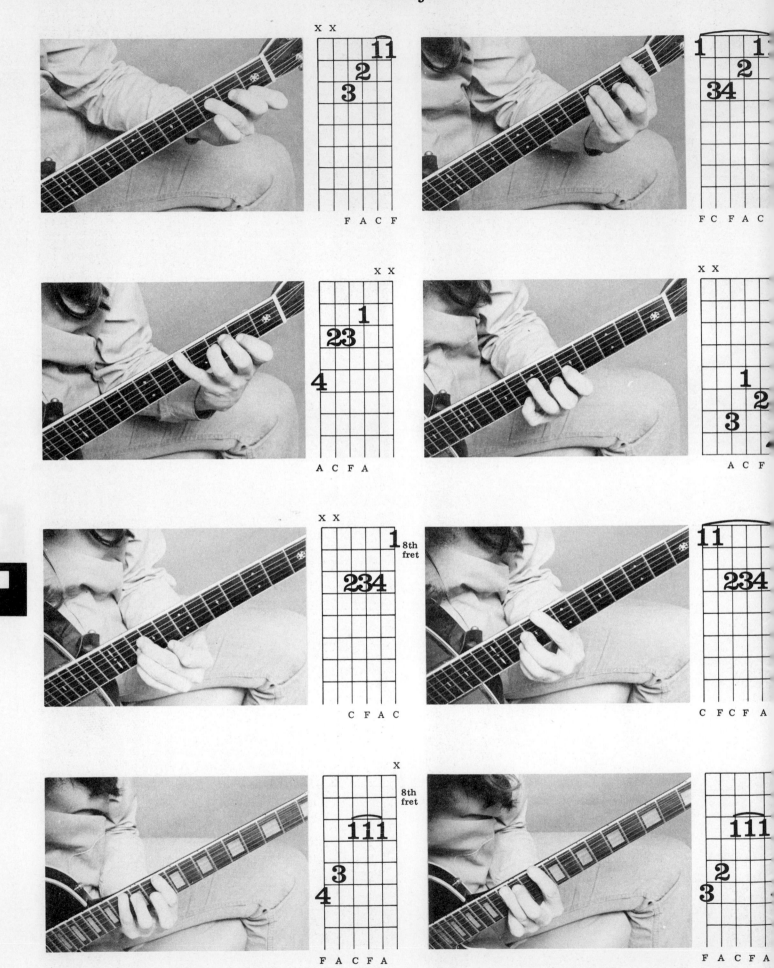

F Minor

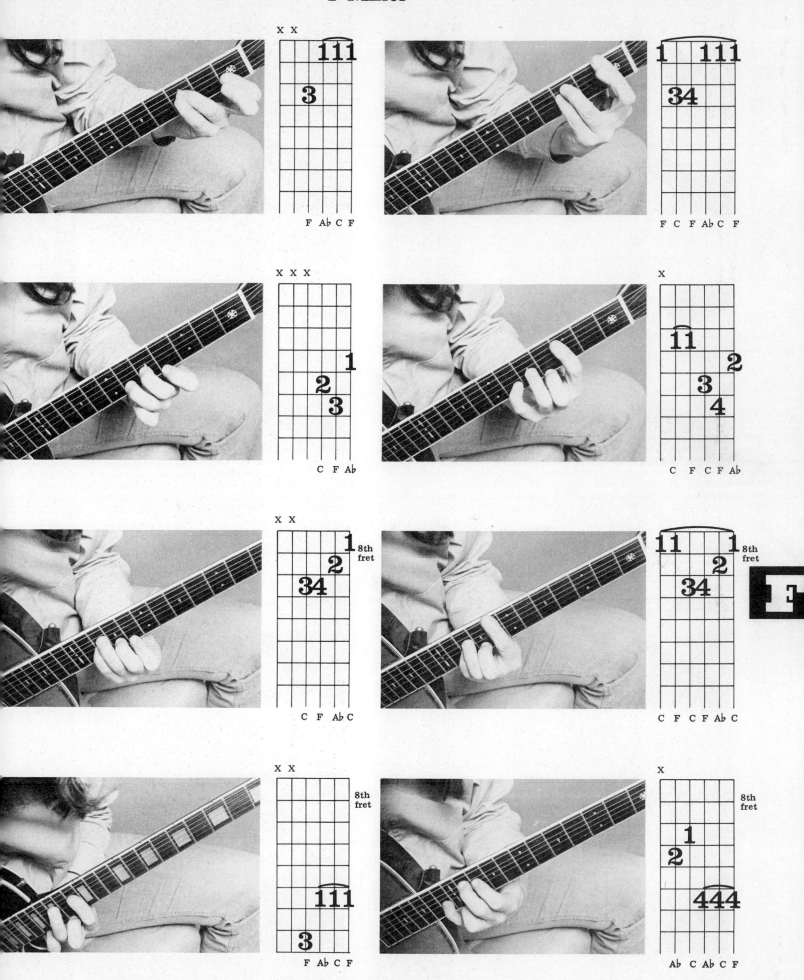

F Major Sixth

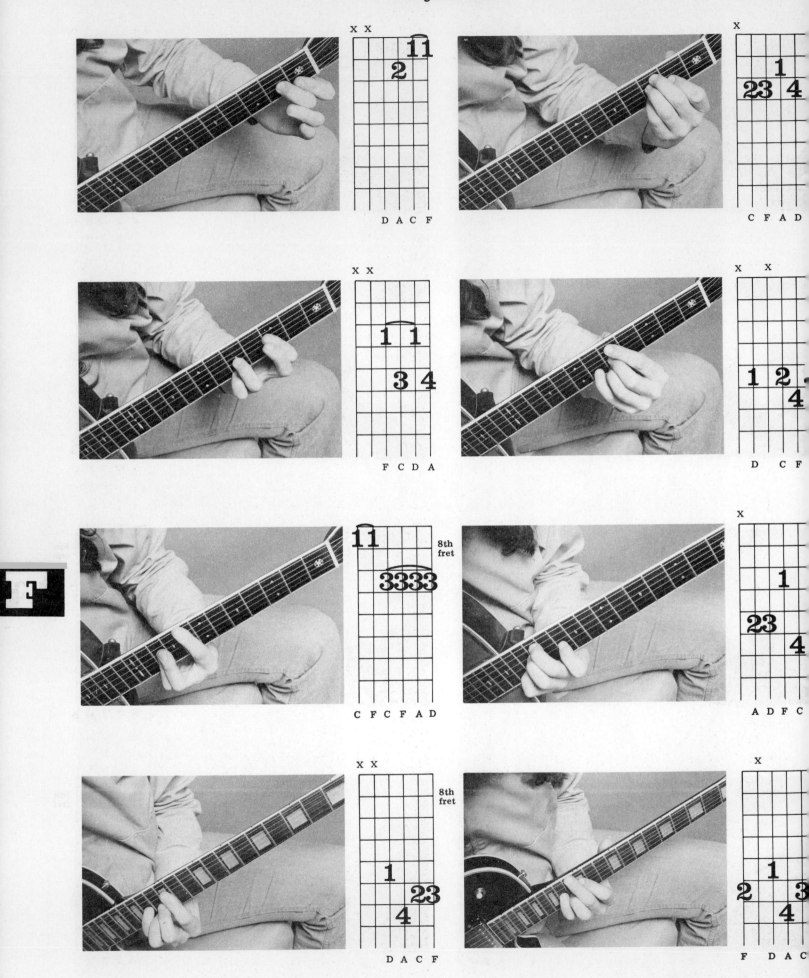

F Minor Sixth

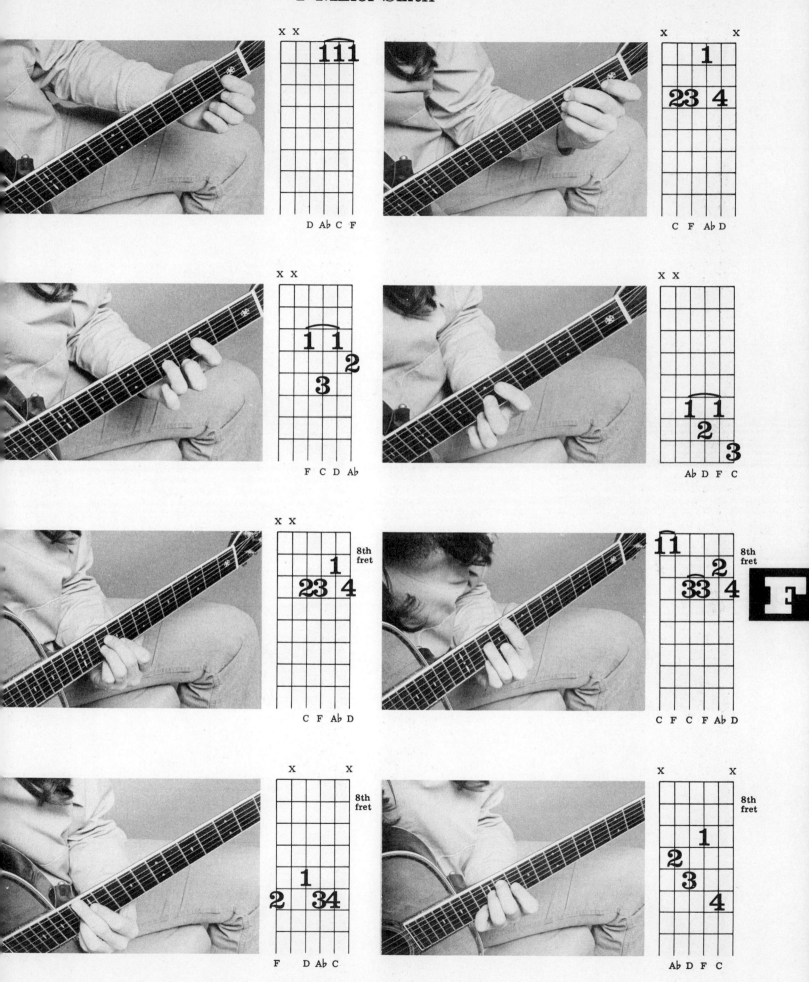

139

F Seventh

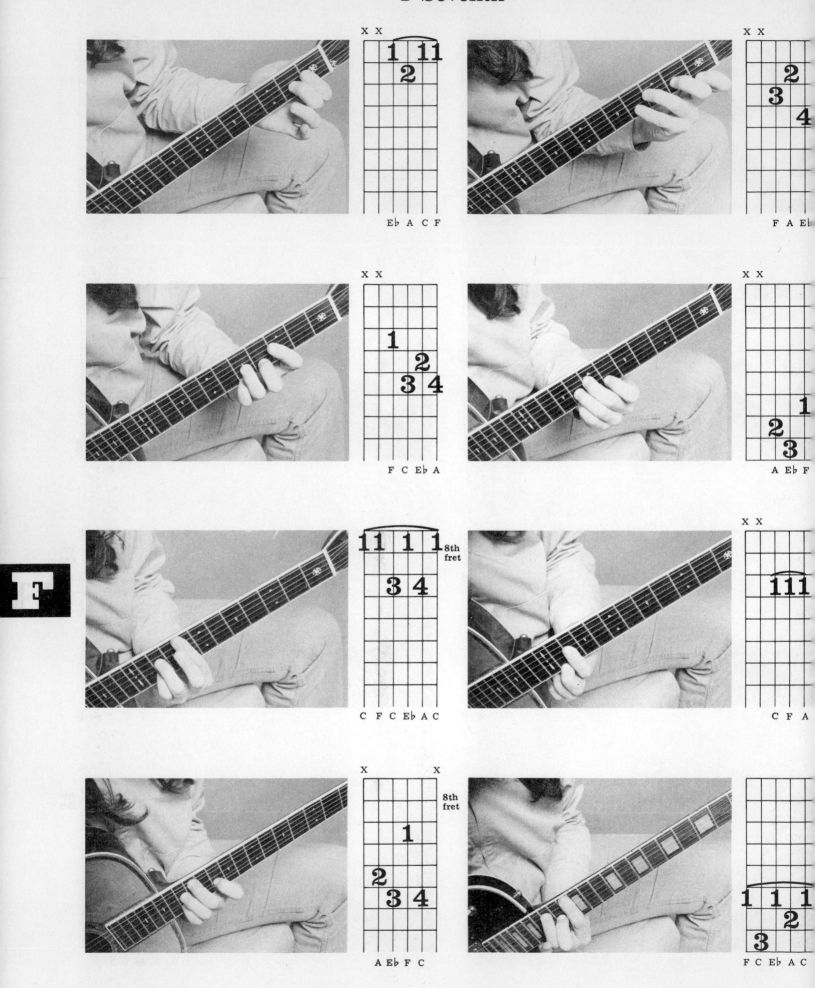

140

F Minor Seventh

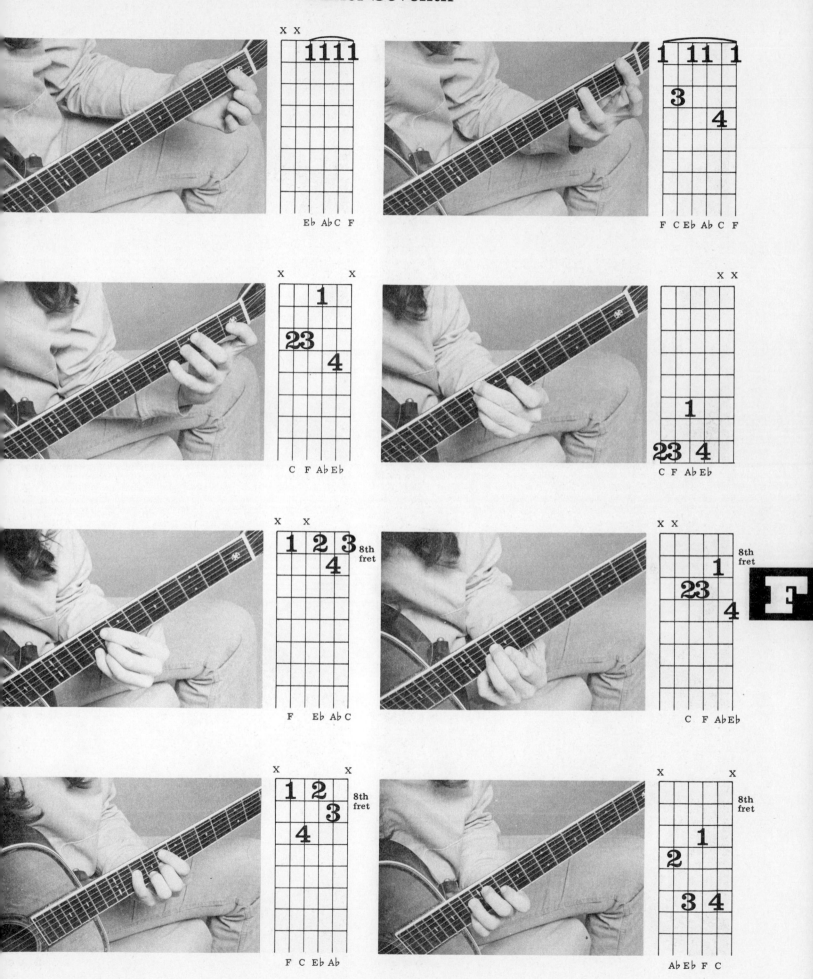

141

F Diminished

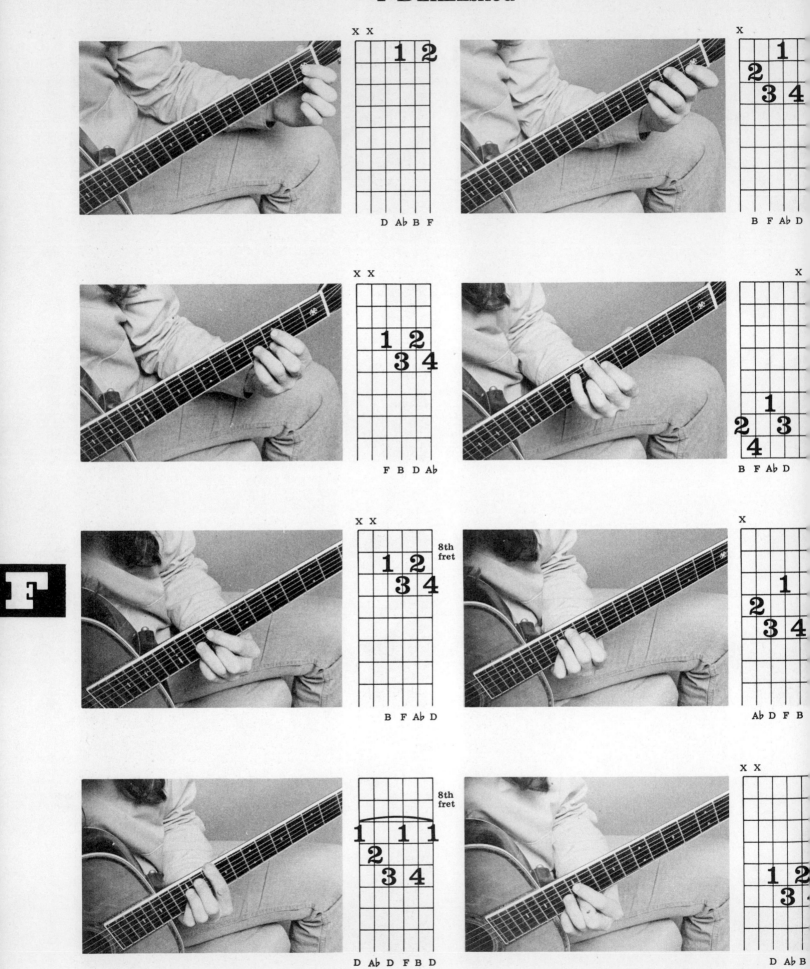

142

F Augmented

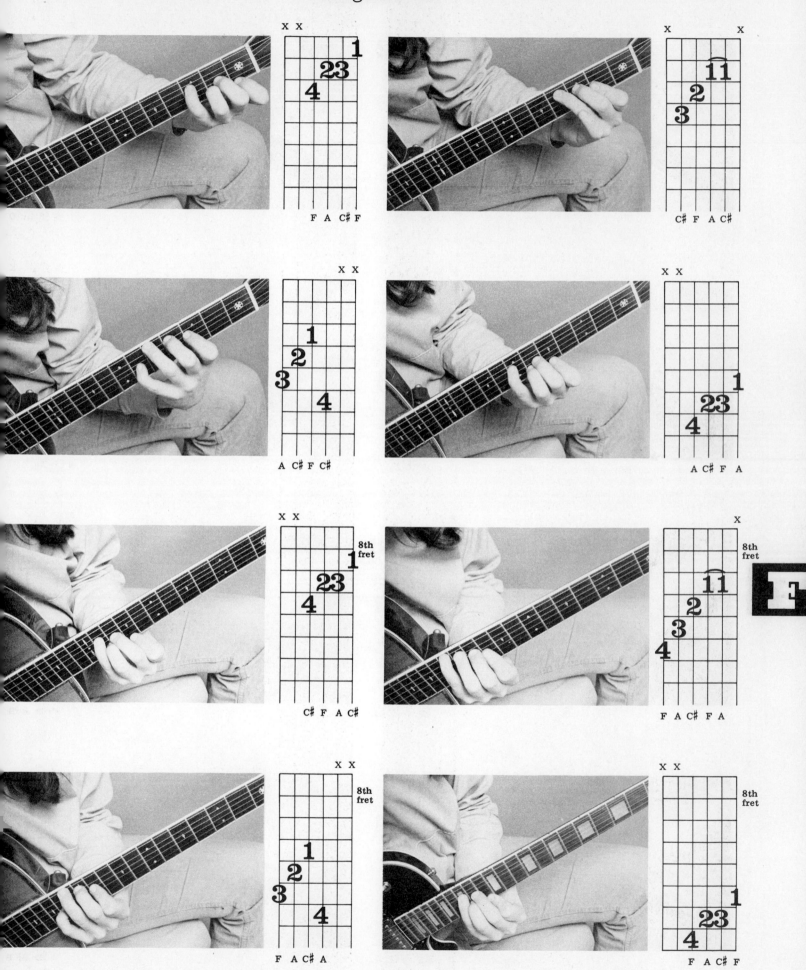

143

F Seventh Augmented Fifth

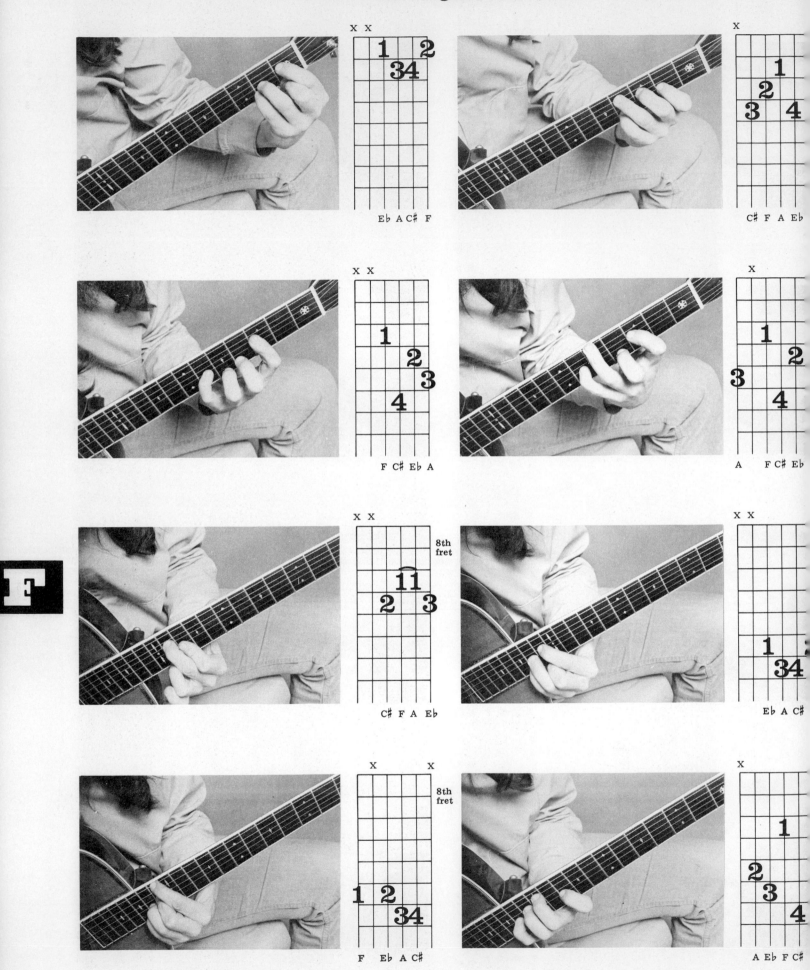

144

F Seventh Flat Five

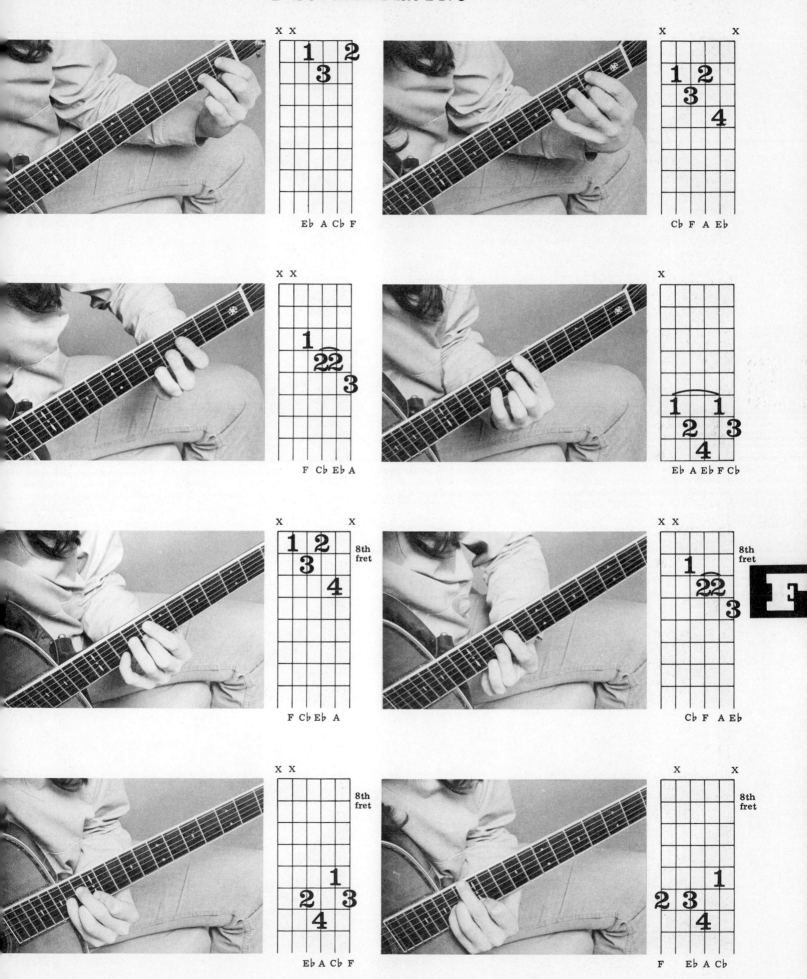

145

F Seventh Flat Nine

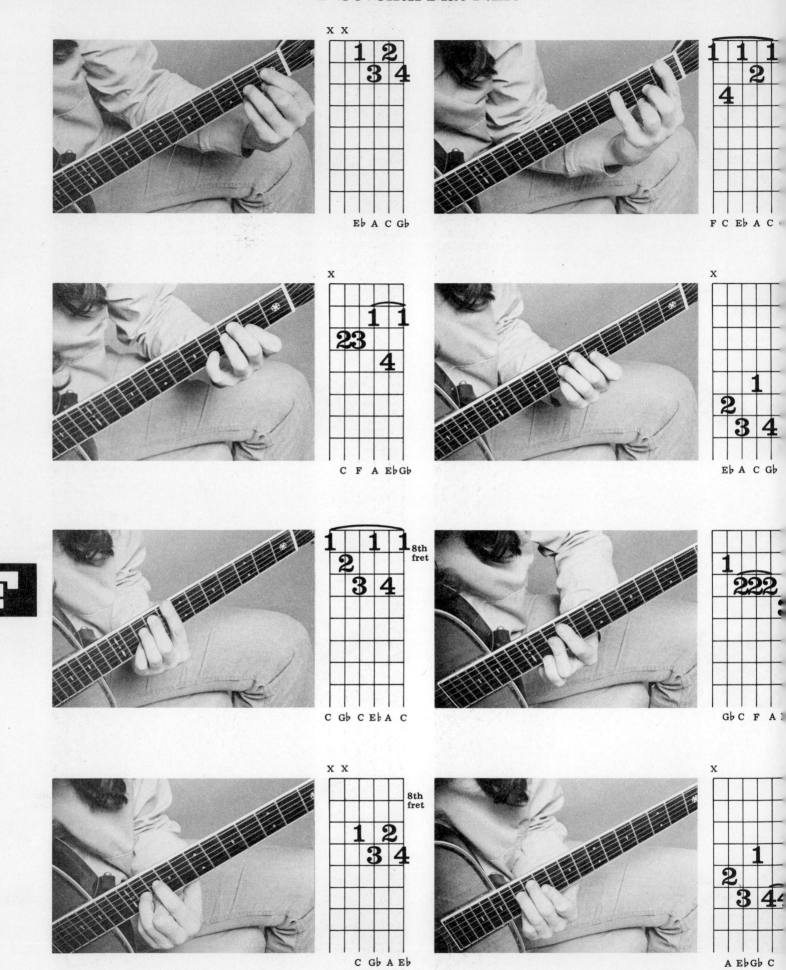

F Major Seventh

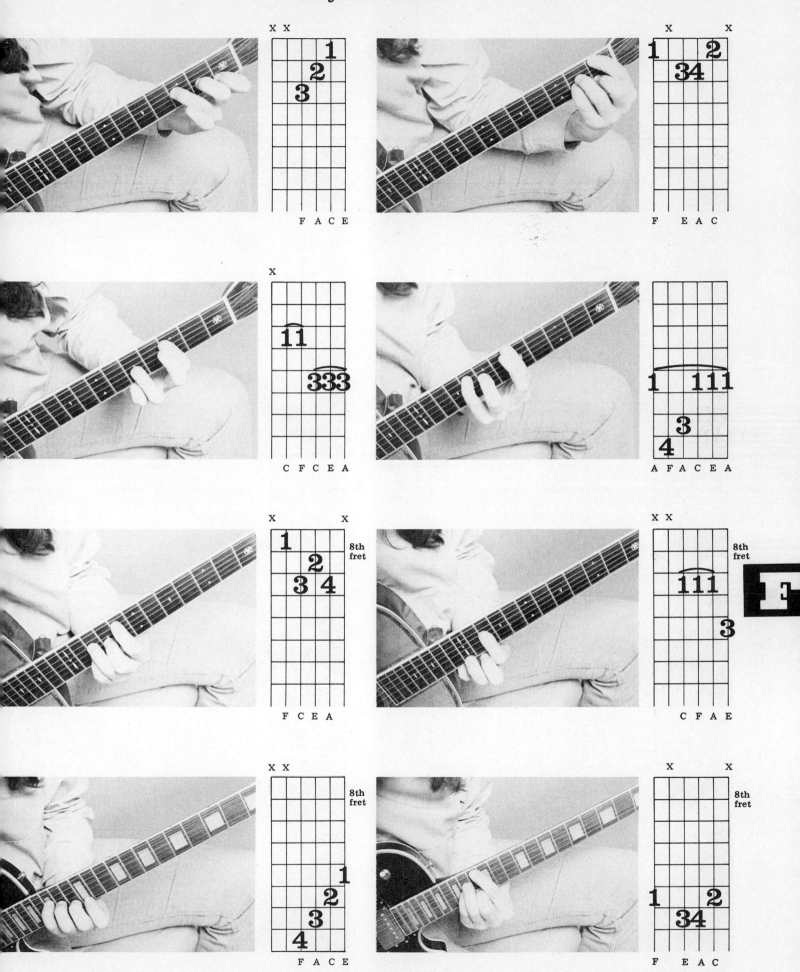

F Minor Seventh Flat Five

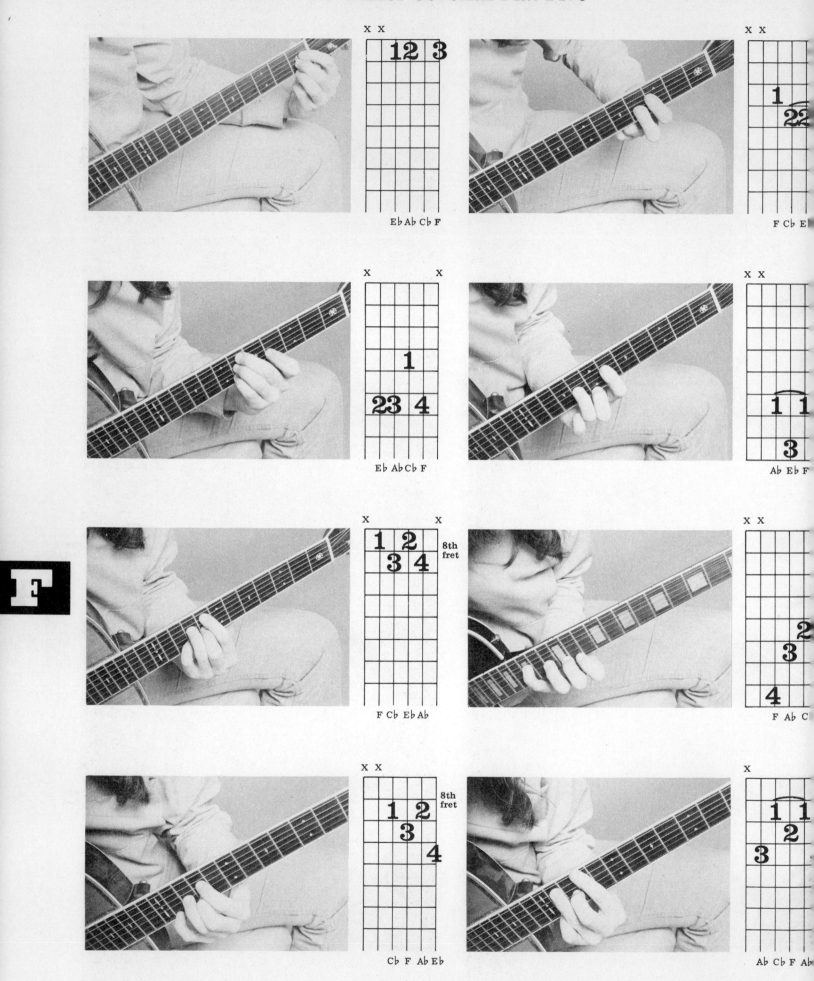

148

F Seventh Suspension Four

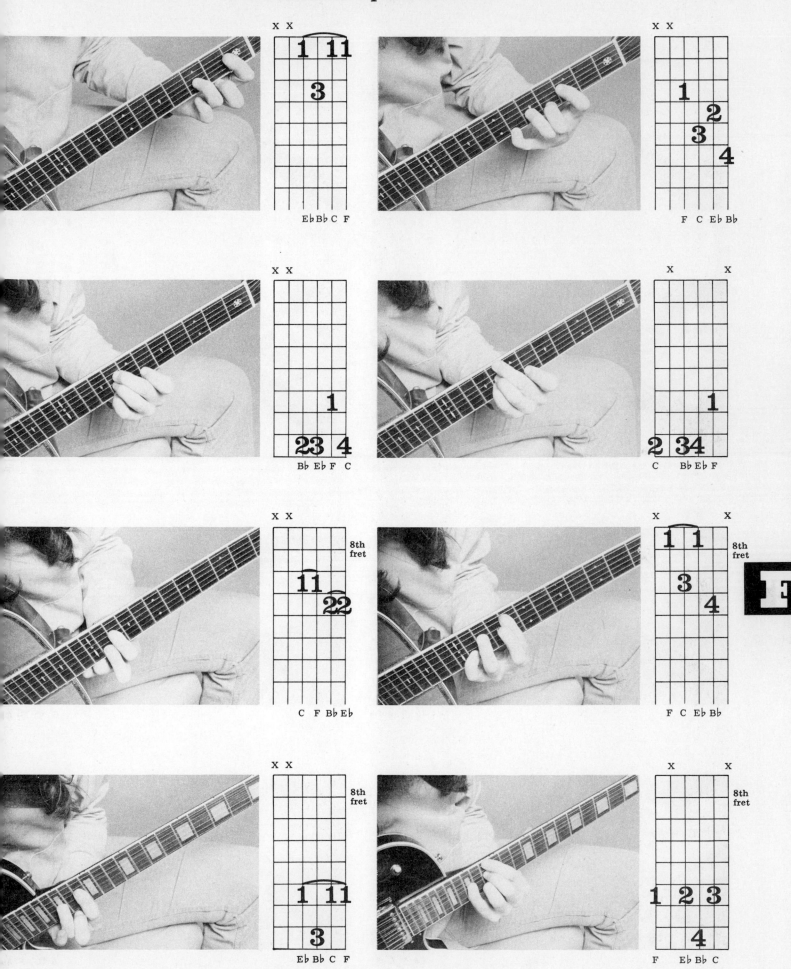

149

F Ninth

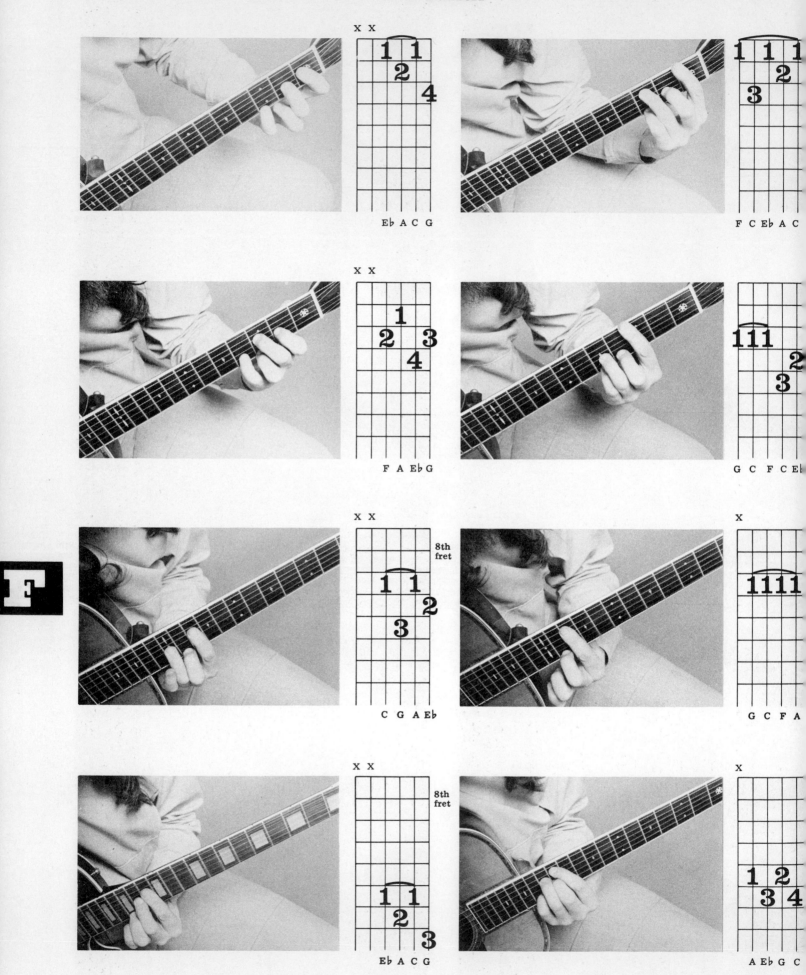

150

F Minor Ninth

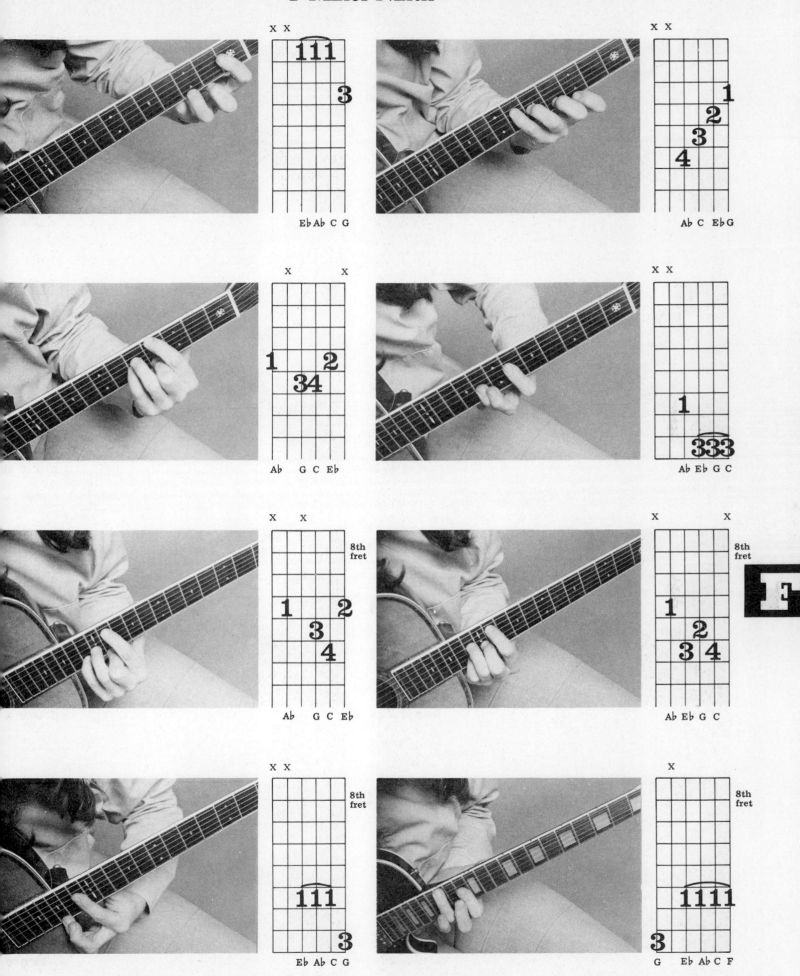

151

F Ninth Augmented Fifth

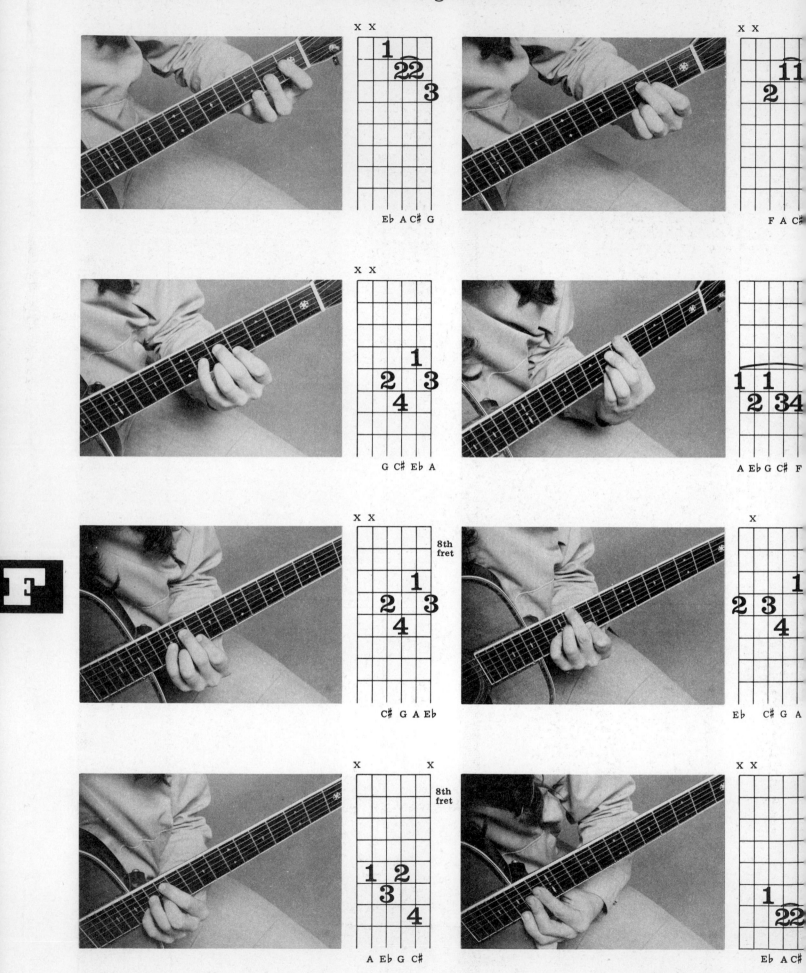

152

F Ninth Flat Five

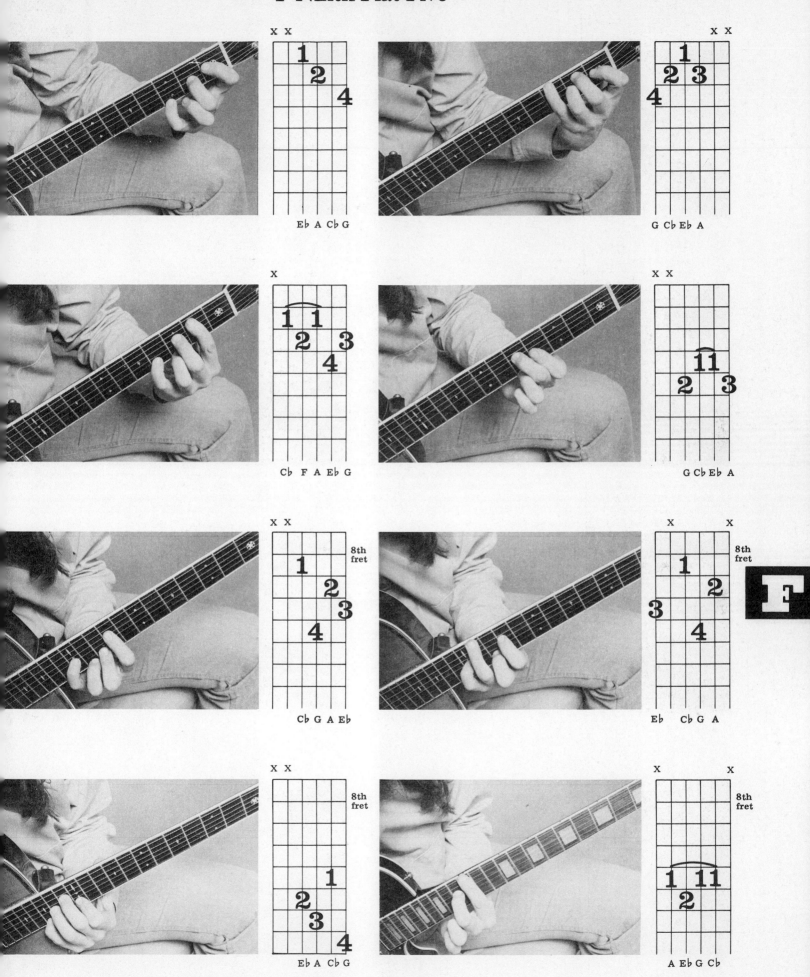

F Major Ninth

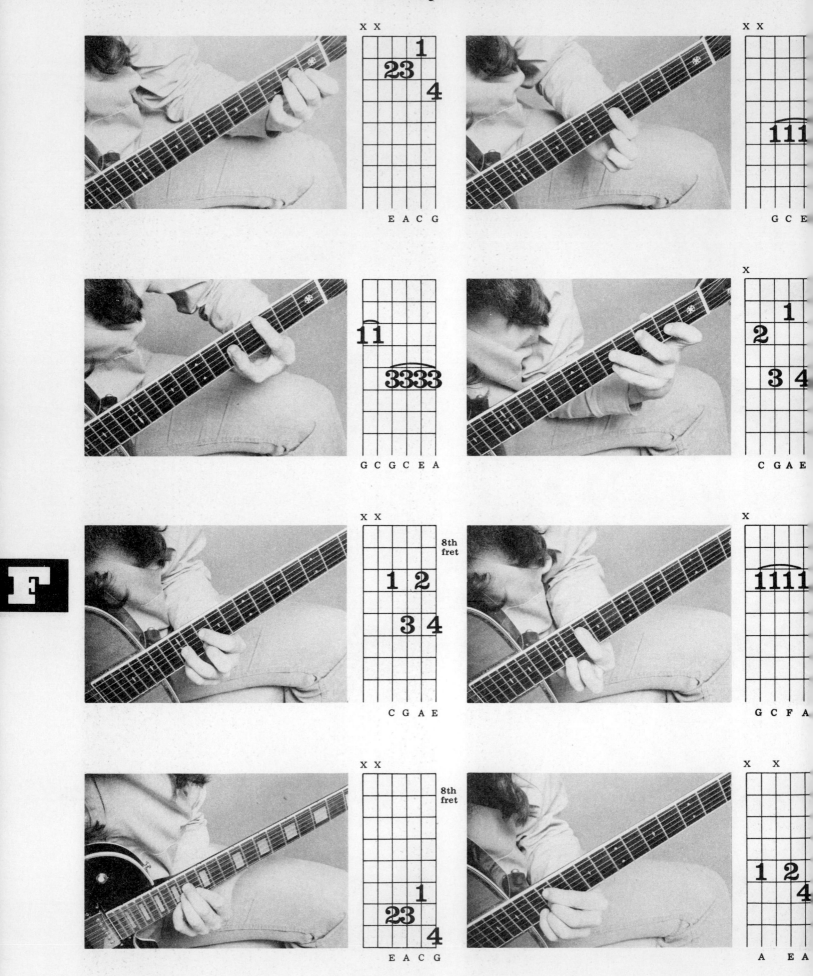

F Eleventh

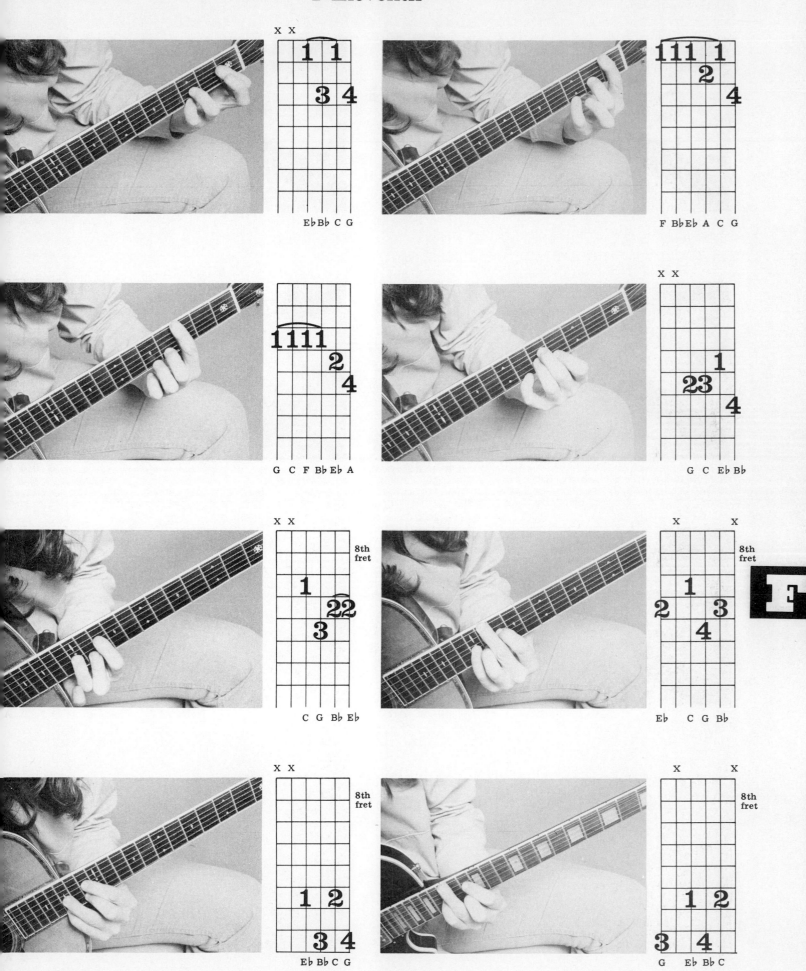

155

F Augmented Eleventh

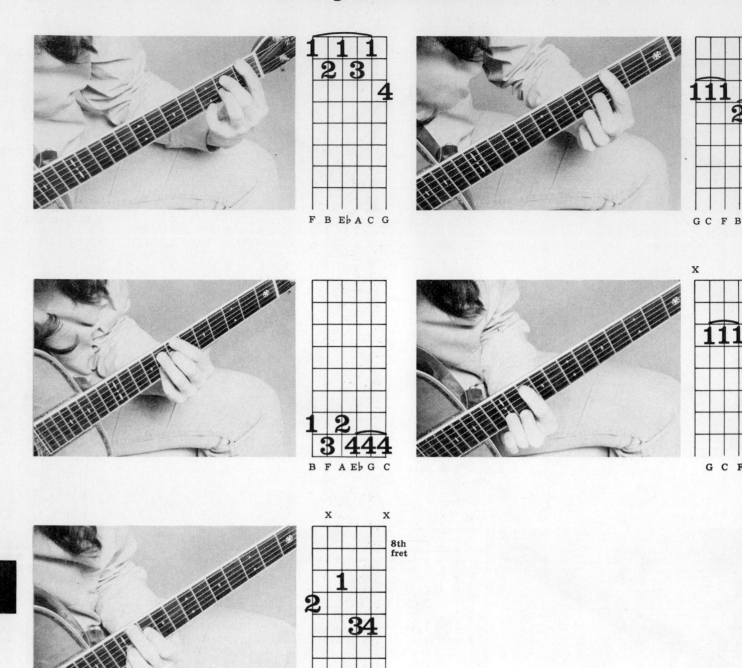

F Thirteenth

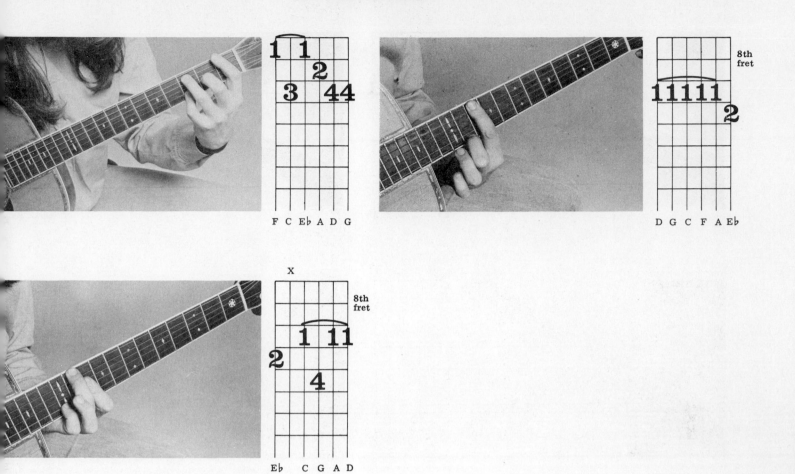

F C E♭ A D G

8th fret

D G C F A E♭

X

8th fret

E♭ C G A D

F Thirteenth Flat Nine

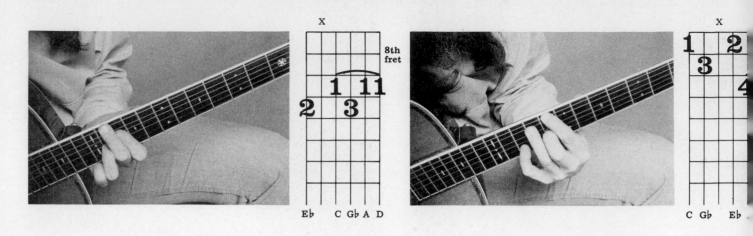

F Seven Six

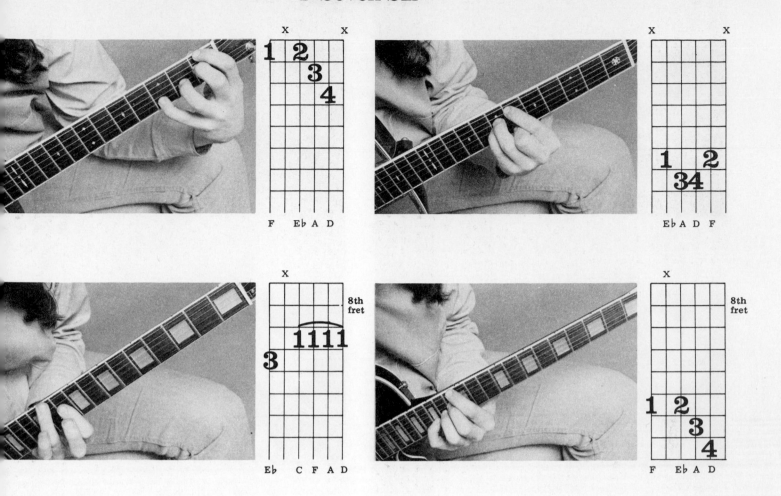

F Nine Six

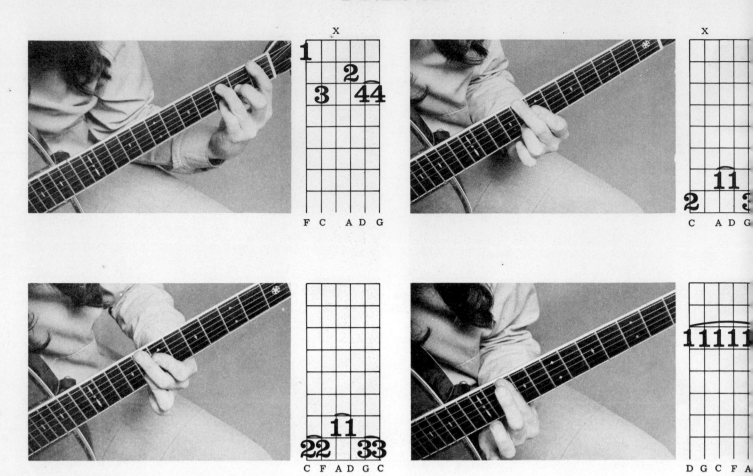

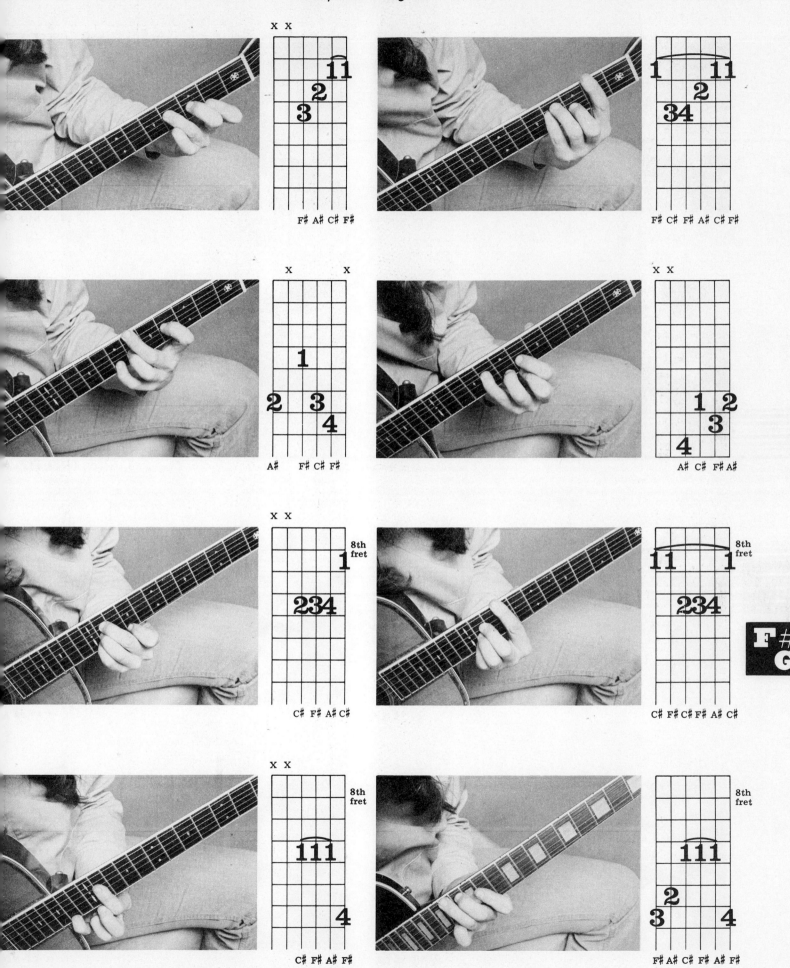

F#/Gb Minor

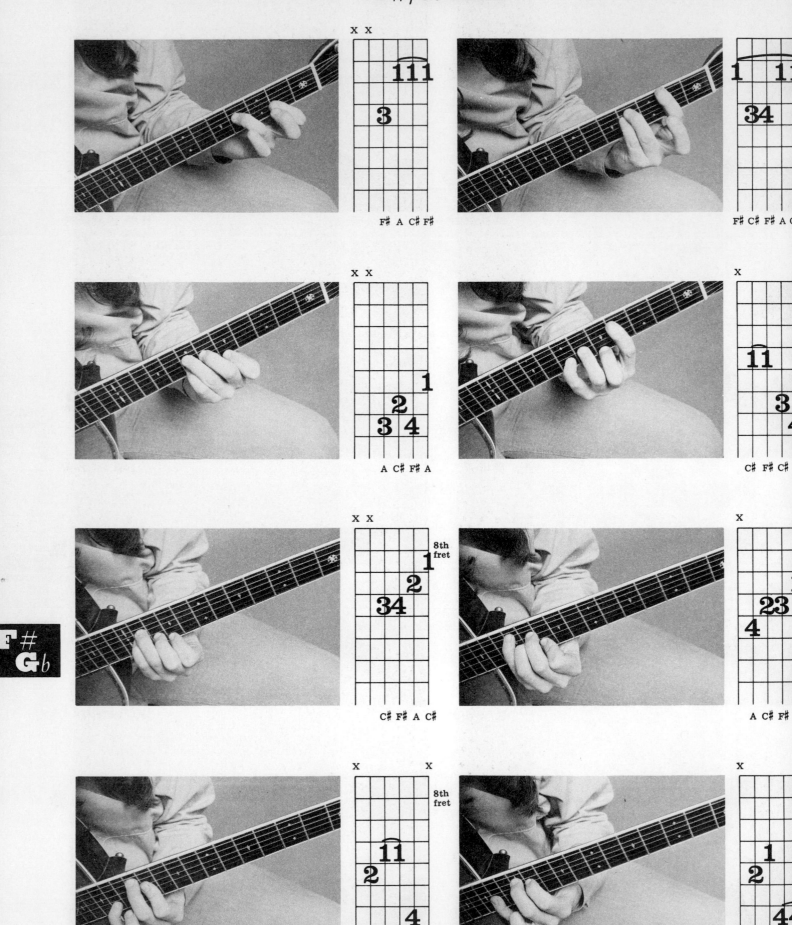

F#/Gb Major Sixth

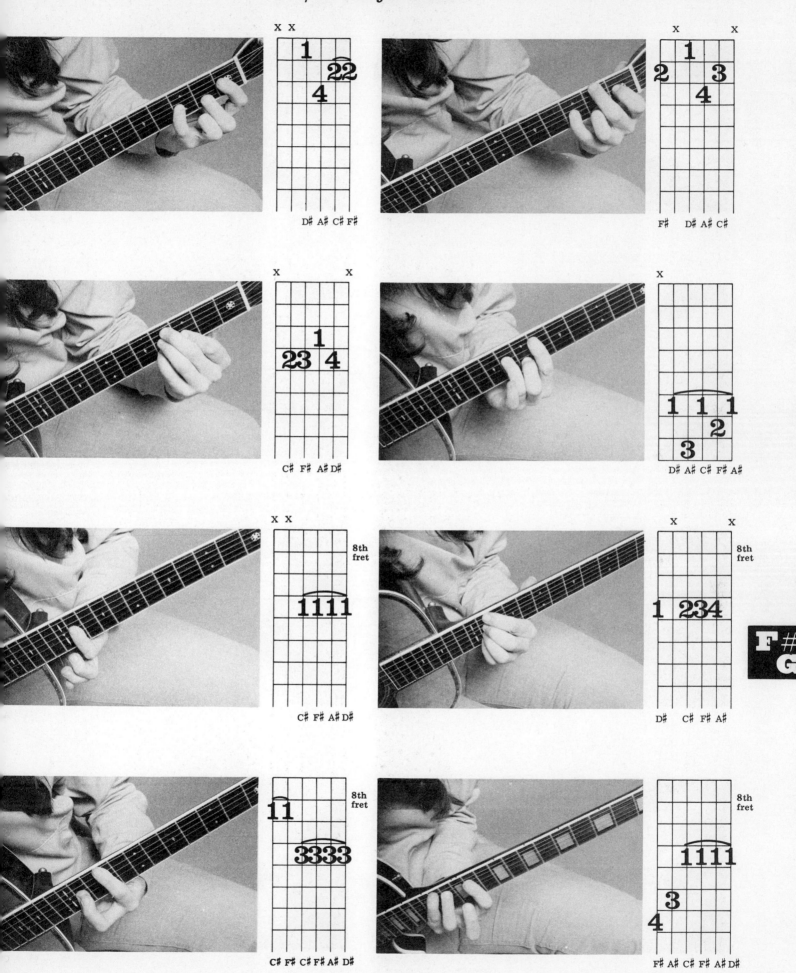

163

F#
Gb

F#/Gb Seventh

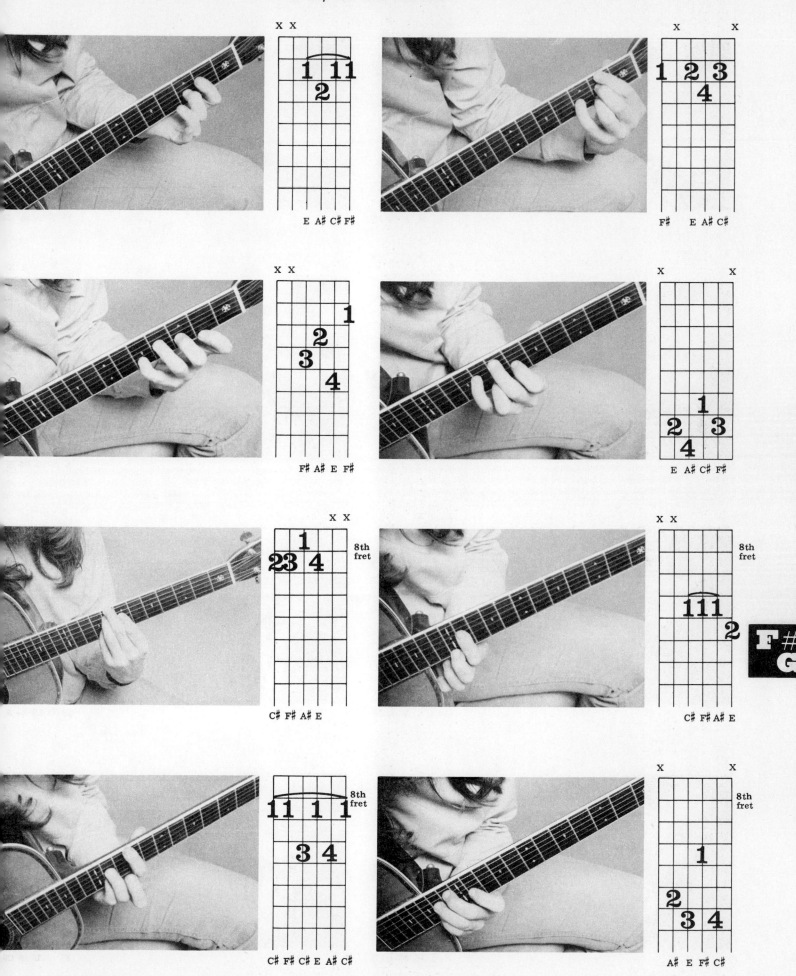

165

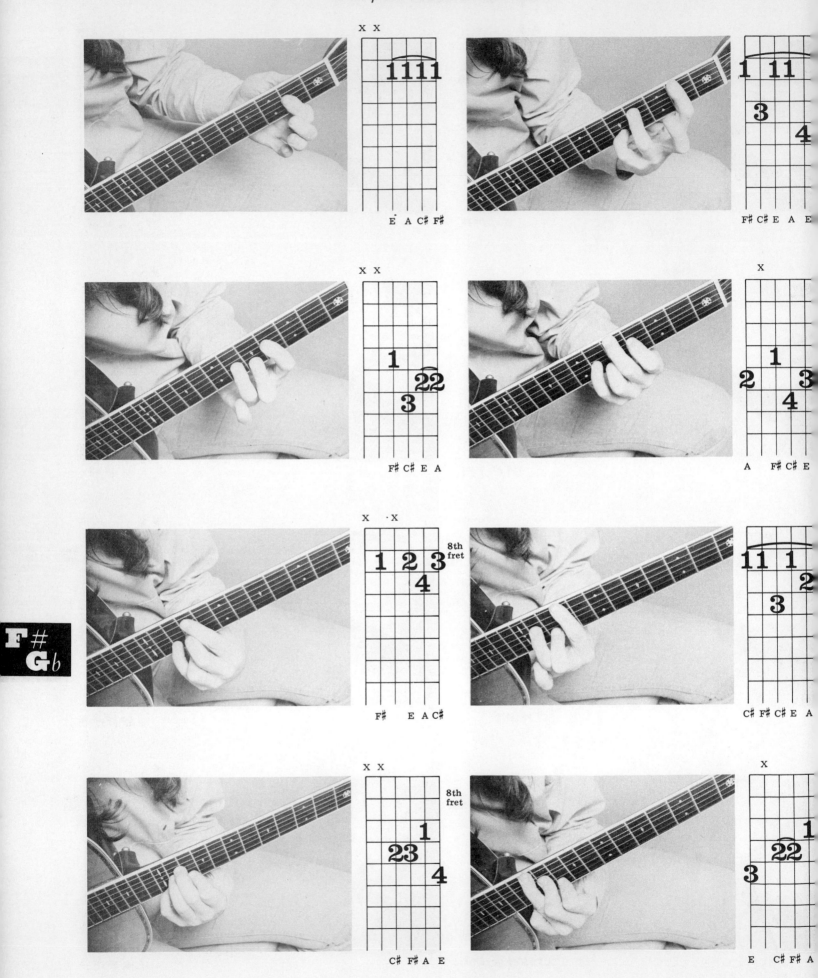

F#/G♭ Diminished

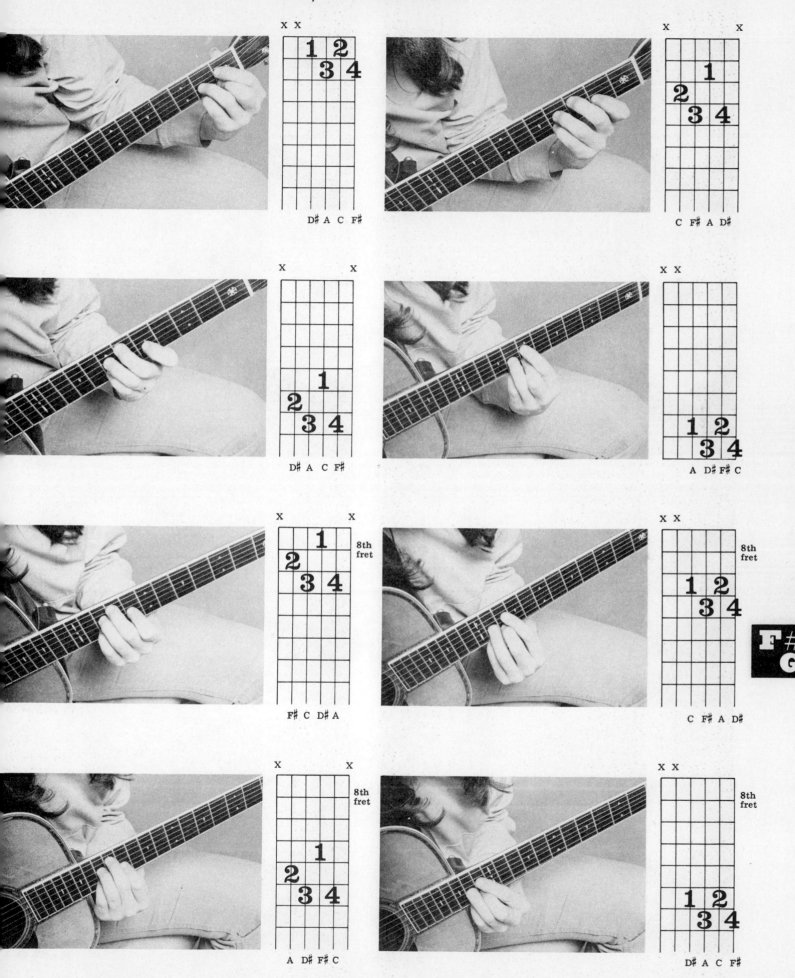

167

F#/Gb Augmented

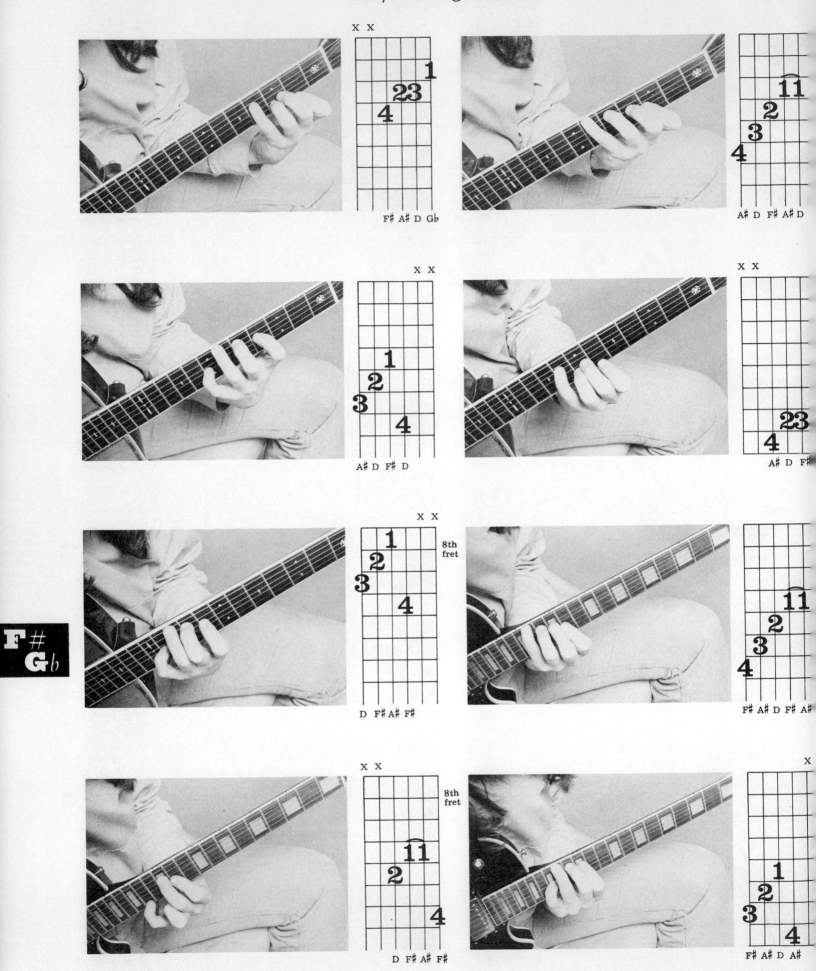

F#/G♭ Seventh Augmented Fifth

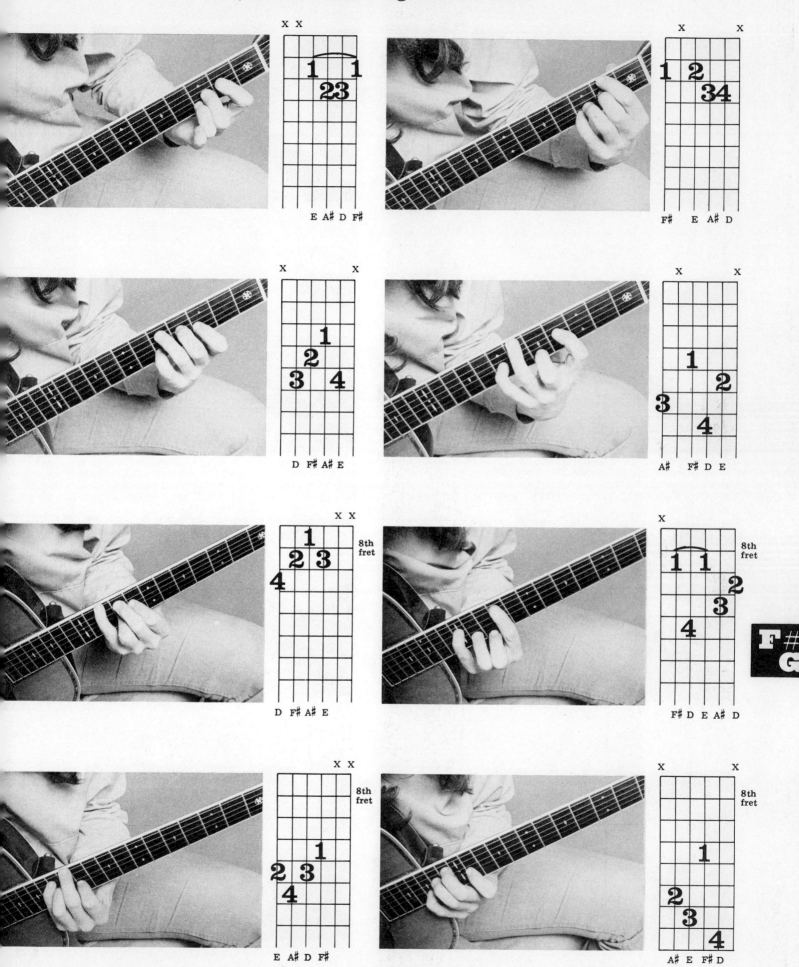

169

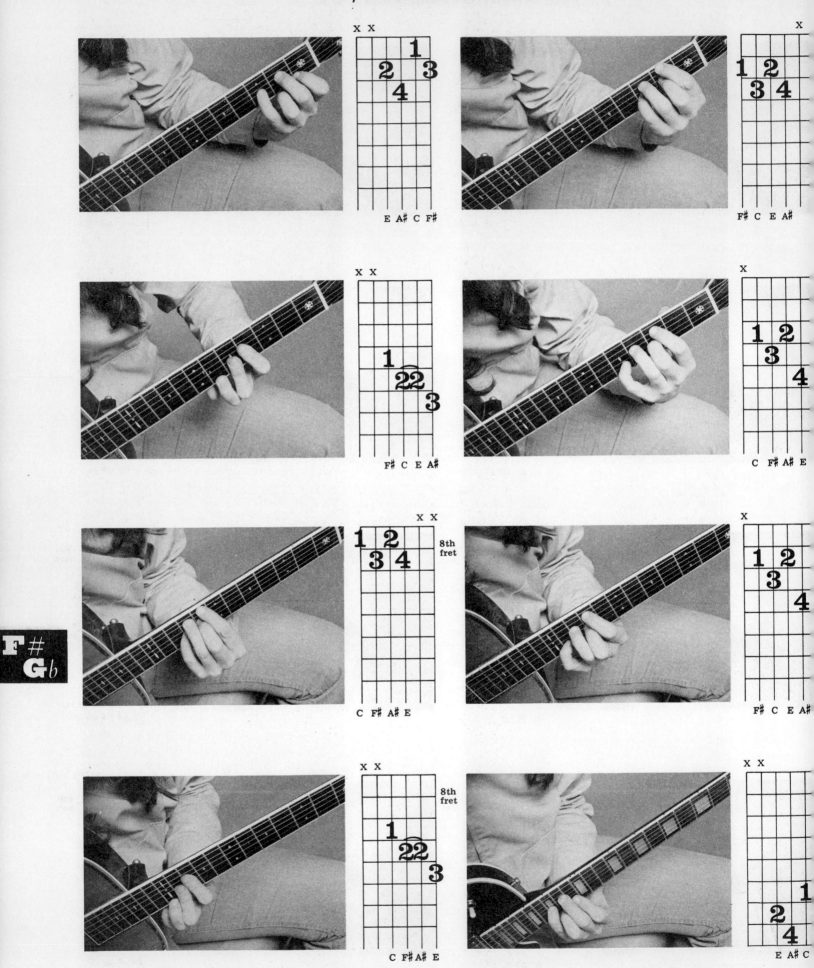

F#/Gb Seventh Flat Nine

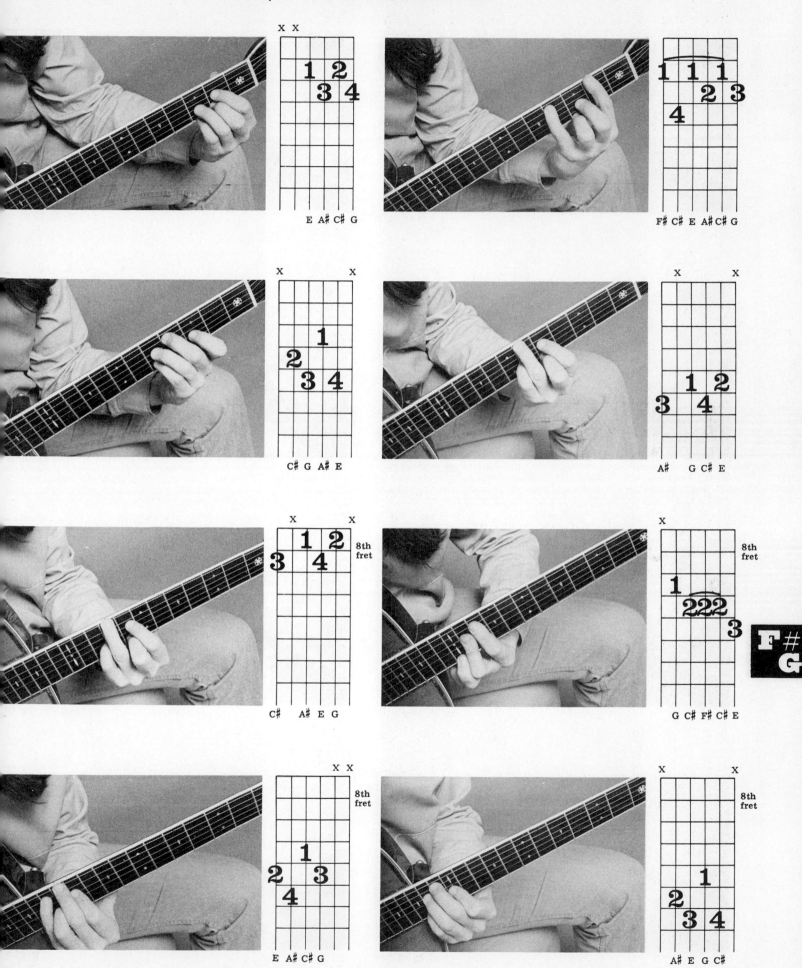

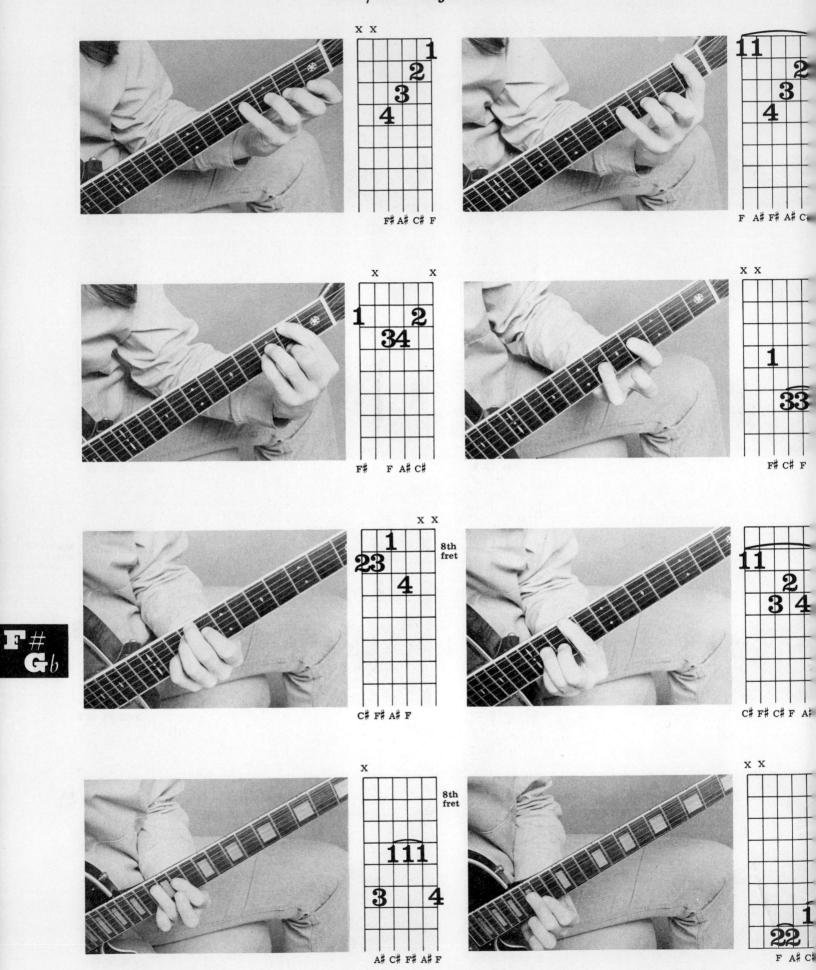

F#/Gb Minor Seventh Flat Five

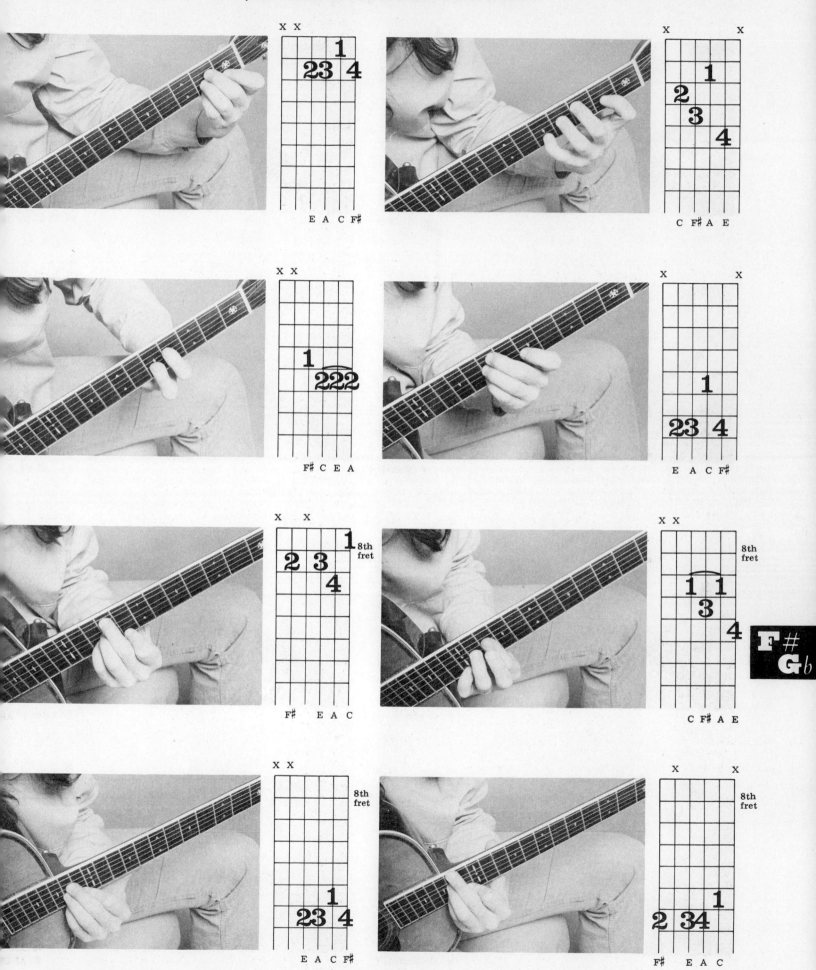

173

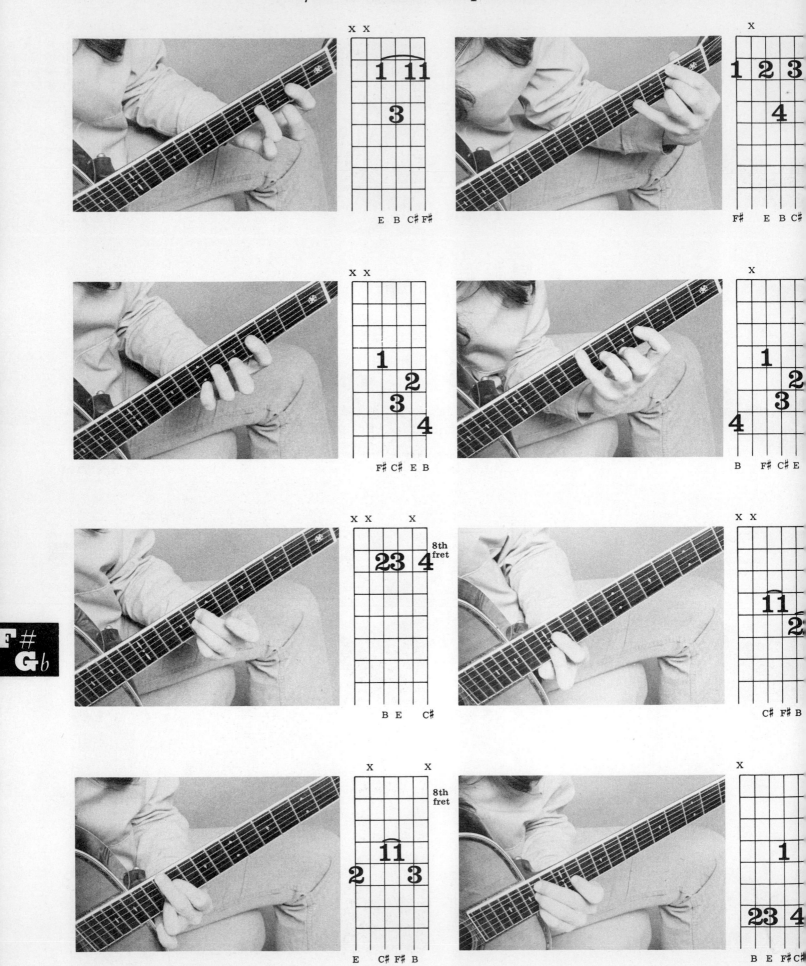

F#/Gb Ninth

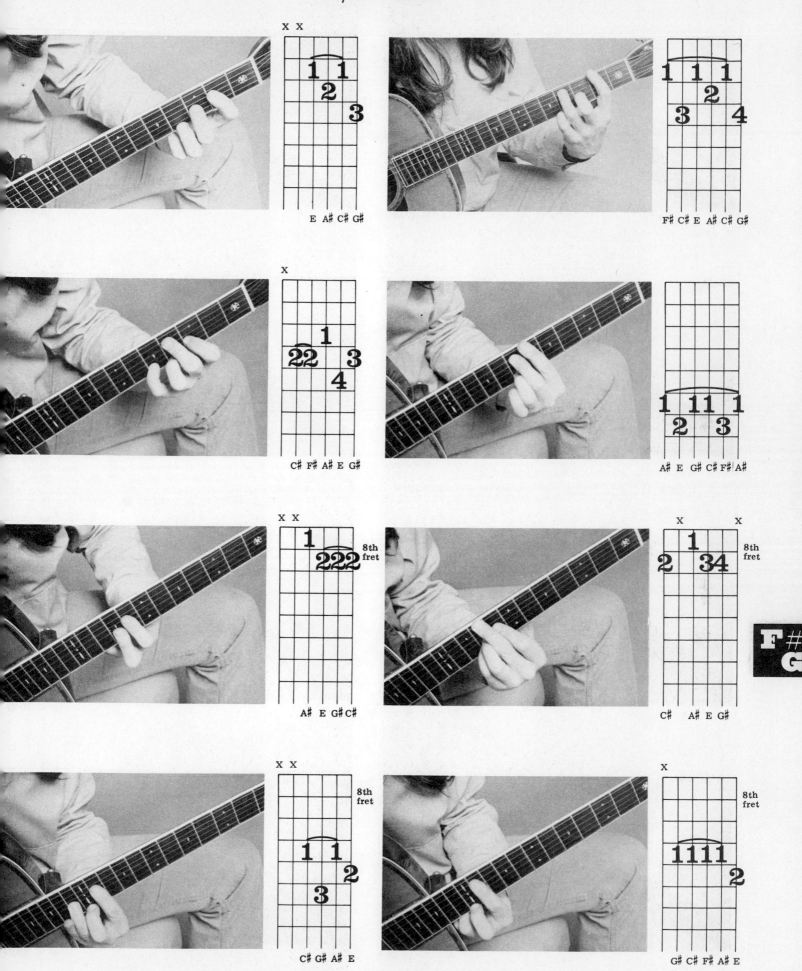

175

F#/Gb Minor Ninth

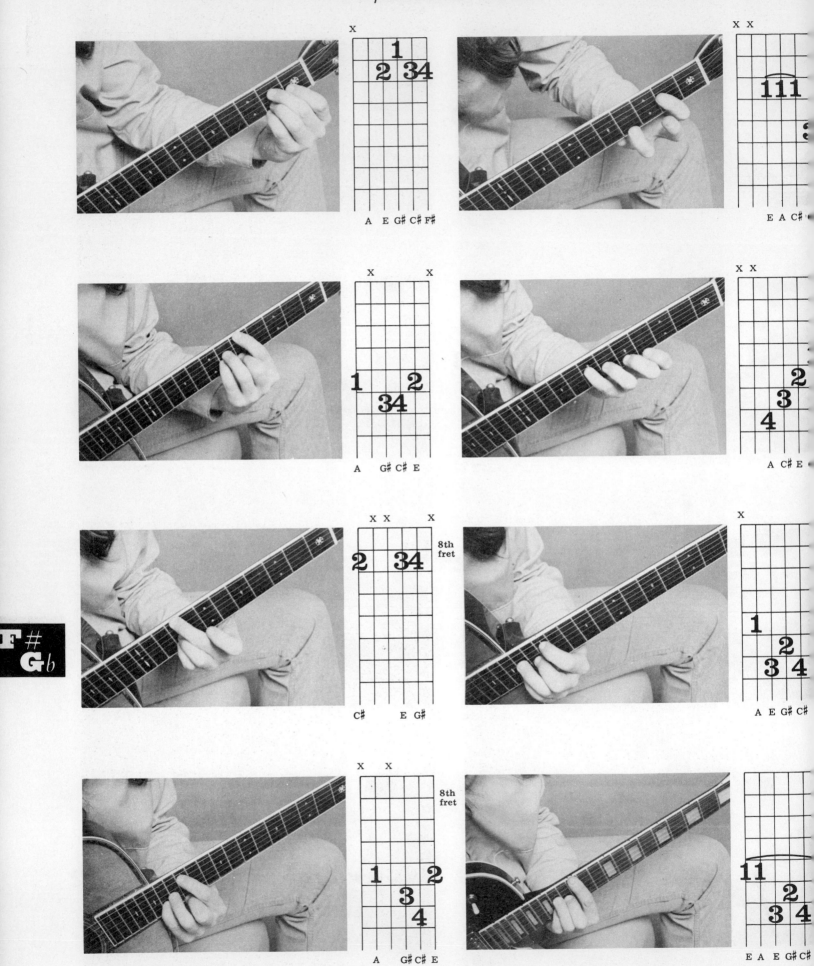

F#
Gb

176

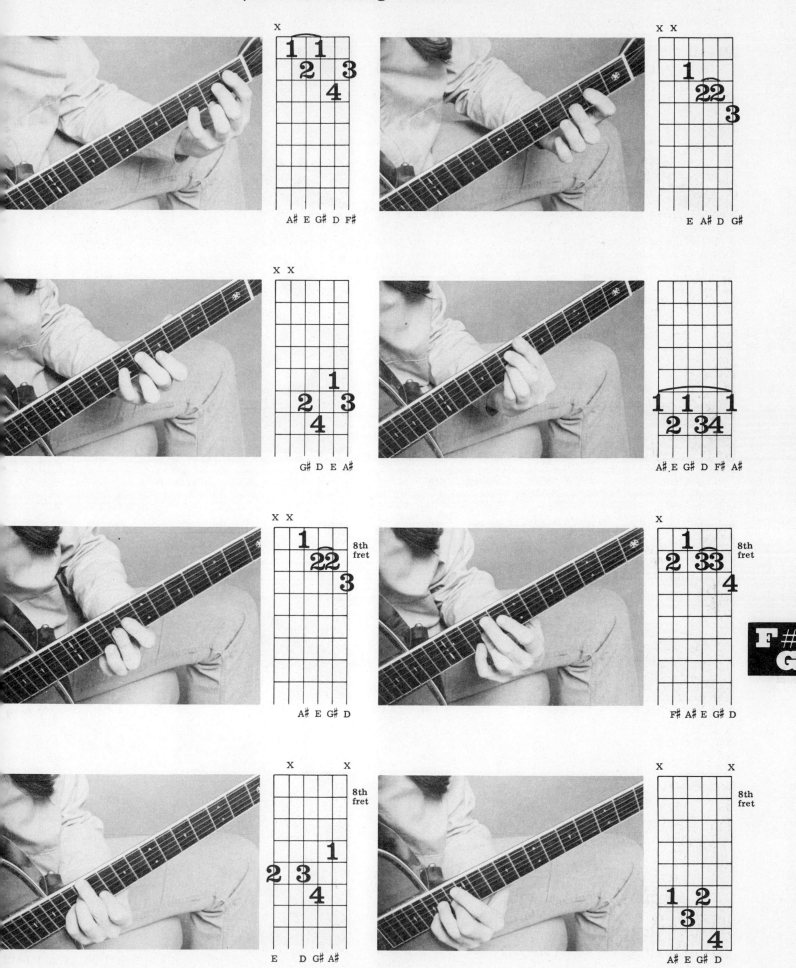

F#/Gb Ninth Flat Five

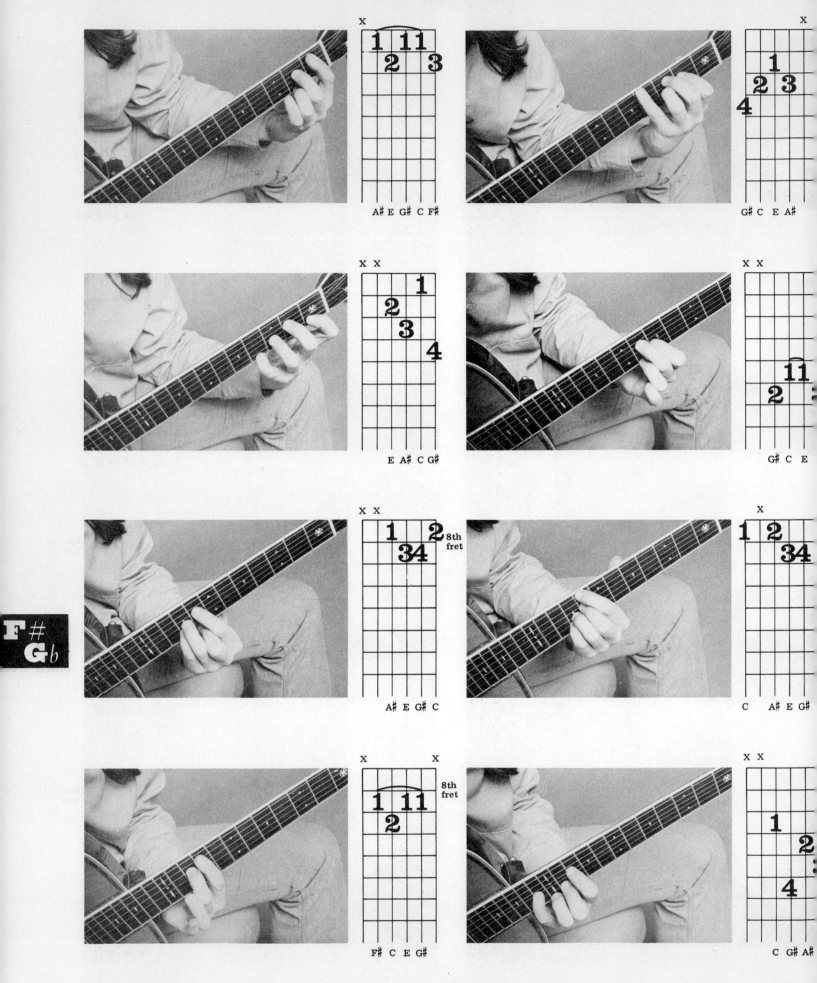

178

F#/Gb Major Ninth

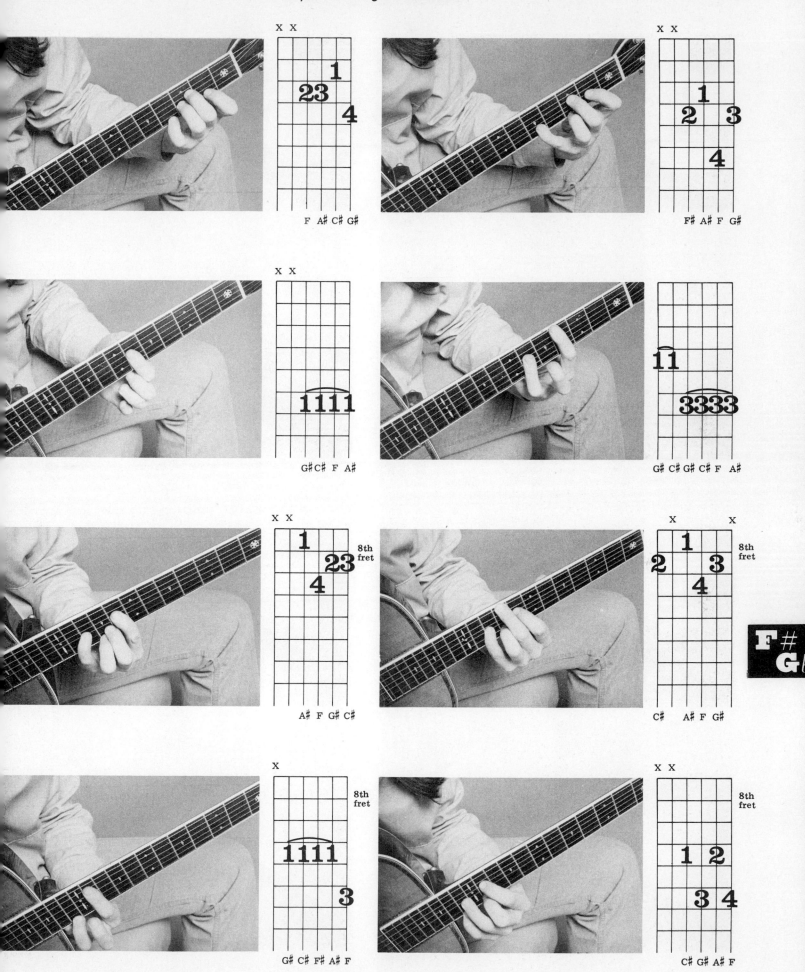

179

F#/Gb Eleventh

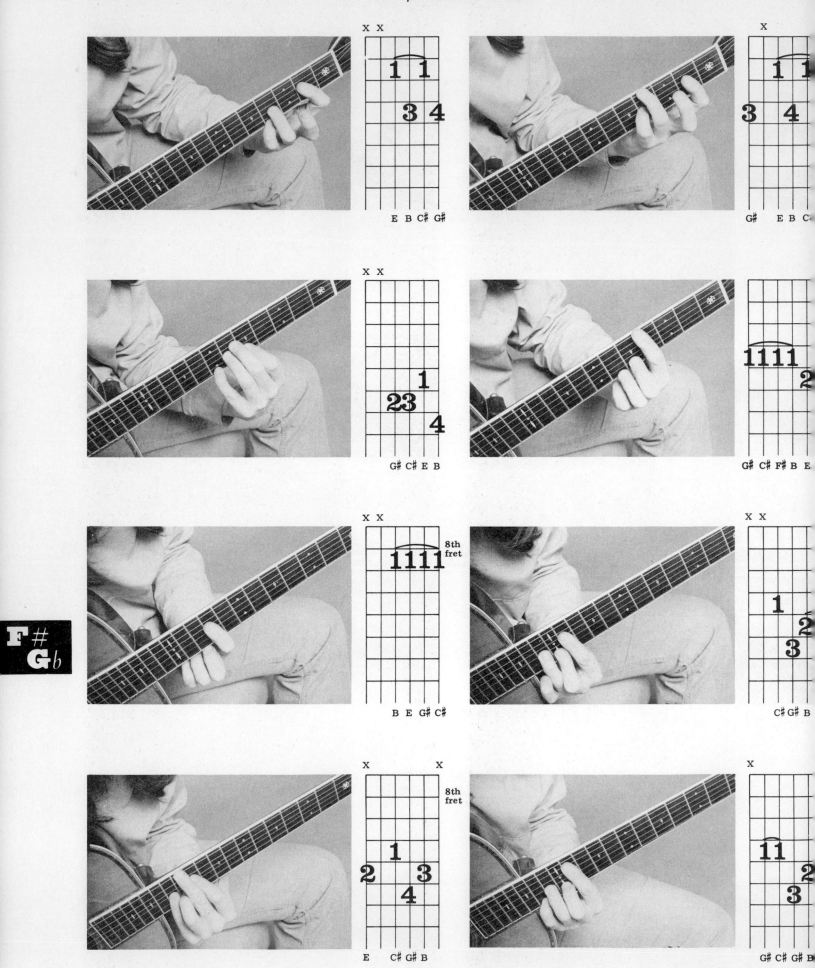

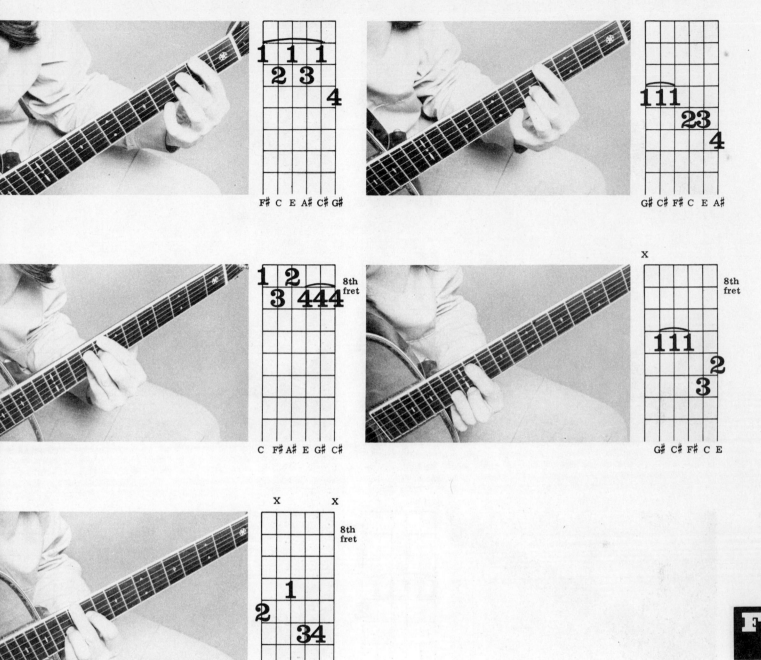

F# C E A# C# G#

G# C# F# C E A#

C F#A# E G# C#

8th fret

X

8th fret

G# C# F# C E

X   X

8th fret

E   C# G# C

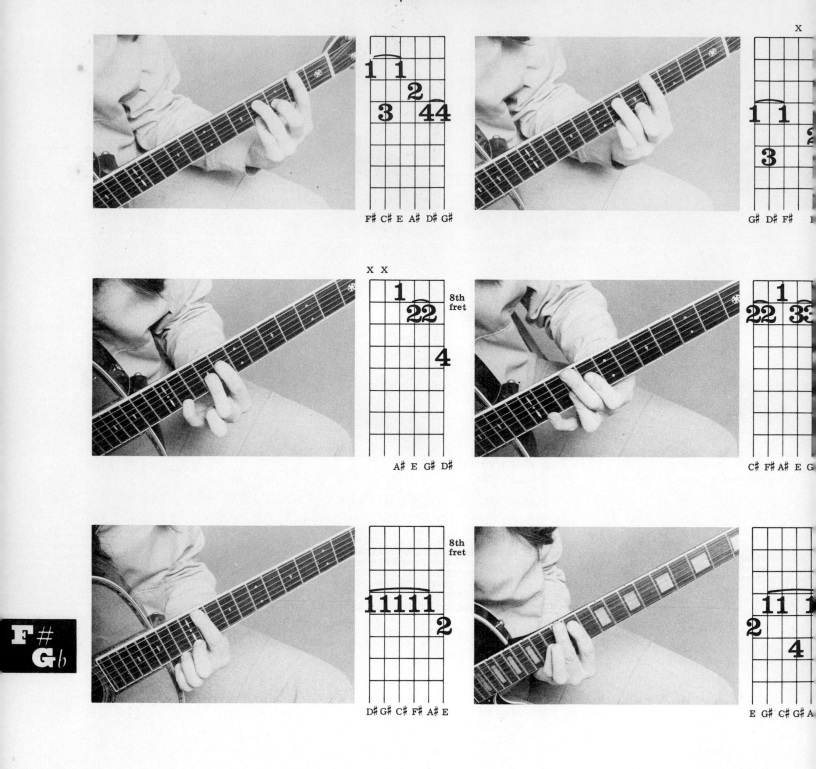

F#
Gb

F#/Gb Thirteenth Flat Nine

F#/Gb Seven Six

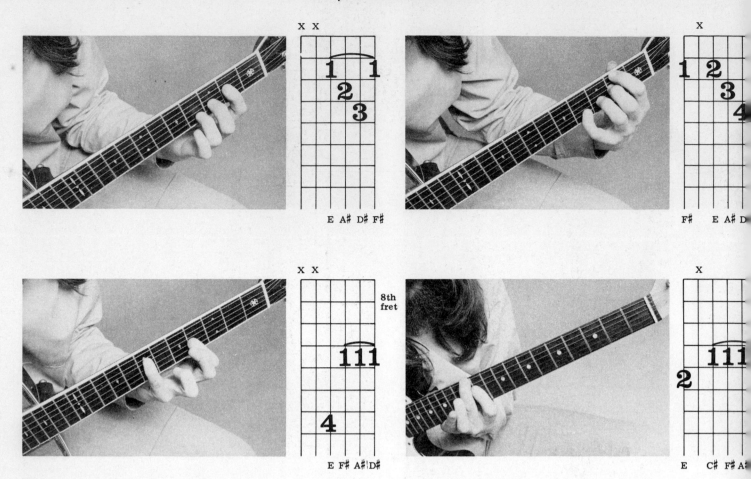

F#/Gb Nine Six

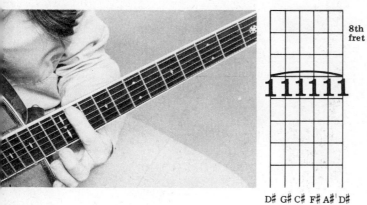

185

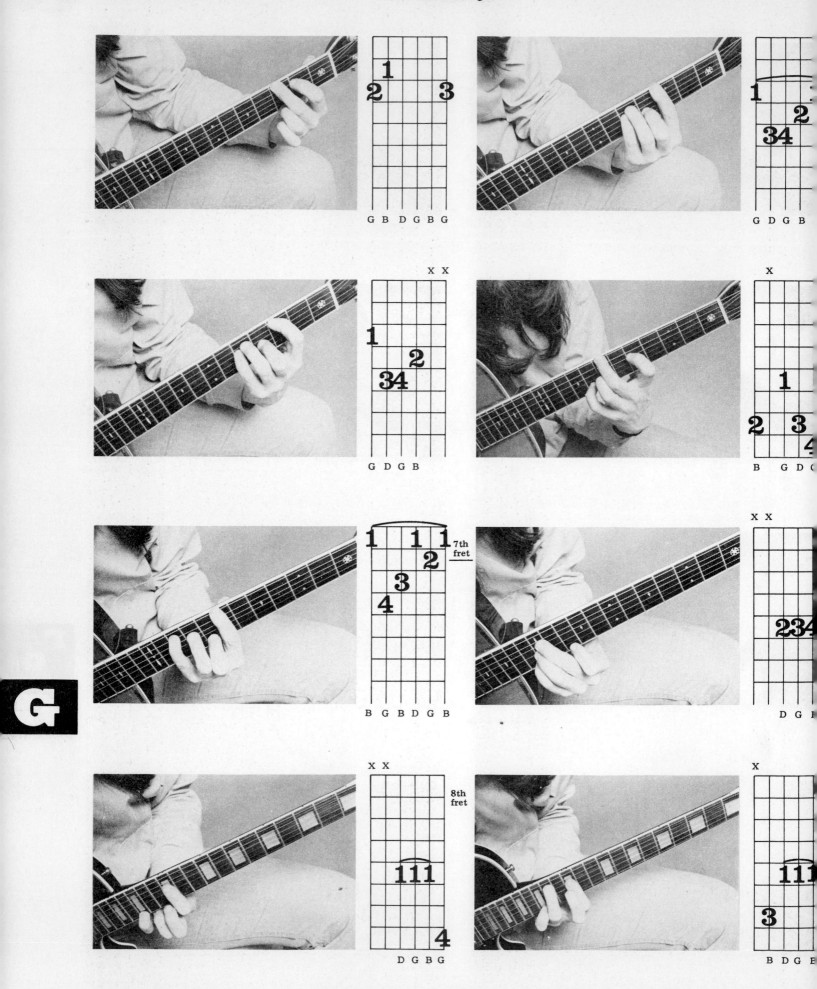

G Minor

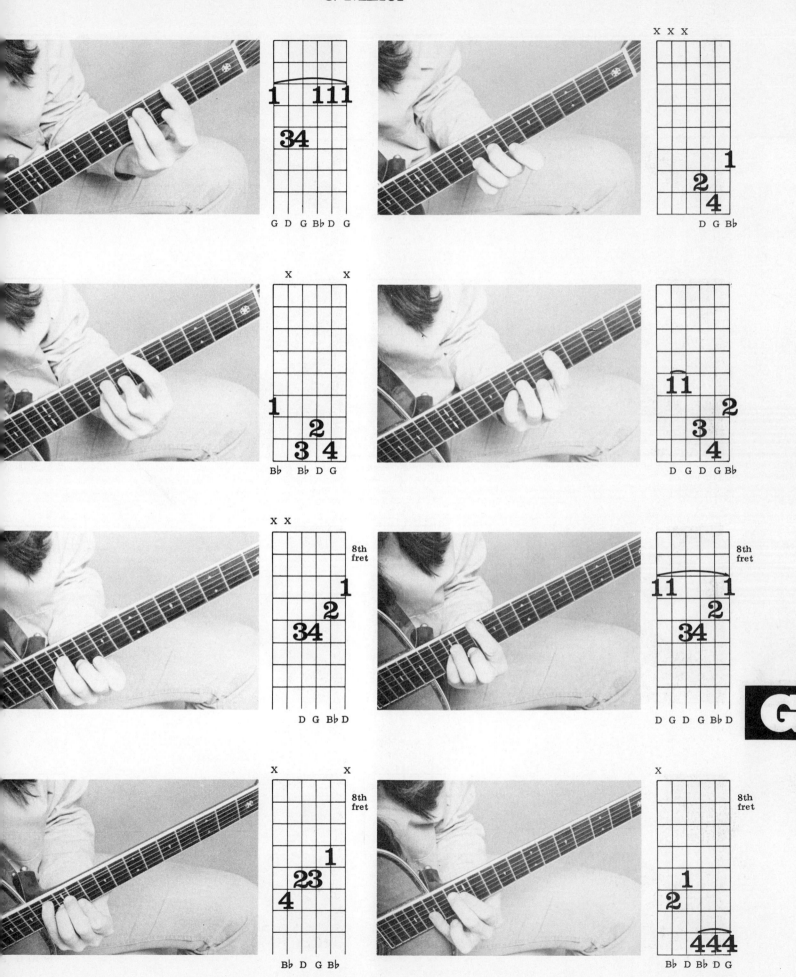

G Major Sixth

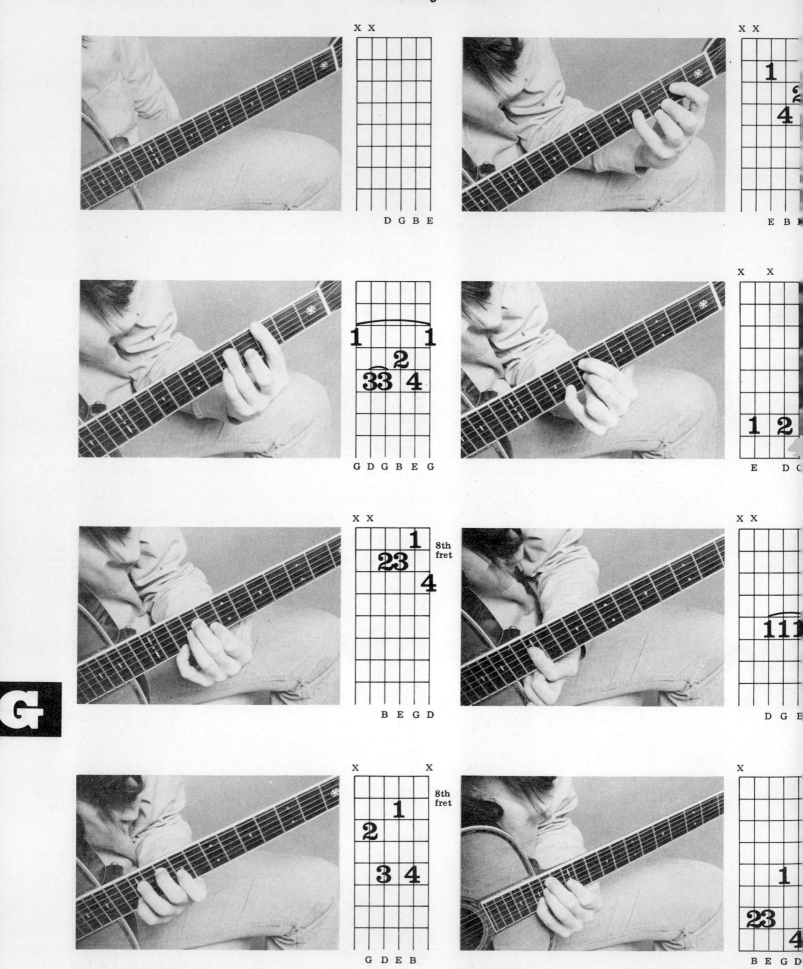

188

G Minor Sixth

189

G Seventh

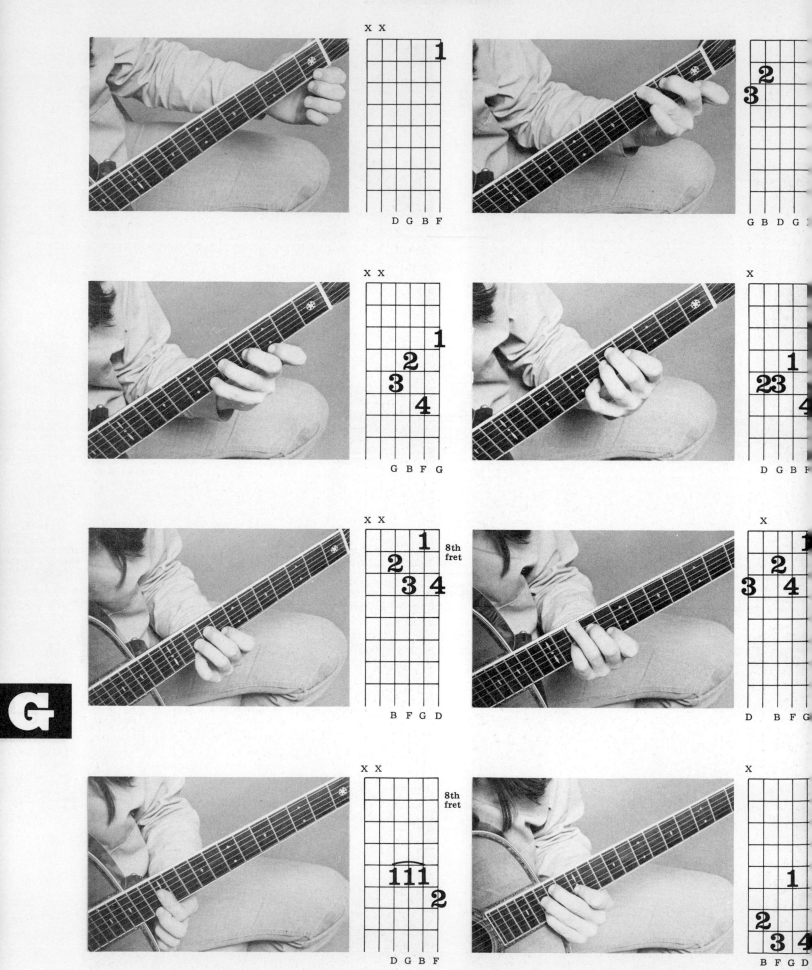

190

G Minor Seventh

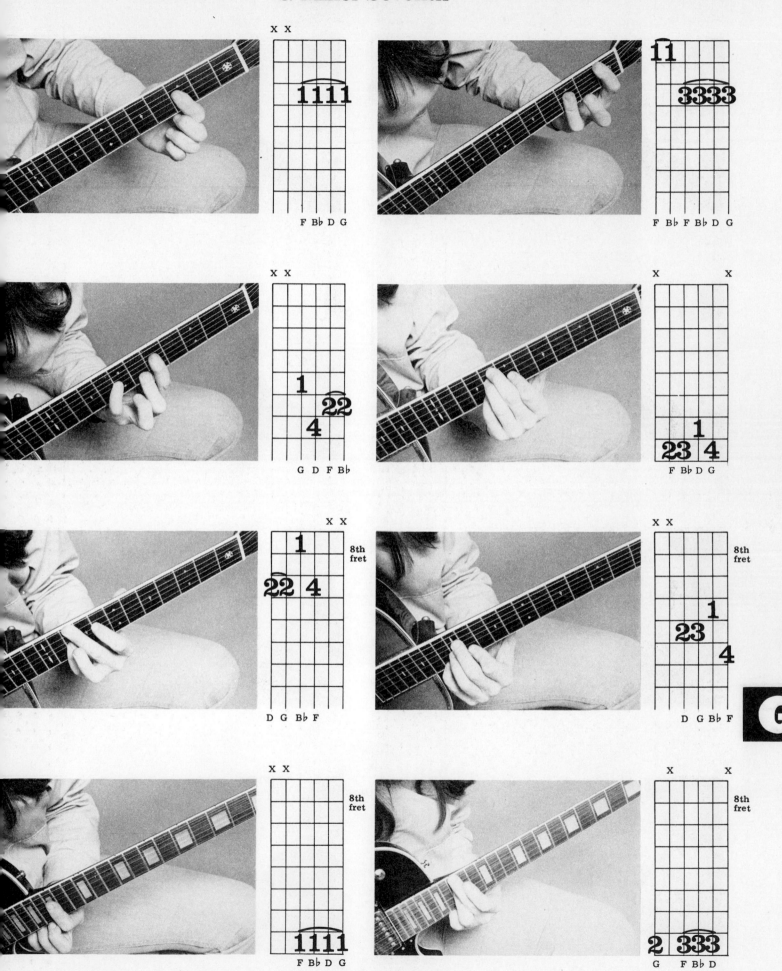

G Diminished

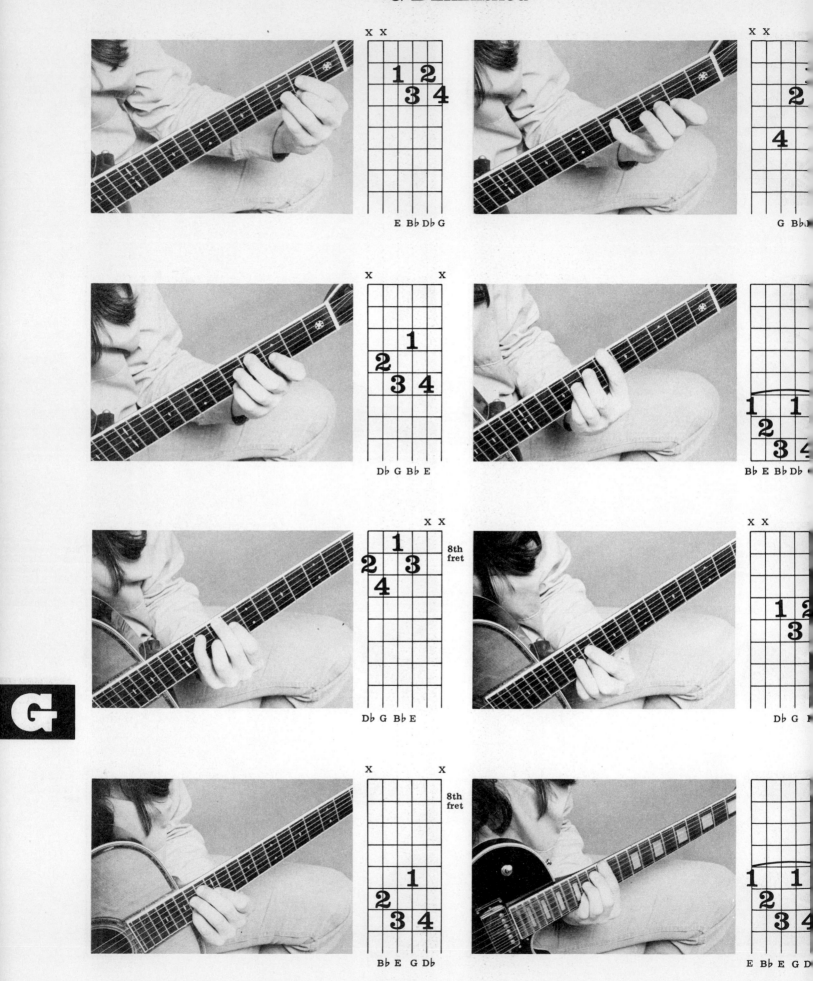

E Bb Db G

G Bb

Db G Bb E

Bb E Bb Db

8th
fret

Db G Bb E

Db G

8th
fret

Bb E G Db

E Bb E G D

192

G Augmented

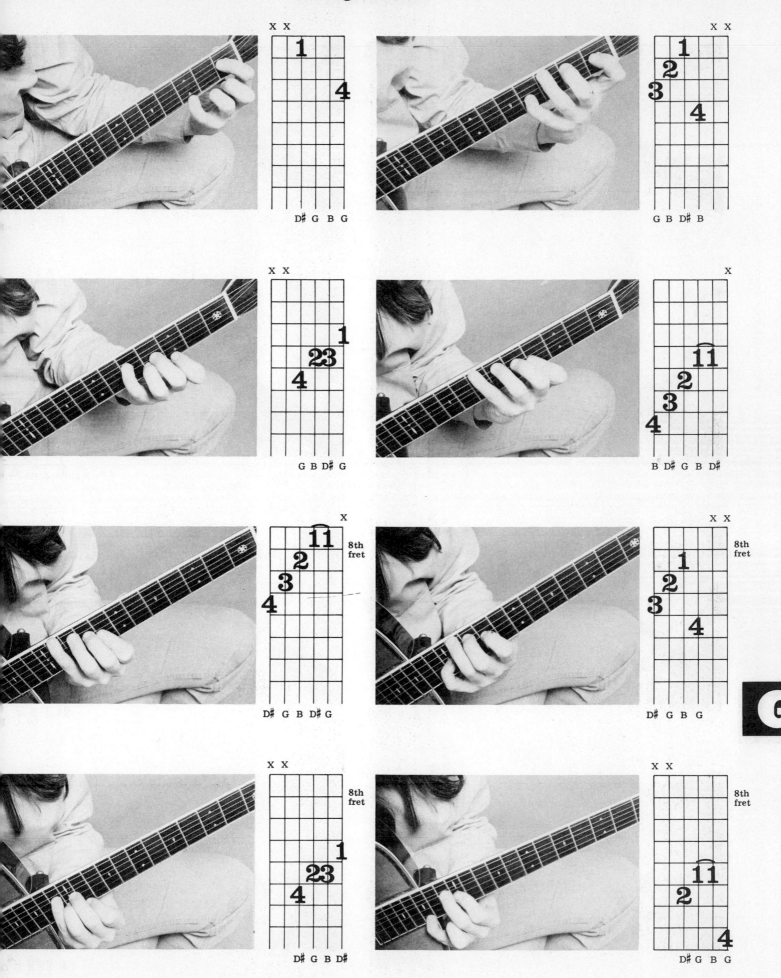

193

G Seventh Augmented Fifth

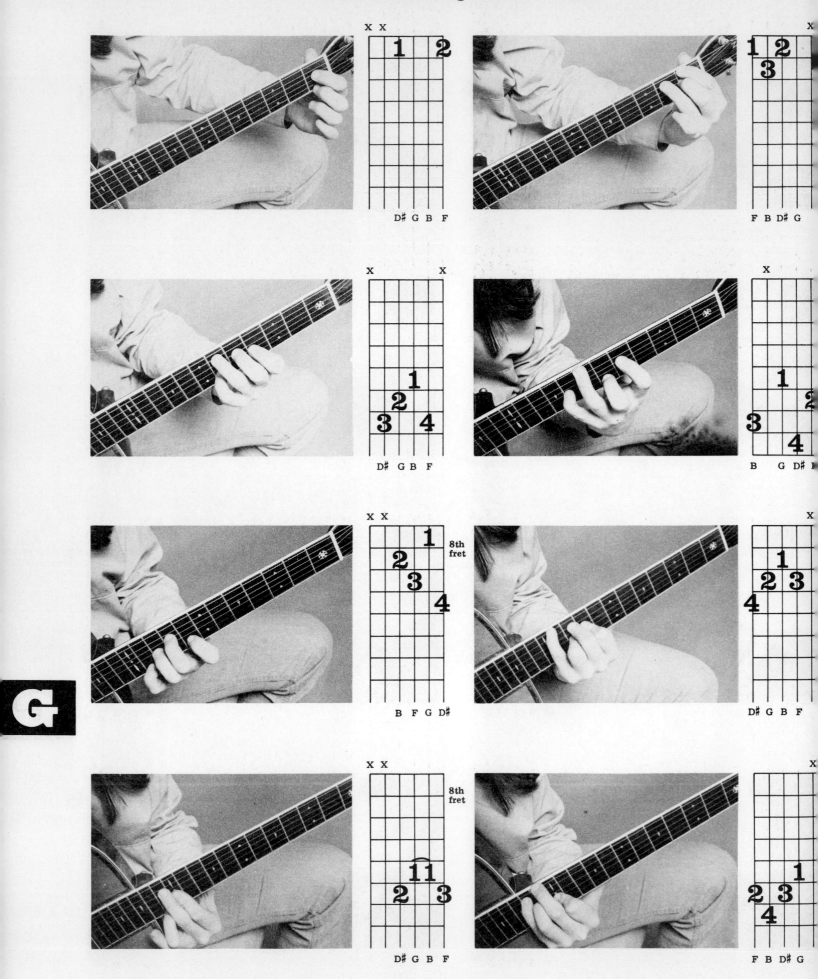

194

G Seventh Flat Five

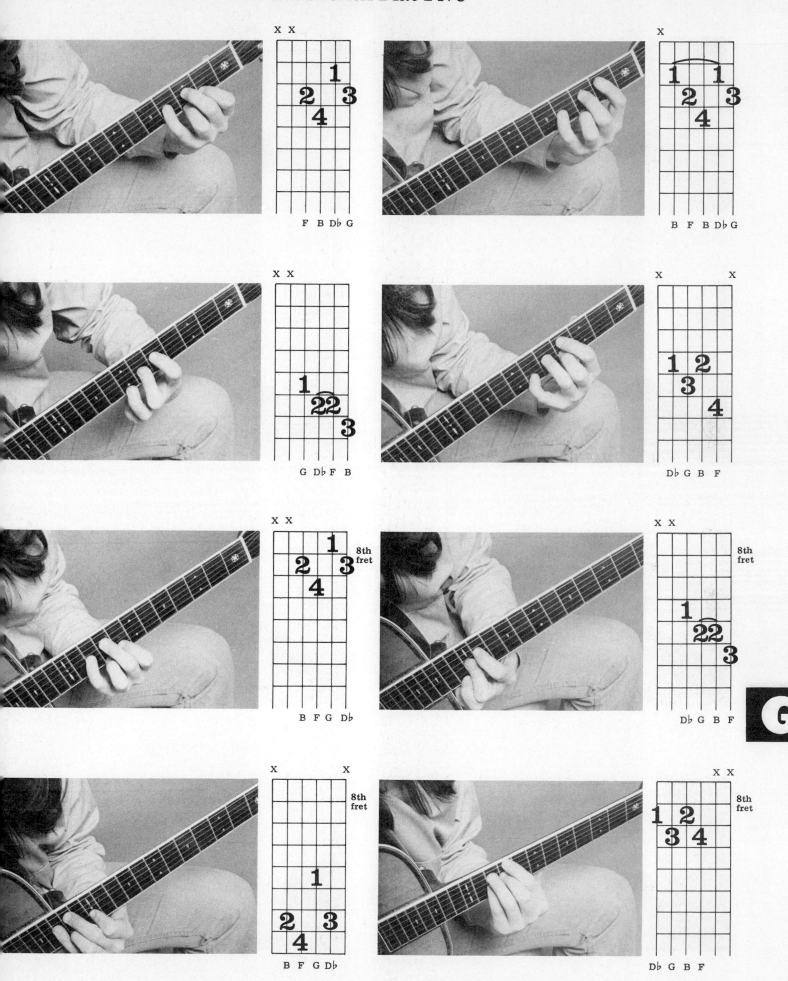

195

G Seventh Flat Nine

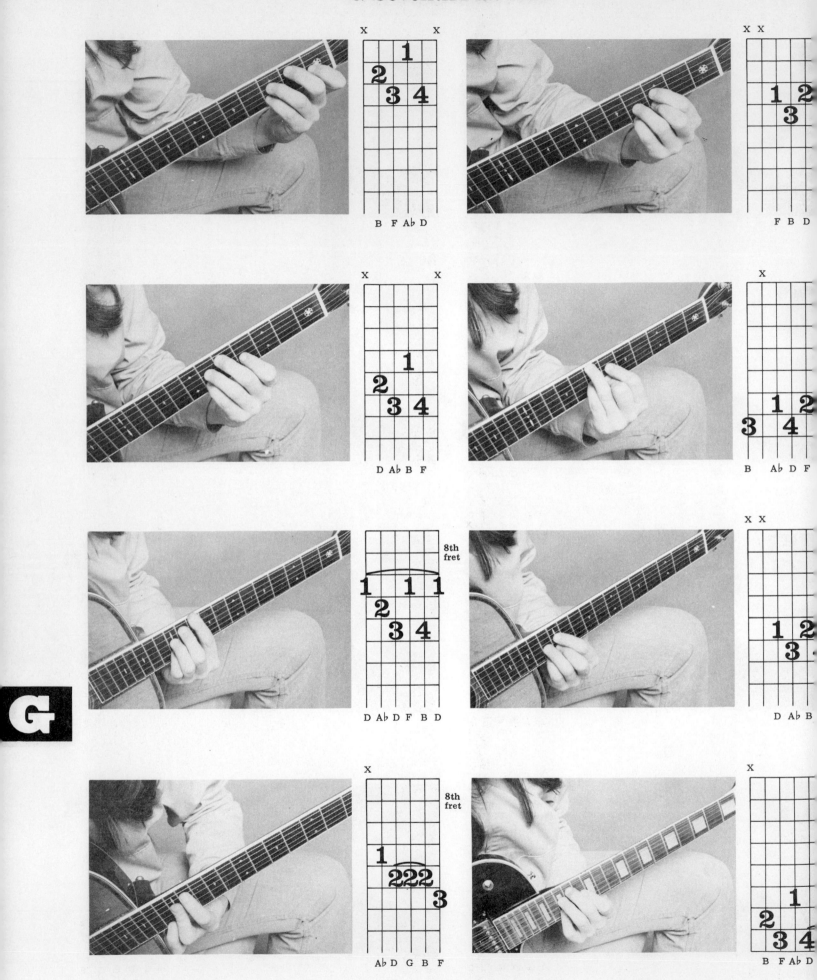

G Major Seventh

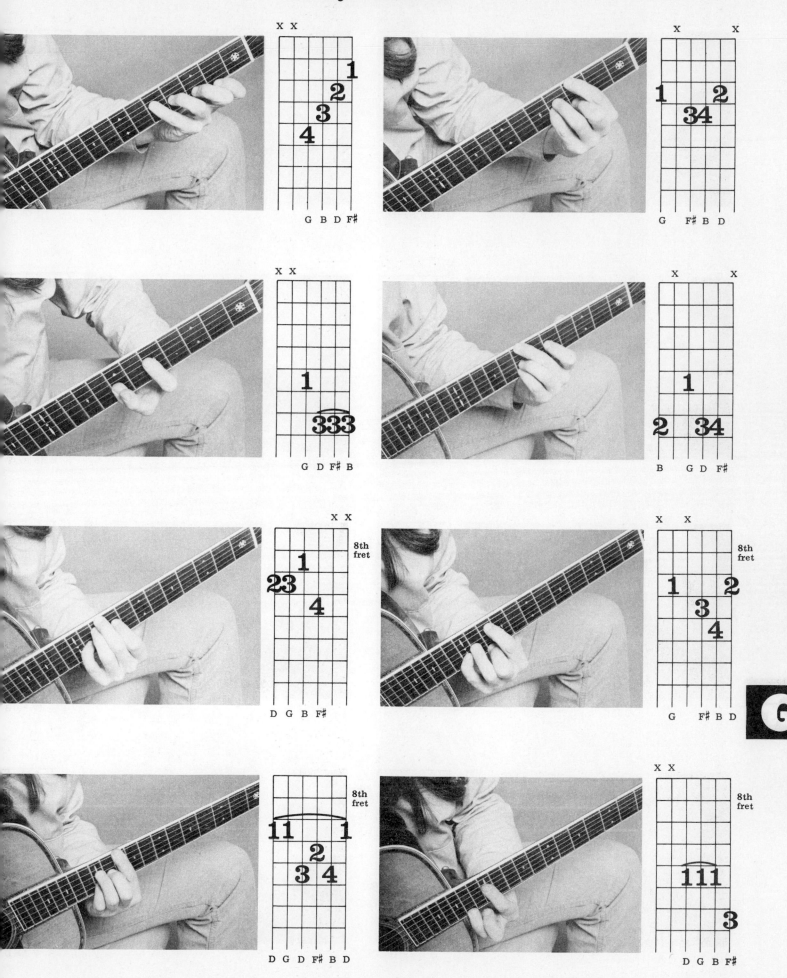

G Minor Seventh Flat Five

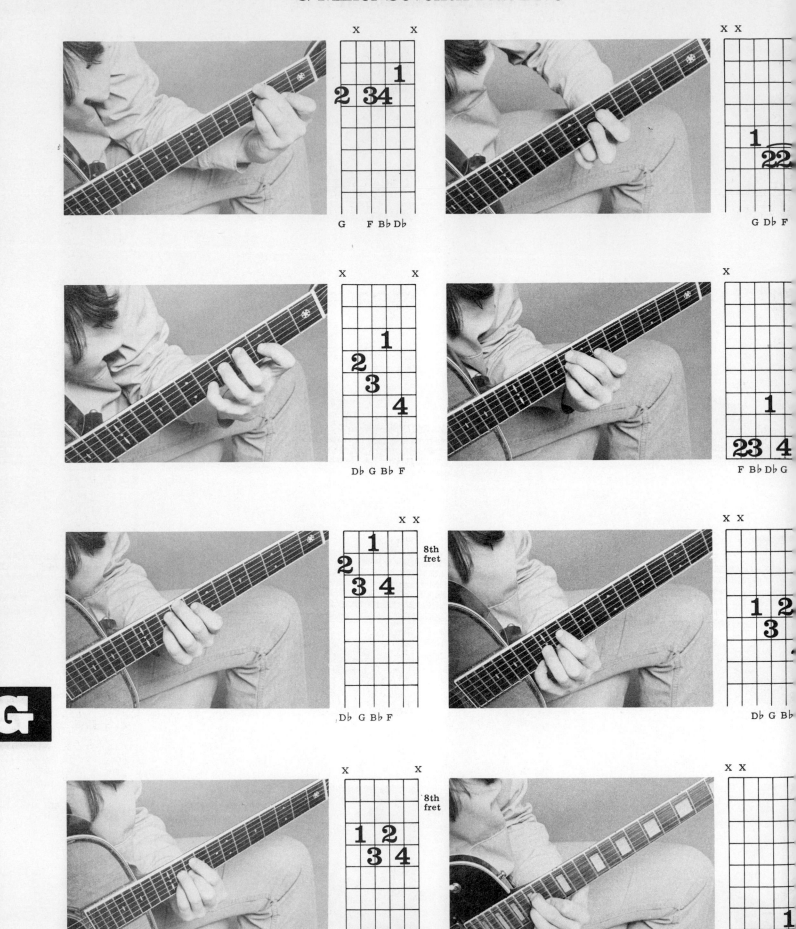

198

G Seventh Suspension Four

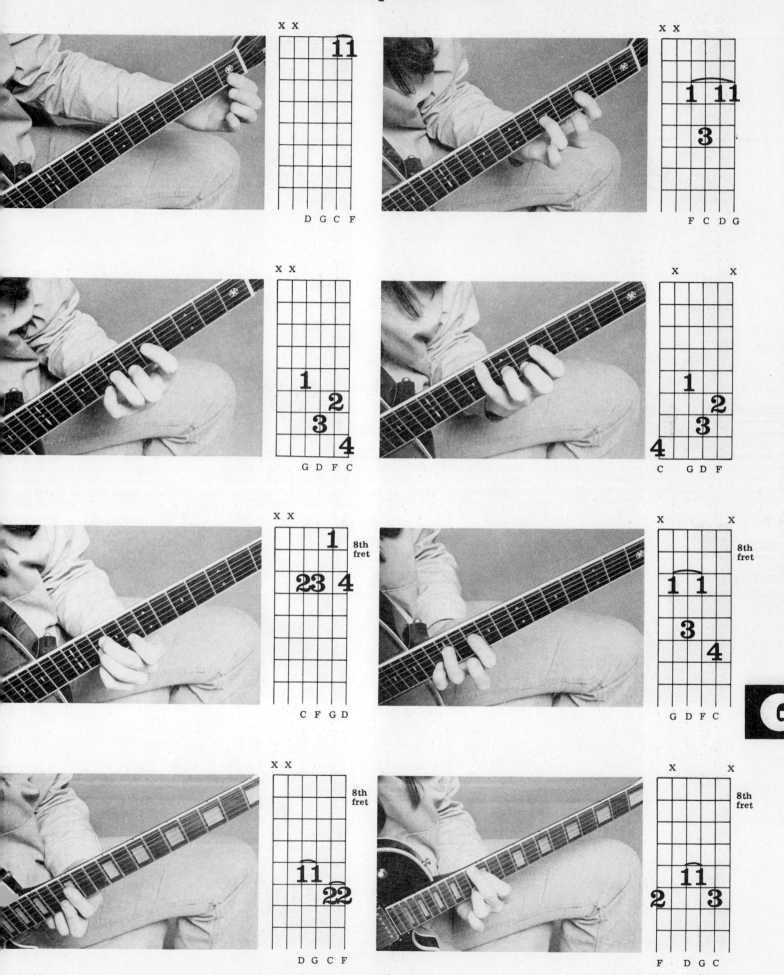

199

G Ninth

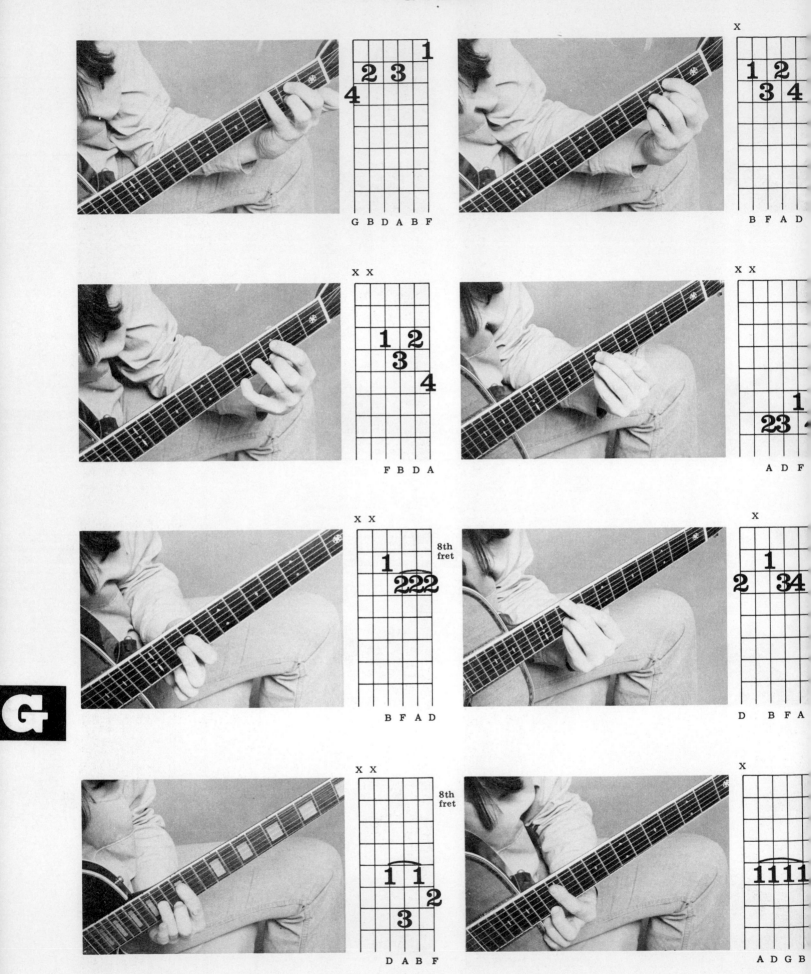

G Minor Ninth

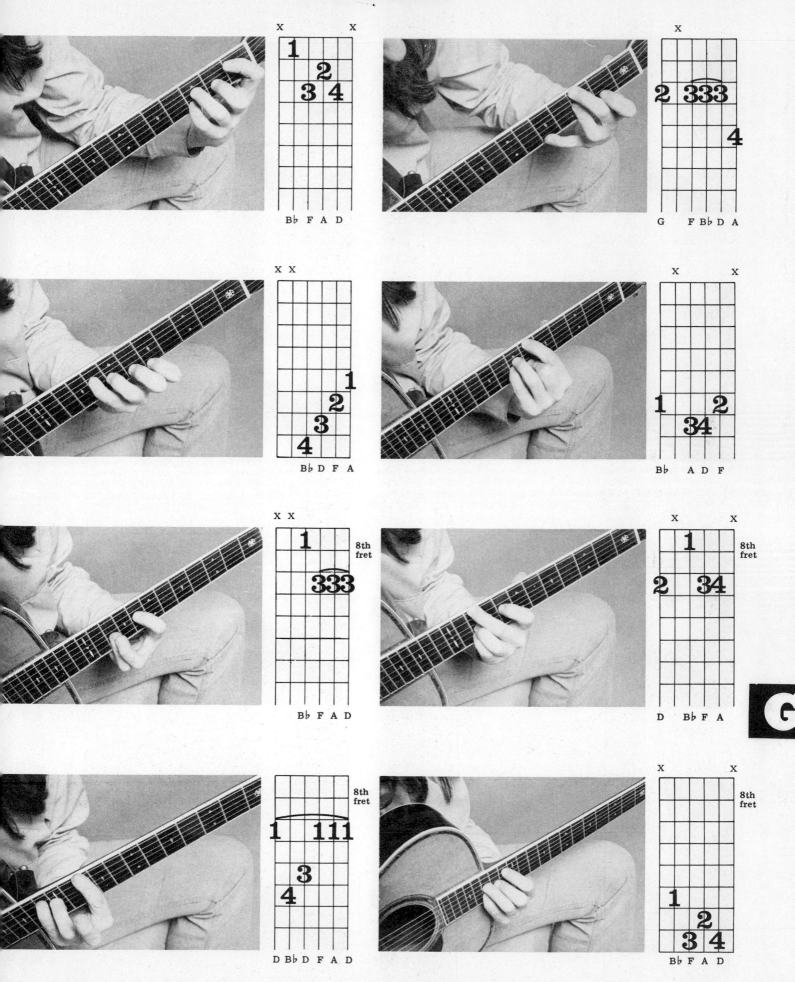

201

G Ninth Augmented Fifth

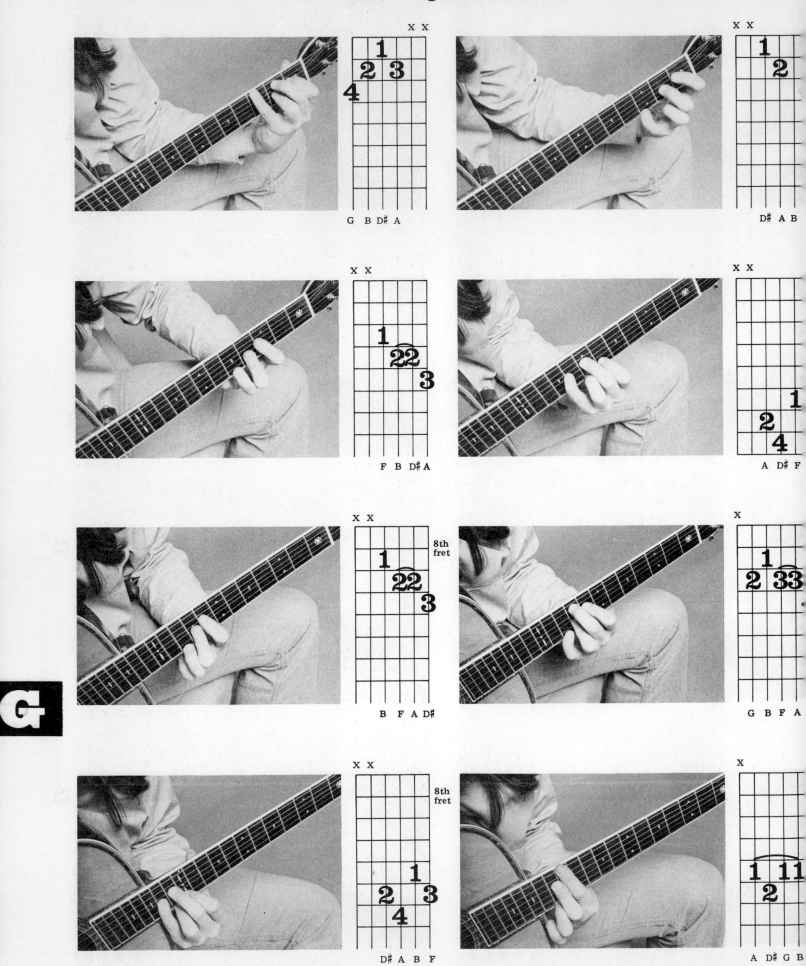

G Ninth Flat Five

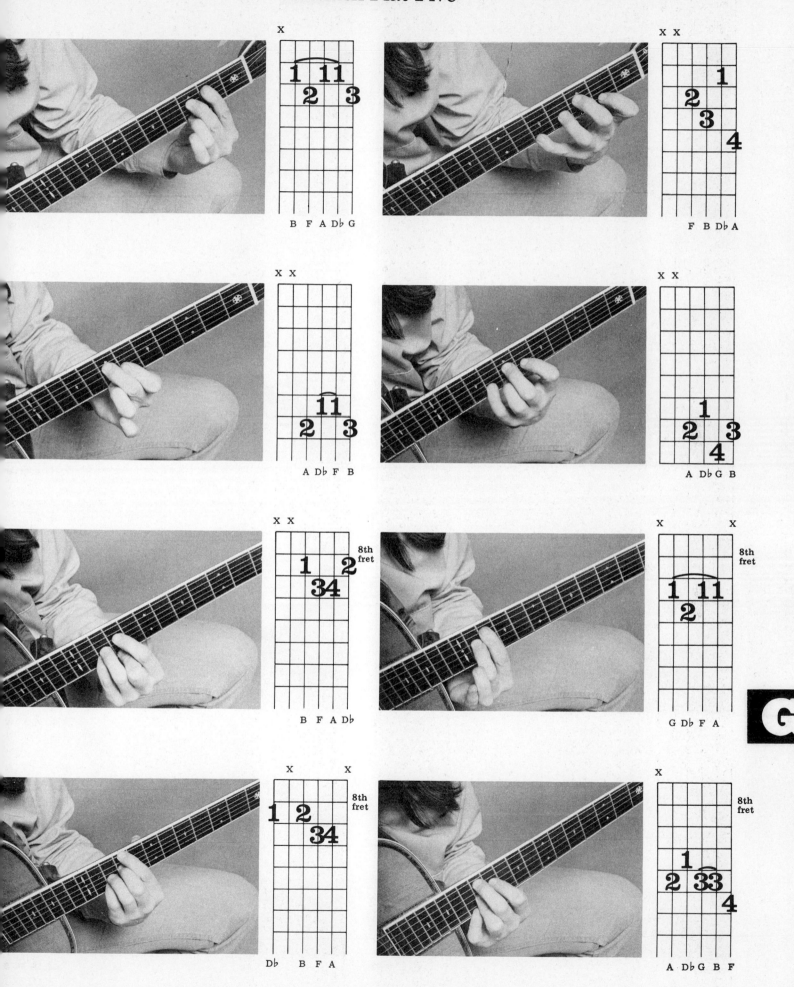

G Major Ninth

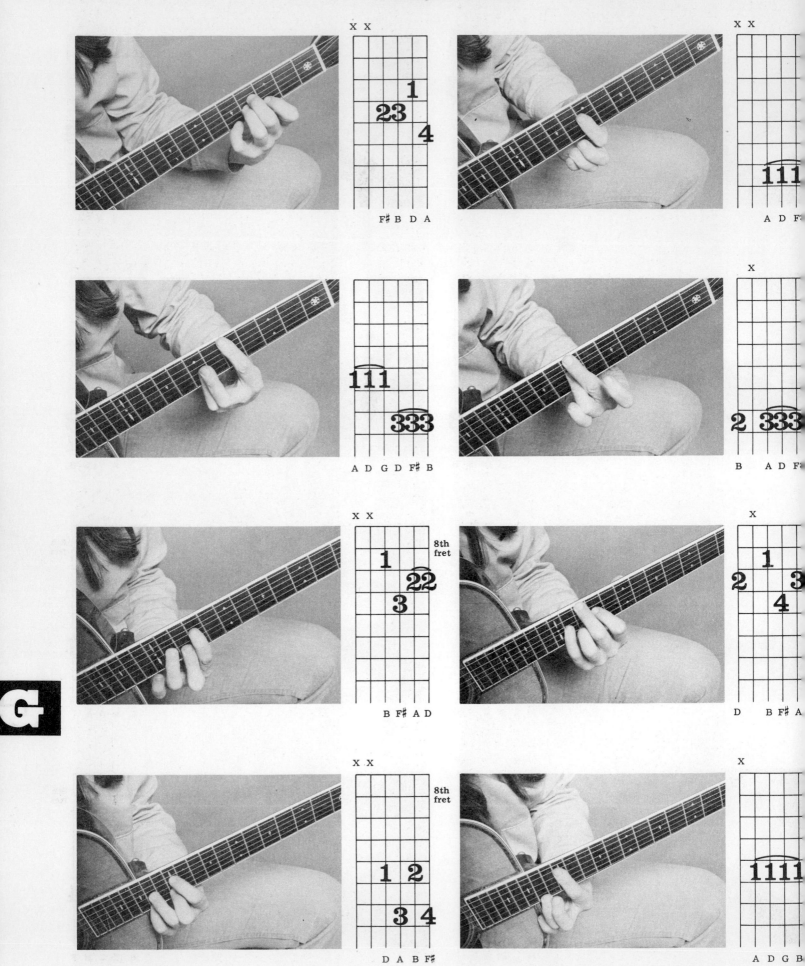

204

G Eleventh

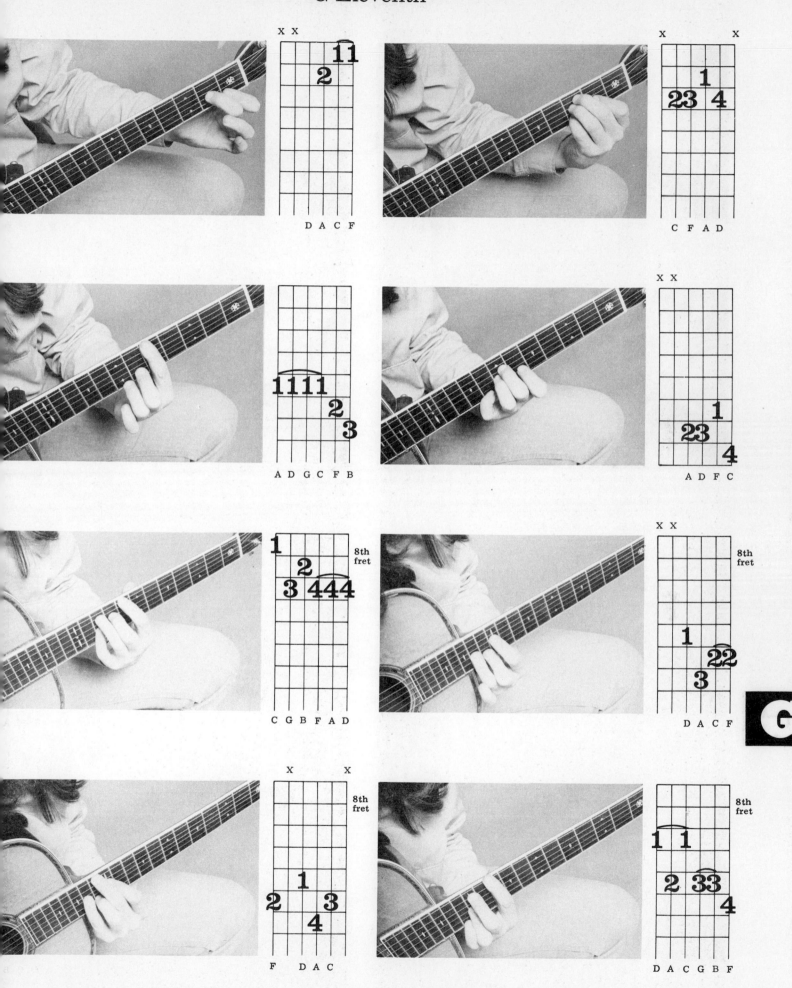

205

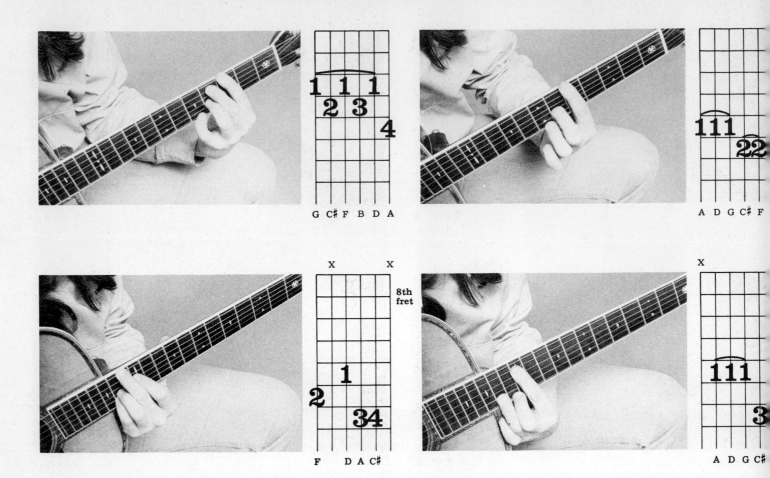

G Thirteenth

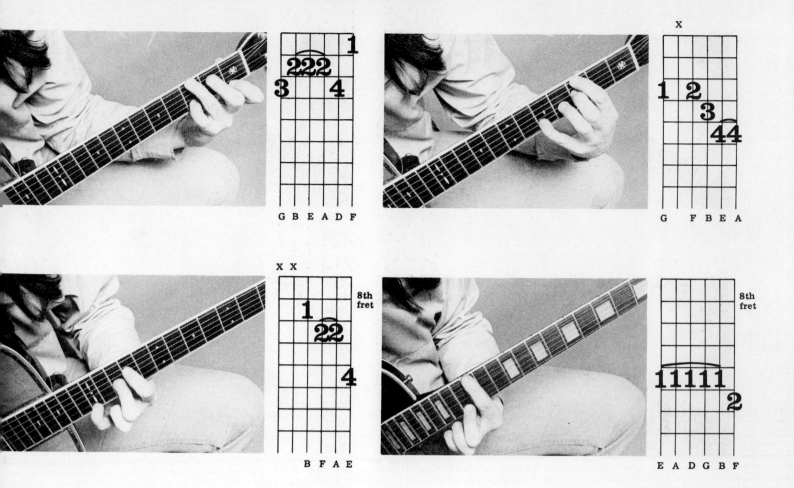

G B E A D F

X
G F B E A

X X   8th fret
B F A E

8th fret
E A D G B F

207

G Thirteenth Flat Nine

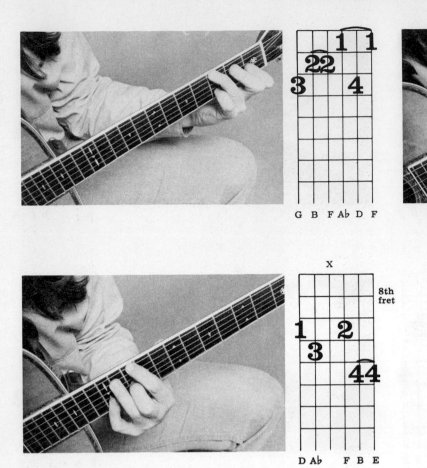

G Seven Six

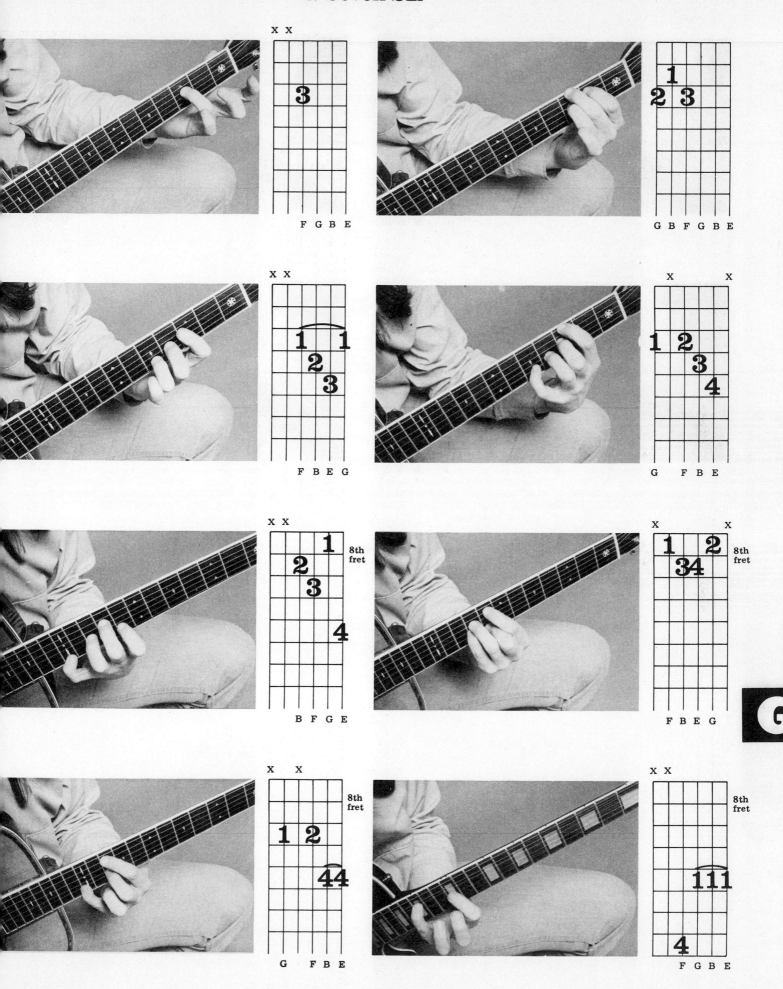

209

G Nine Six

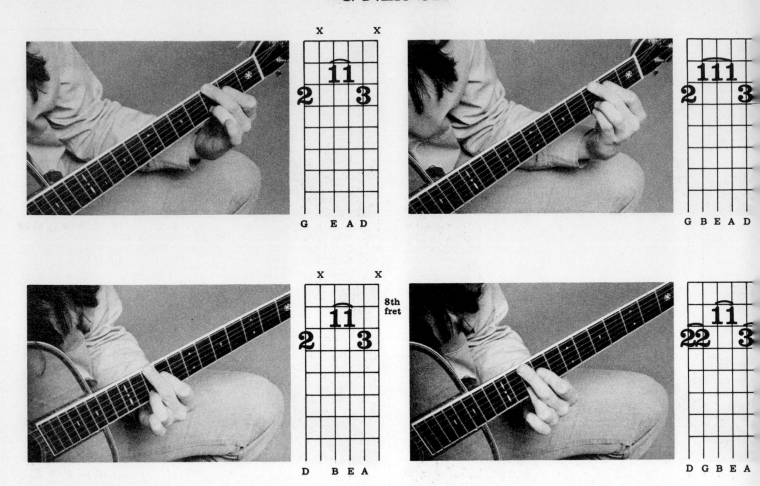

G#/A♭ Major

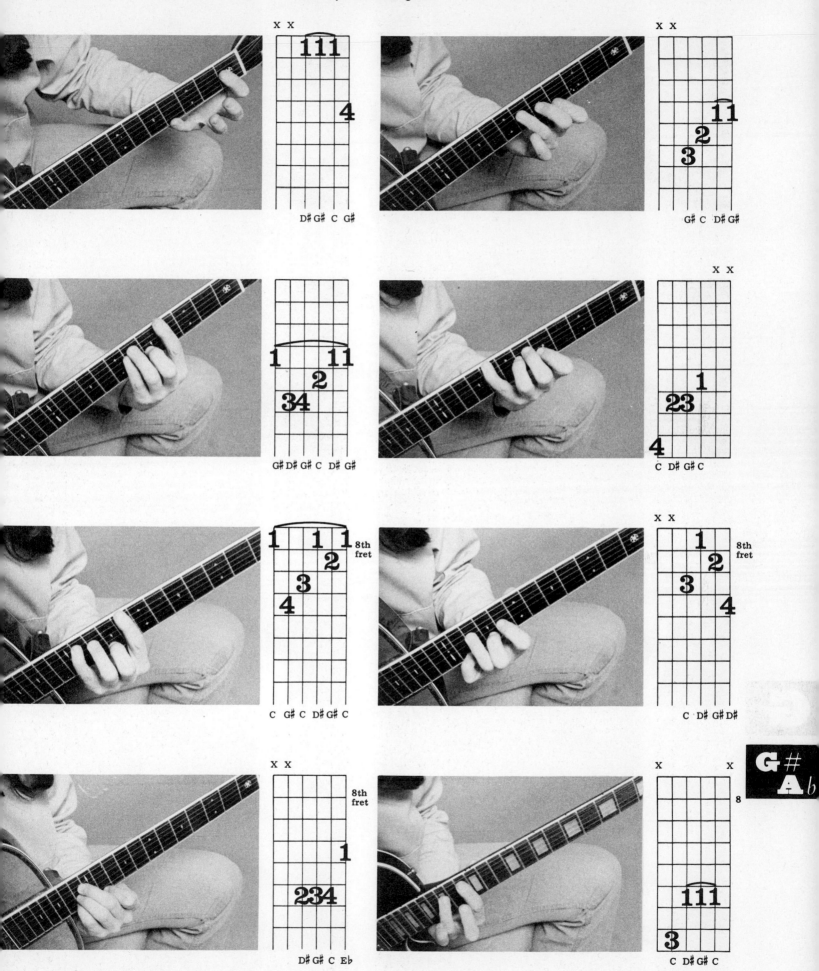

211

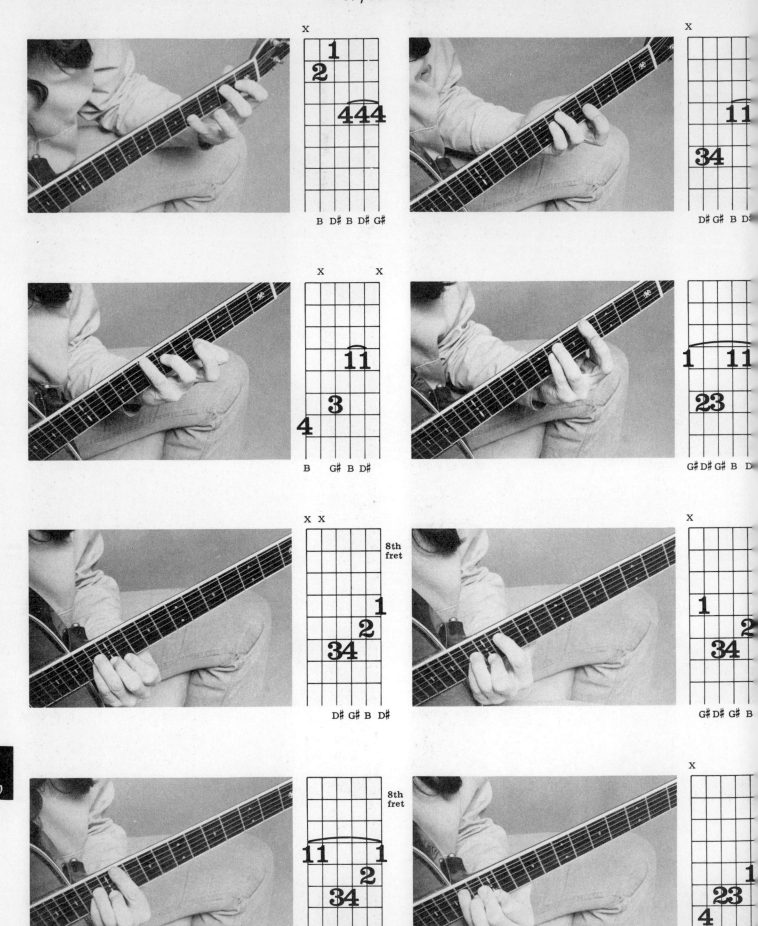

G#/Ab Major Sixth

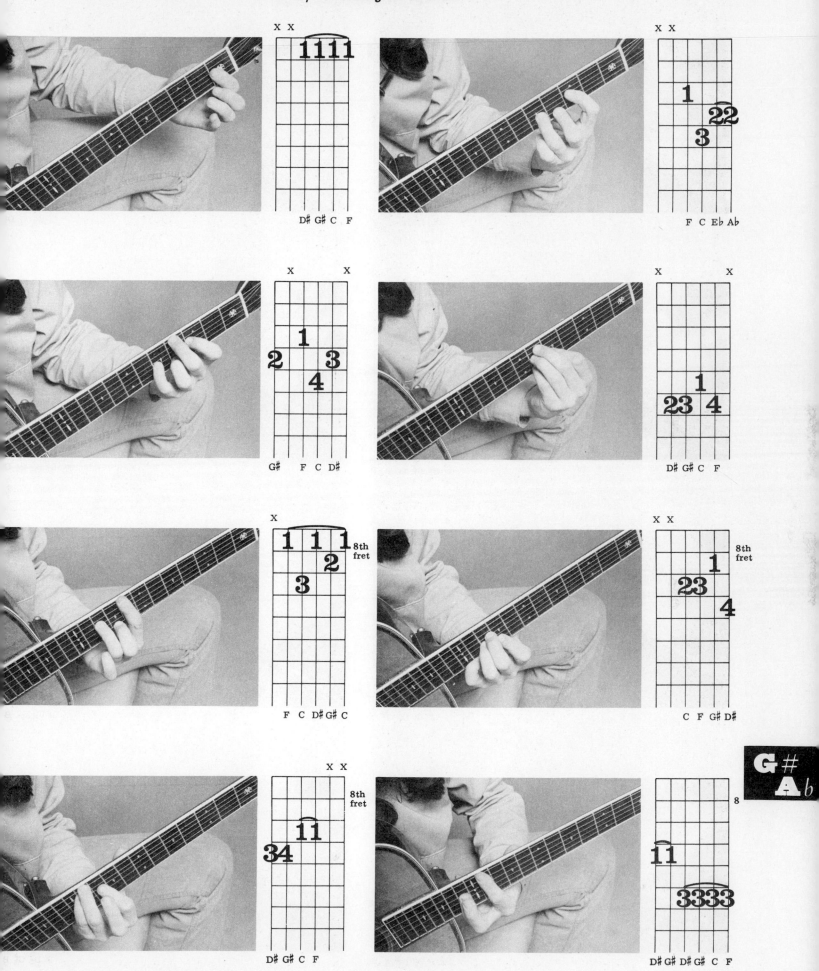

213

G#/Ab Minor Sixth

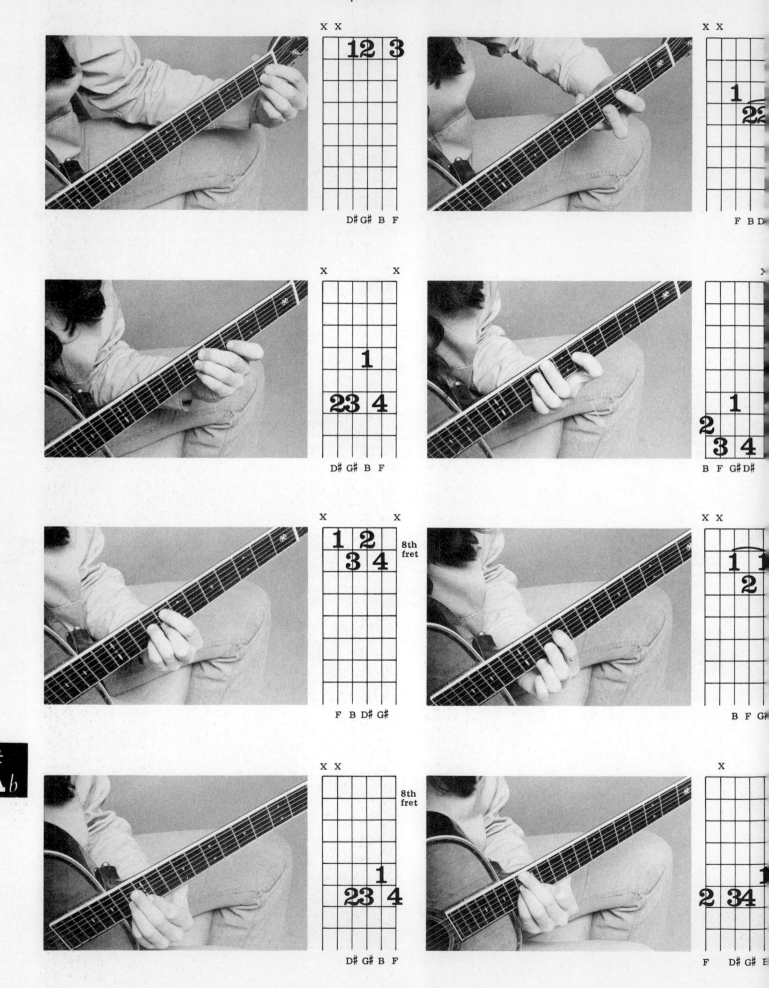

214

G#/Ab Seventh

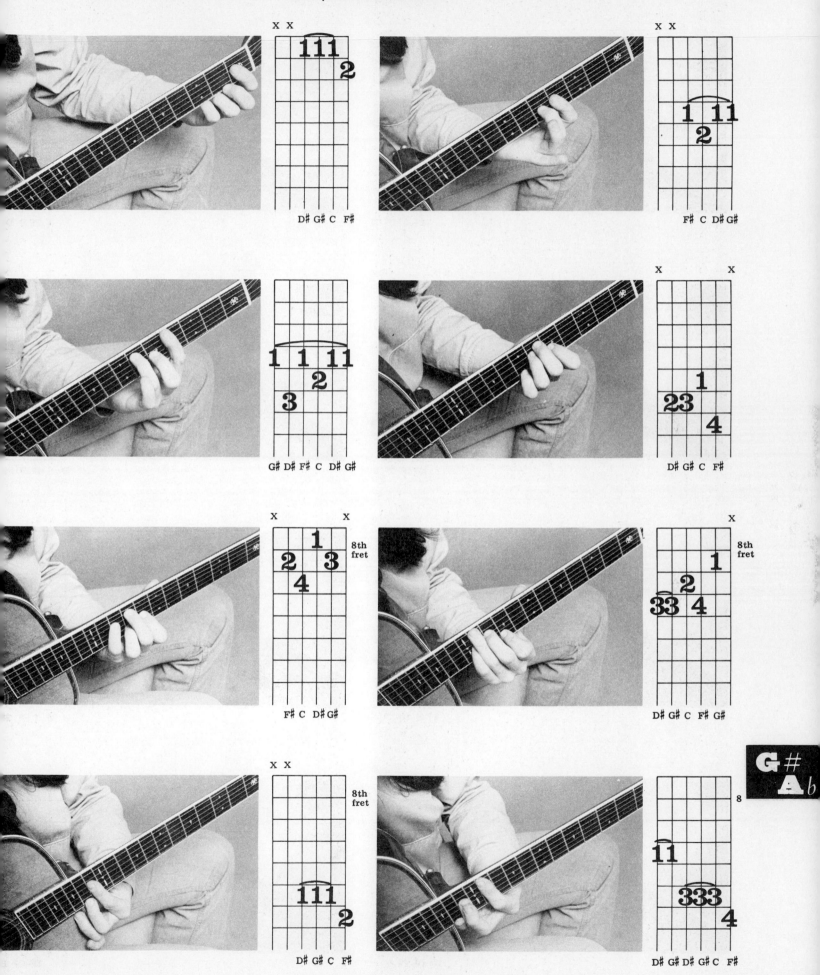

215

G#/Ab Minor Seventh

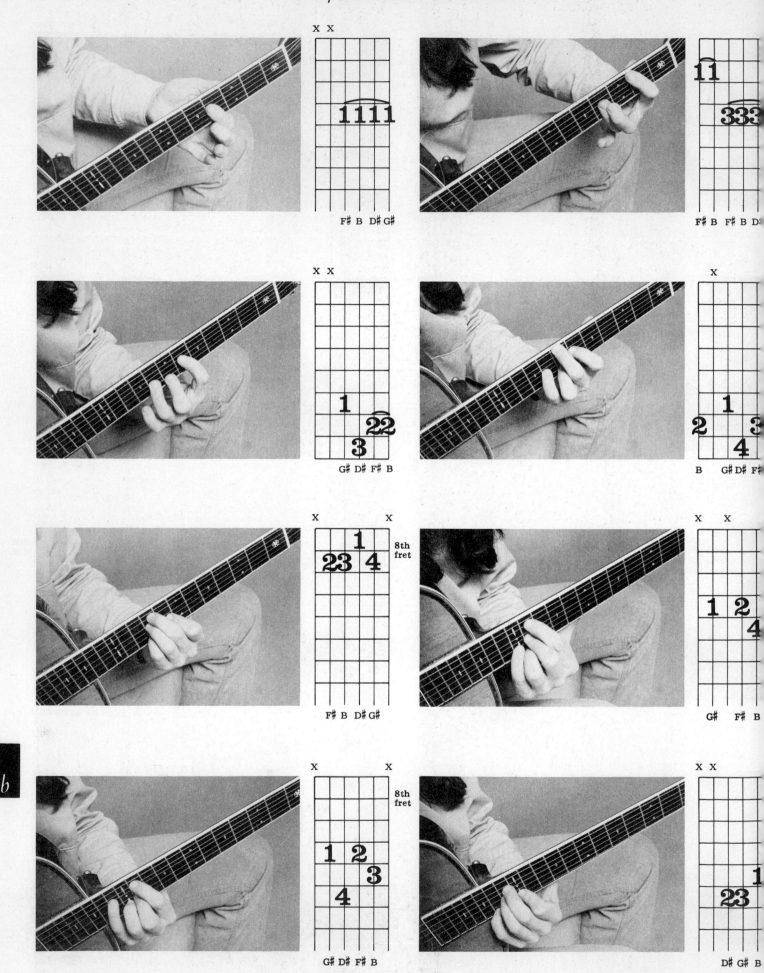

G#/Ab Diminished

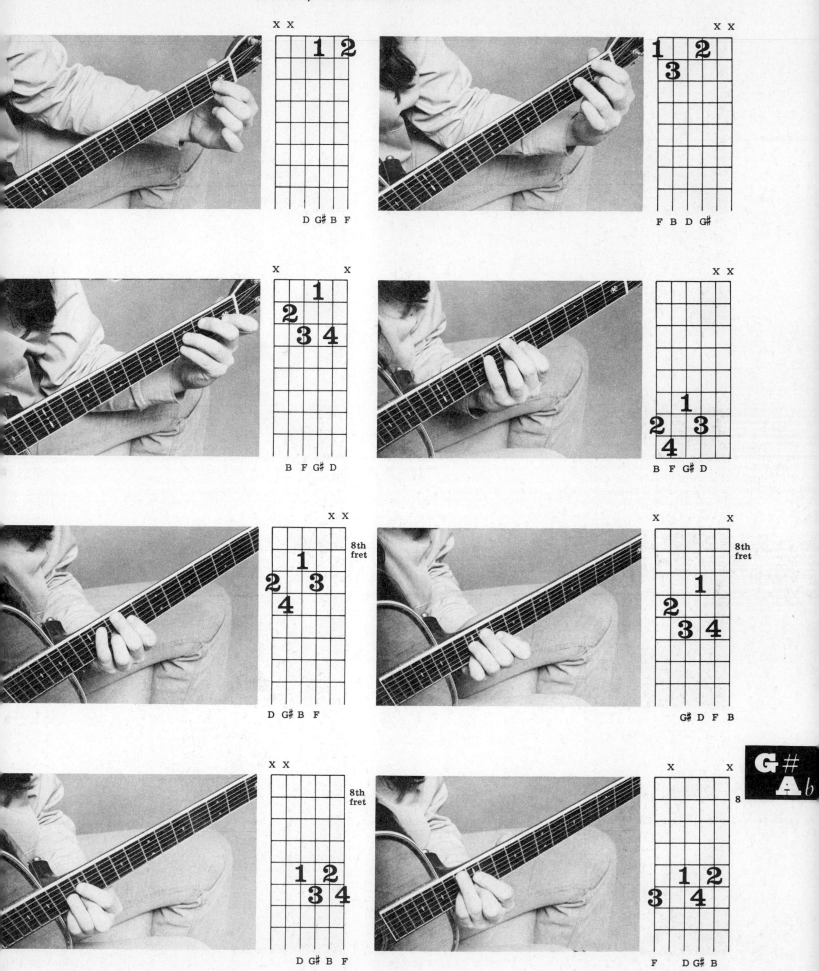

217

G#/Ab Augmented

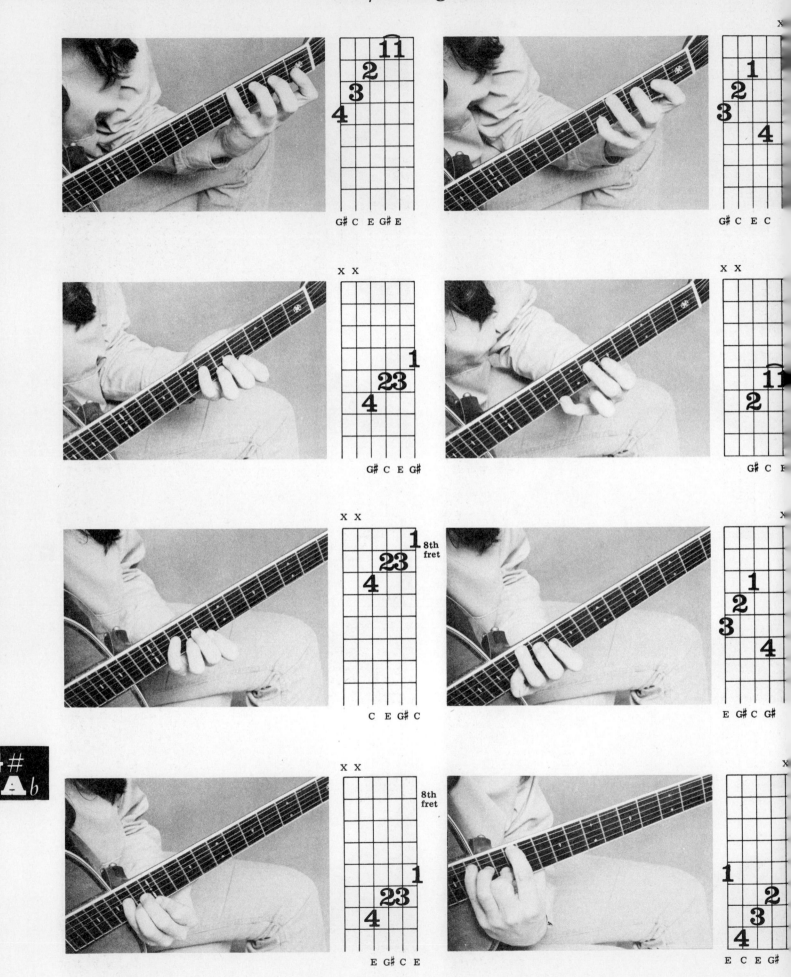

G#/Ab Seventh Augmented Fifth

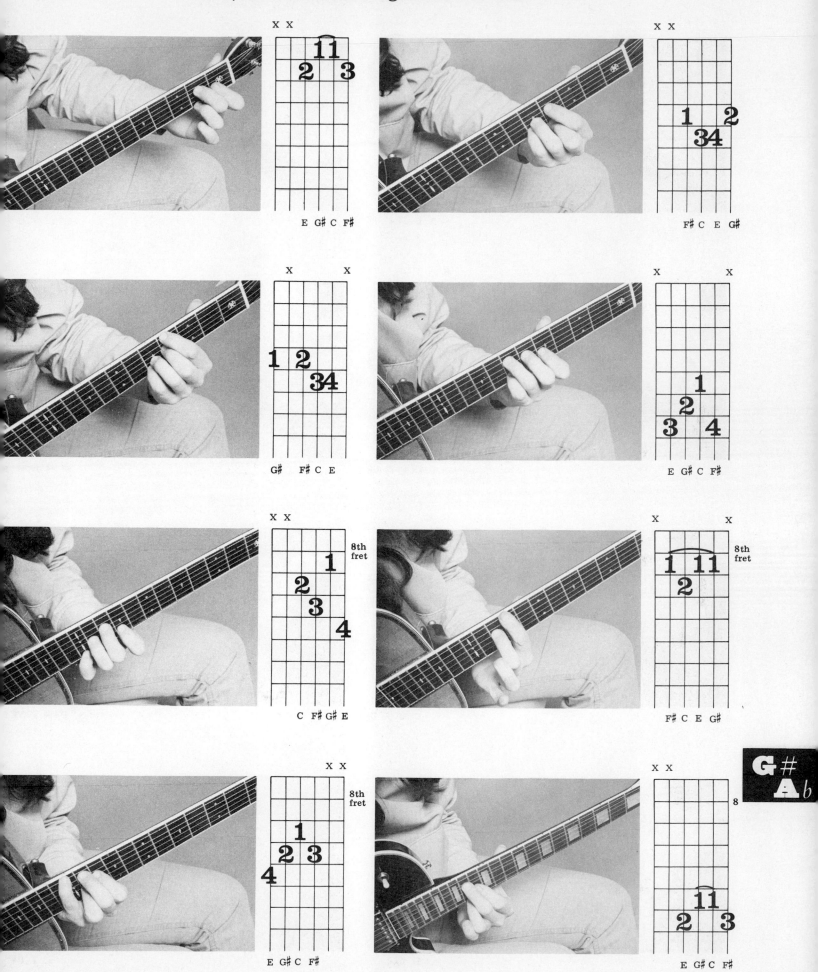

219

G#/Ab Seventh Flat Five

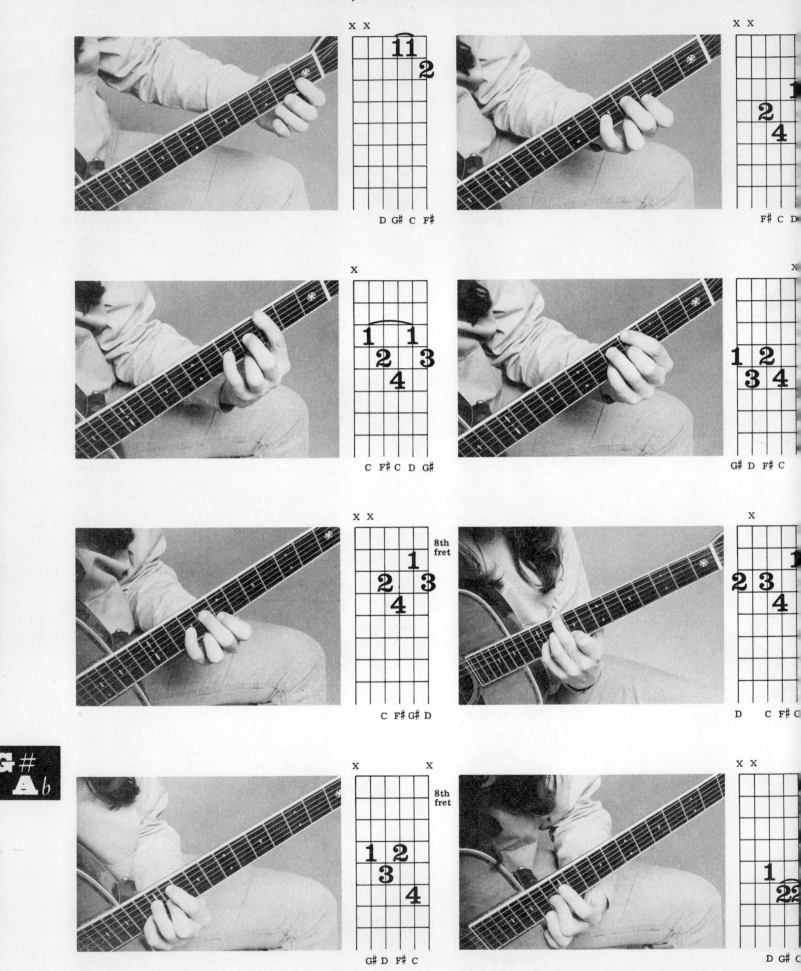

220

G#/Ab Seventh Flat Nine

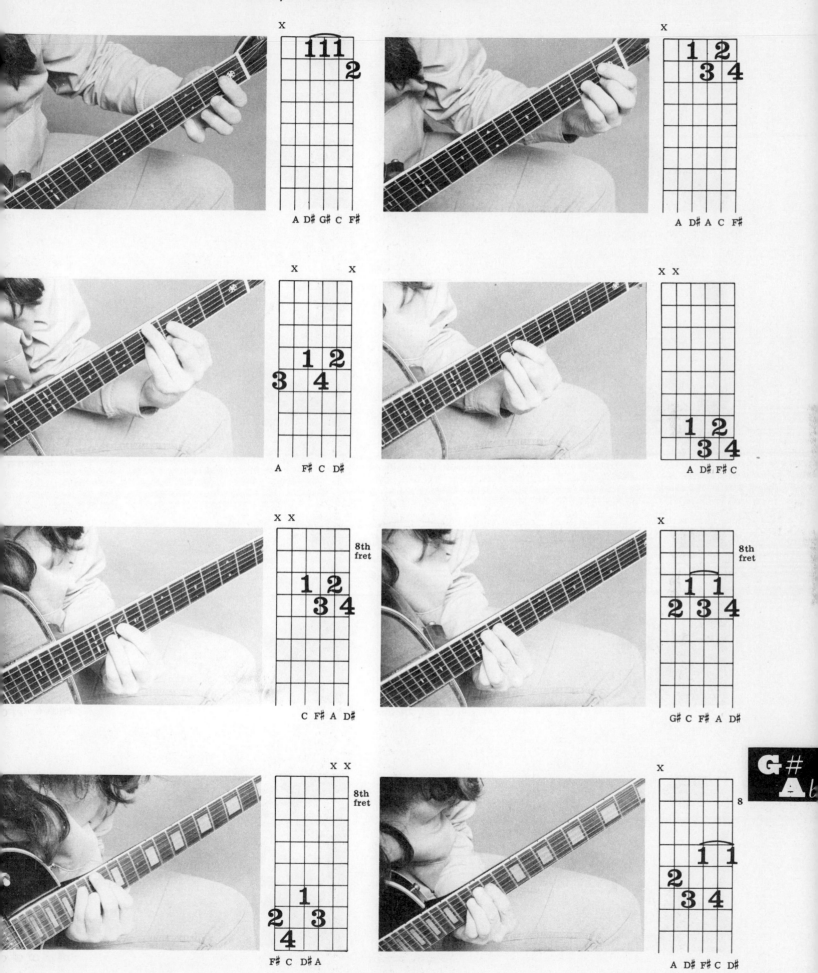

221

G#/Ab Major Seventh

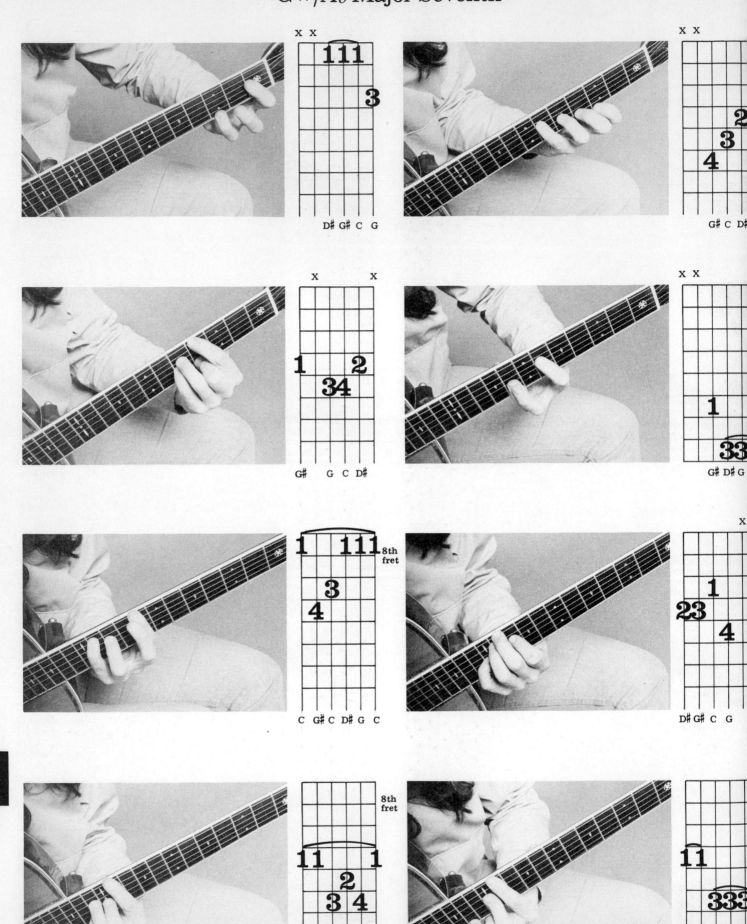

G#/Ab Minor Seventh Flat Five

223

G#/A♭ Seventh Suspension Four

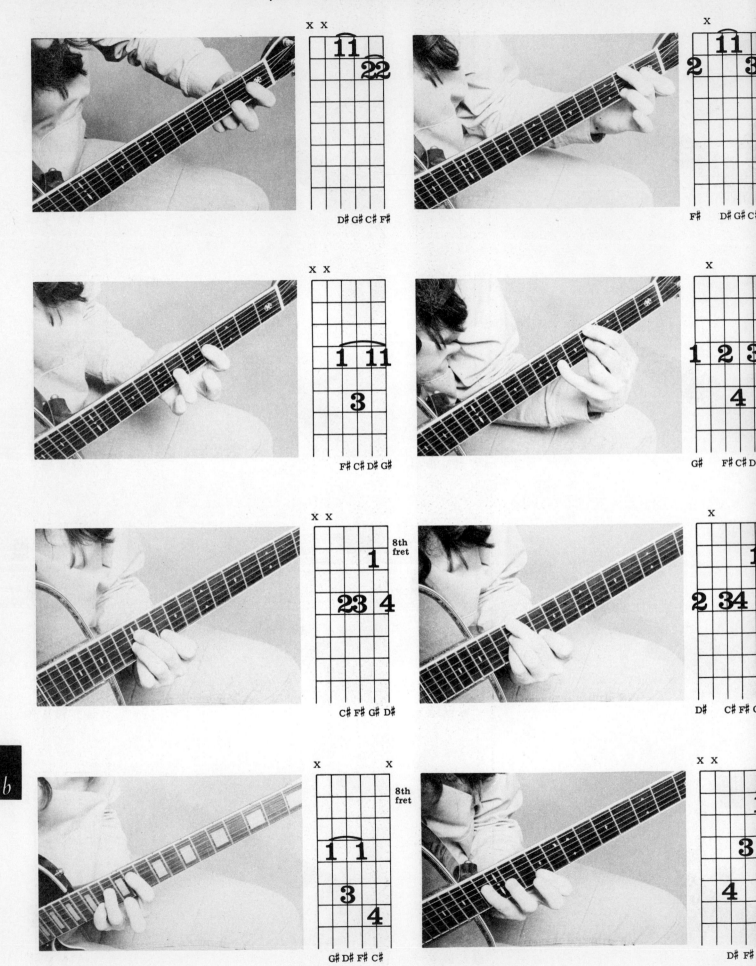

G#/Ab Ninth

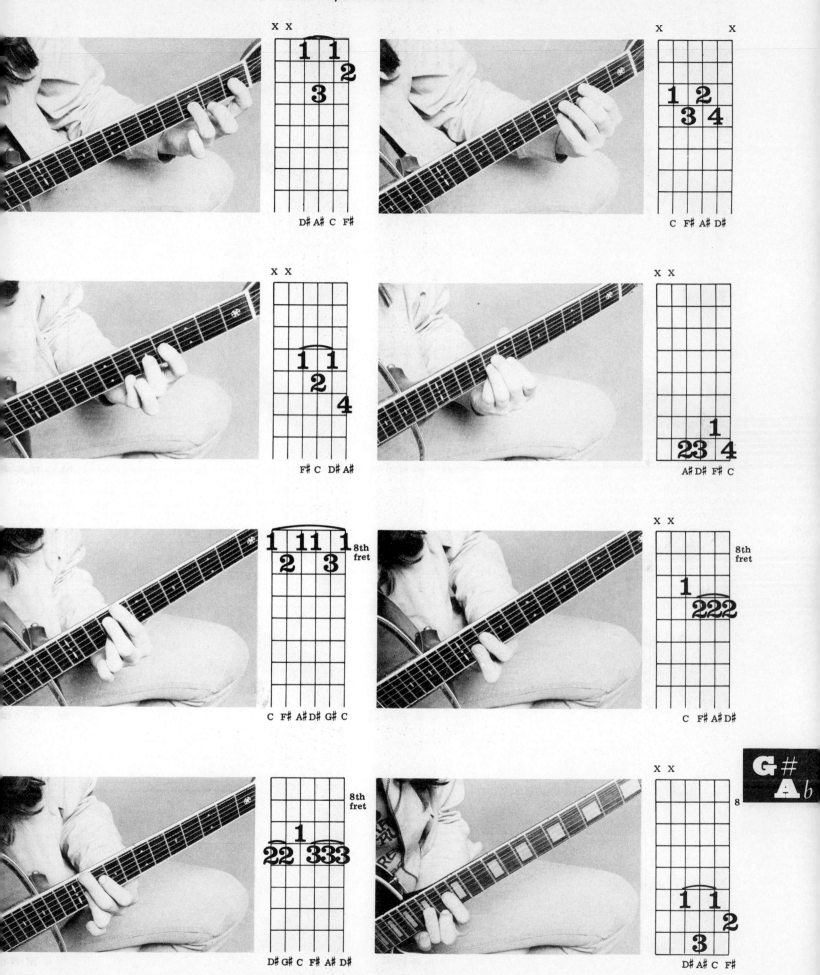

225

G#/Ab Minor Ninth

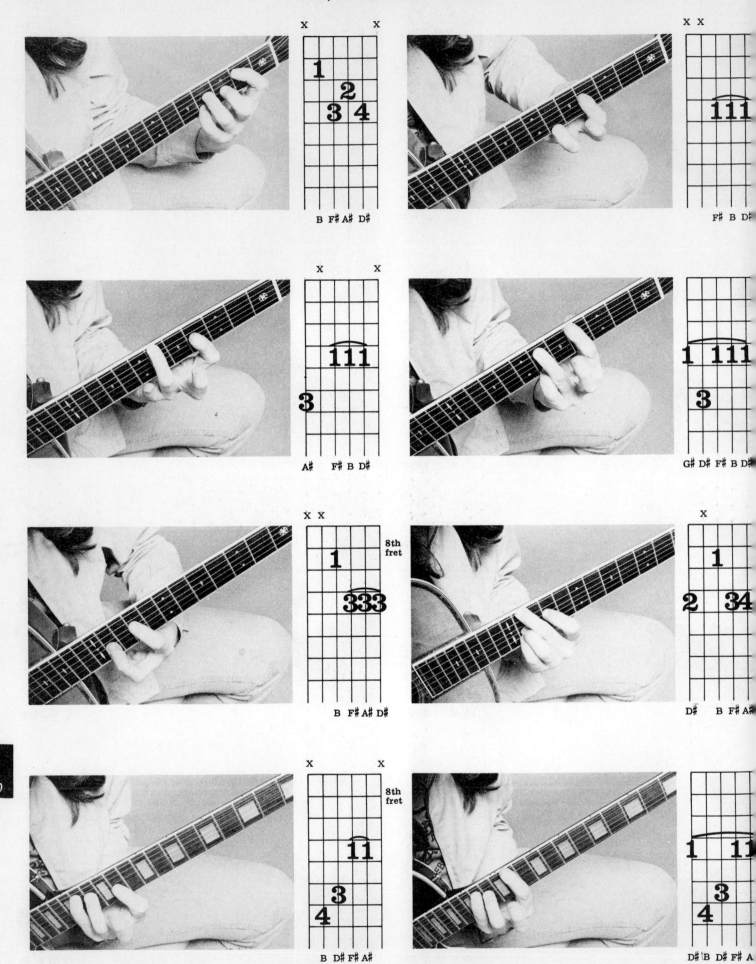

226

G#/Ab Ninth Flat Five

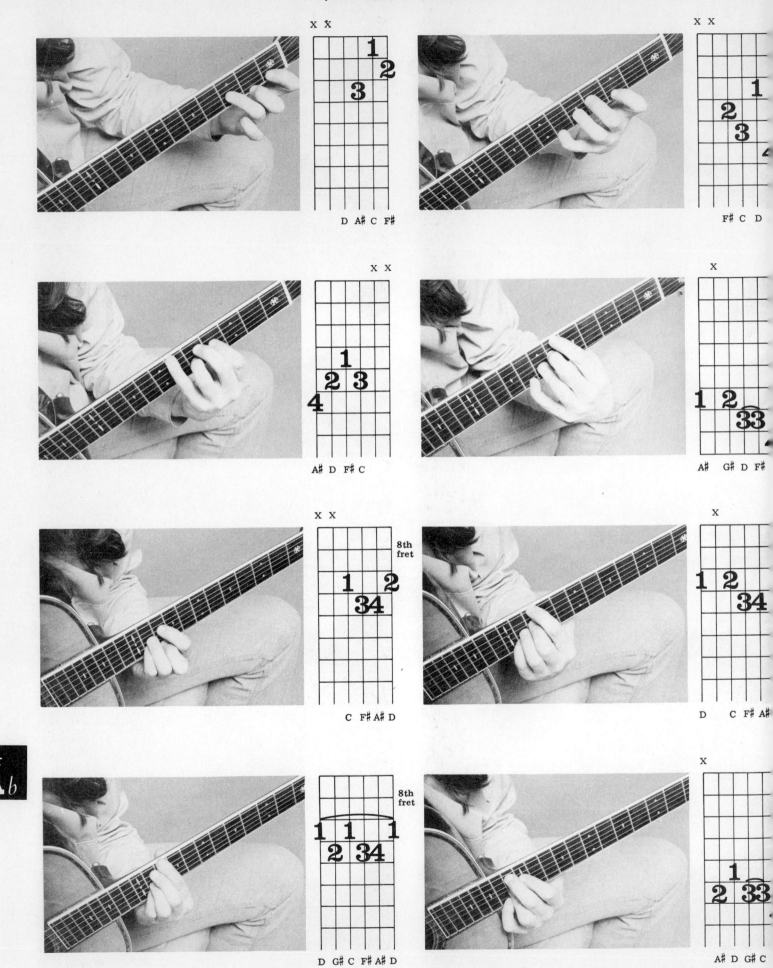

G#/Ab Major Ninth

229

G#/Ab Eleventh

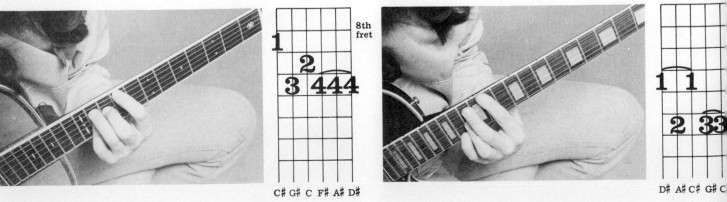

230

G♯/A♭ Augmented Eleventh

F#   D# A# D

A# D# G# D F#

G# D F# C D# A#

A# D# G# D F# C

8th
fret

D G# C F# A# D#

231

G #/Ab Thirteenth

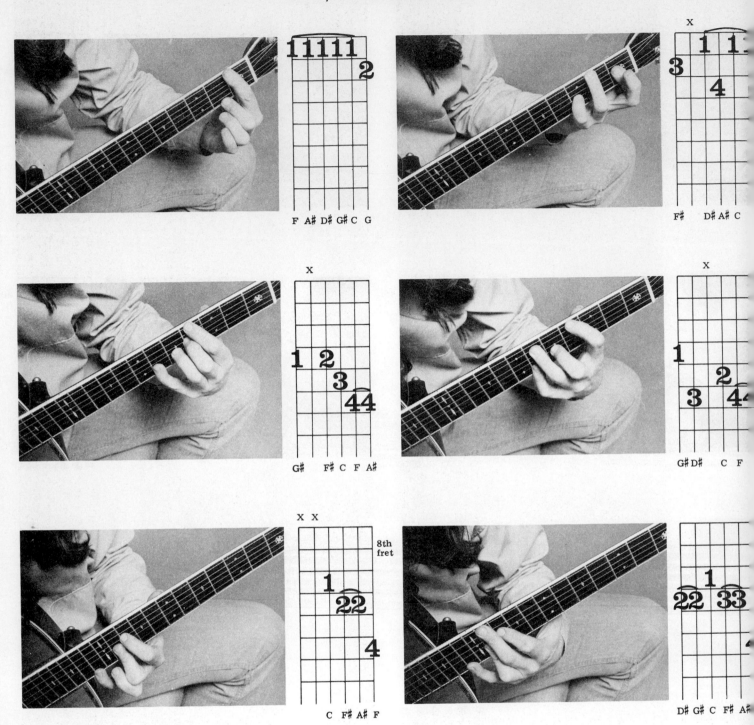

G #/A♭ Thirteenth Flat Nine

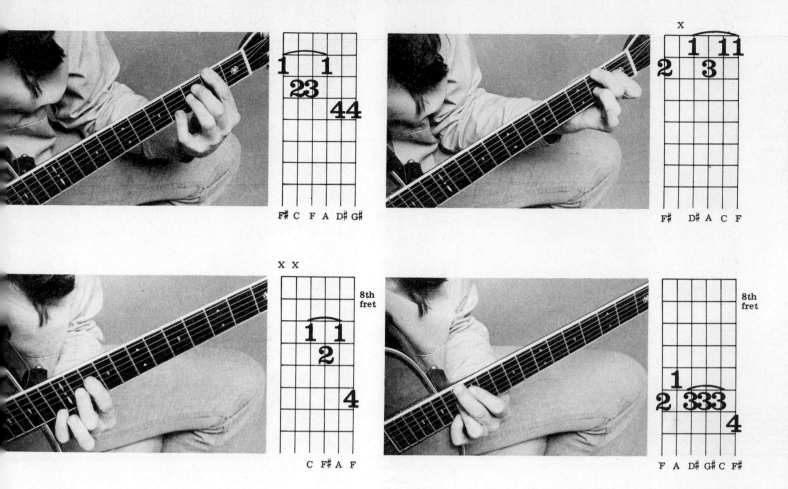

F# C F A D# G#

x
F# D# A C F

x x
8th fret
C F# A F

8th fret
F A D# G# C F#

G#/Ab Seven Six

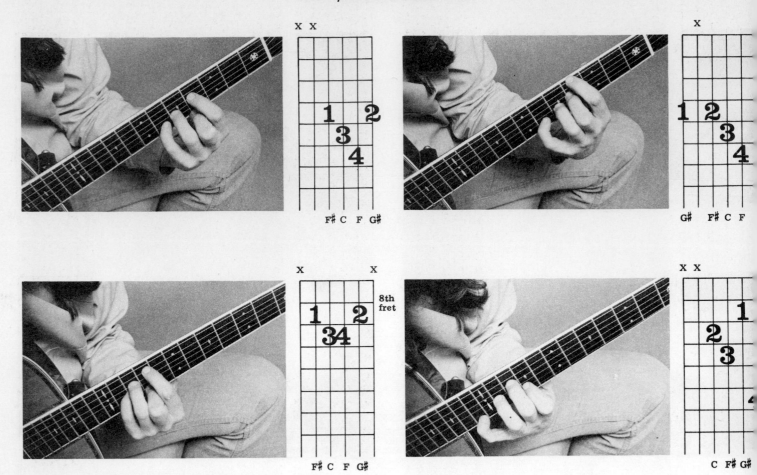

G#/Ab Nine Six

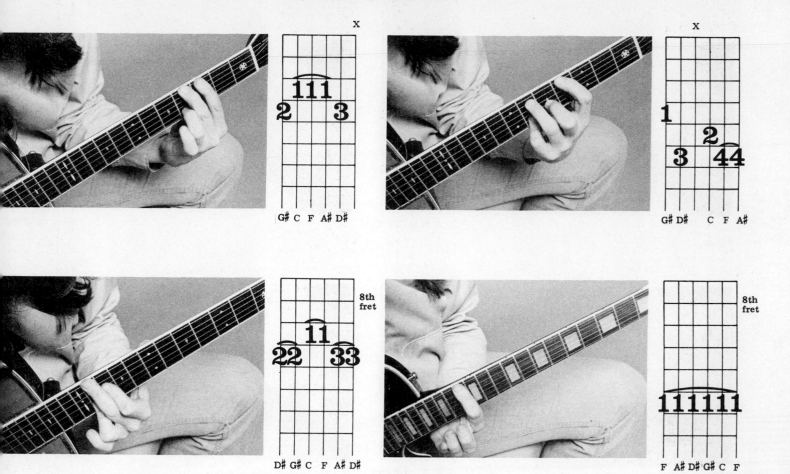

G# C F A# D#

G# D# C F A#

D# G# C F A# D# — 8th fret

F A# D# G# C F — 8th fret

A Major

A Minor

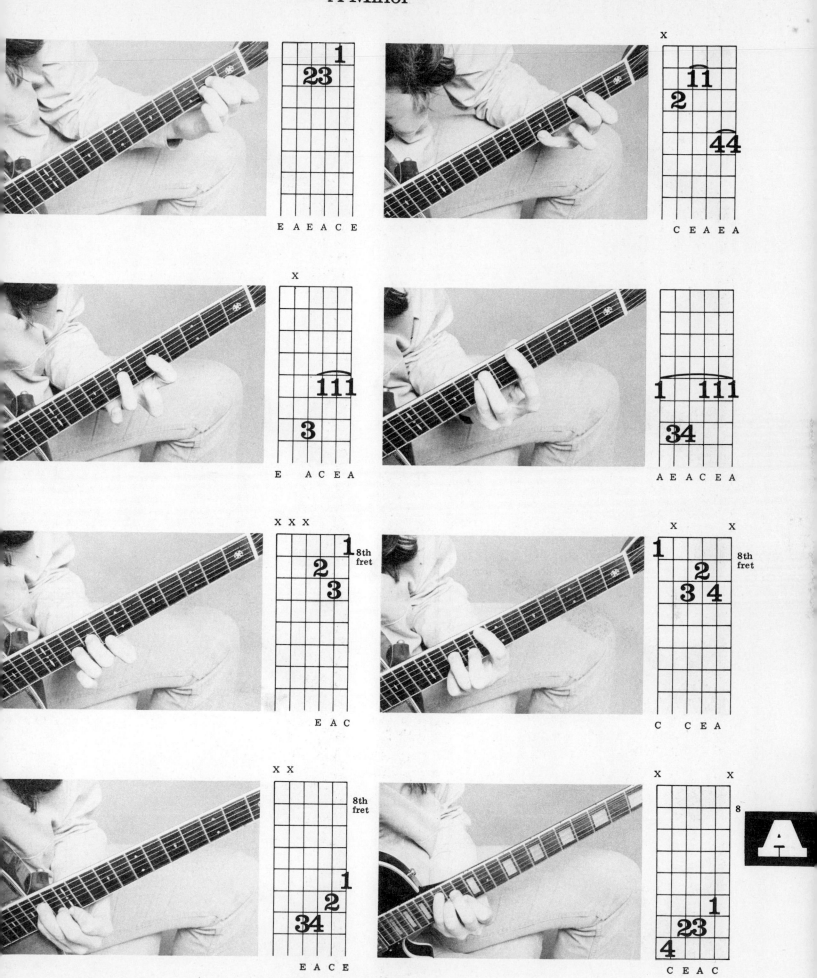

A Major Sixth

238

A Minor Sixth

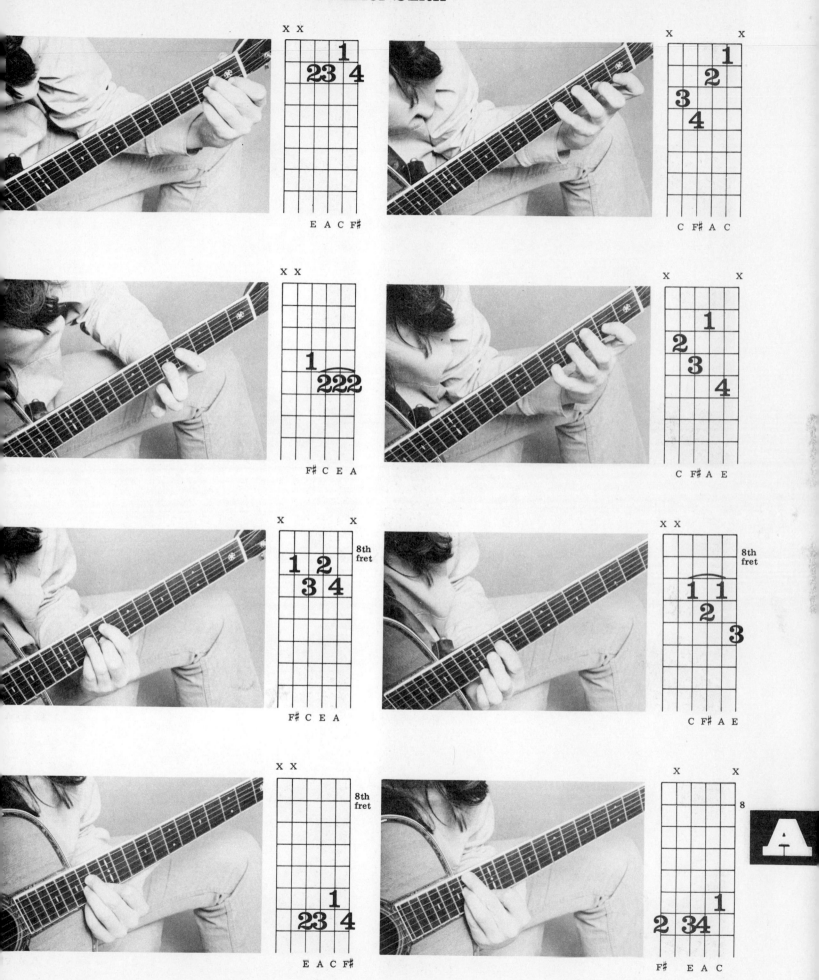

239

A Seventh

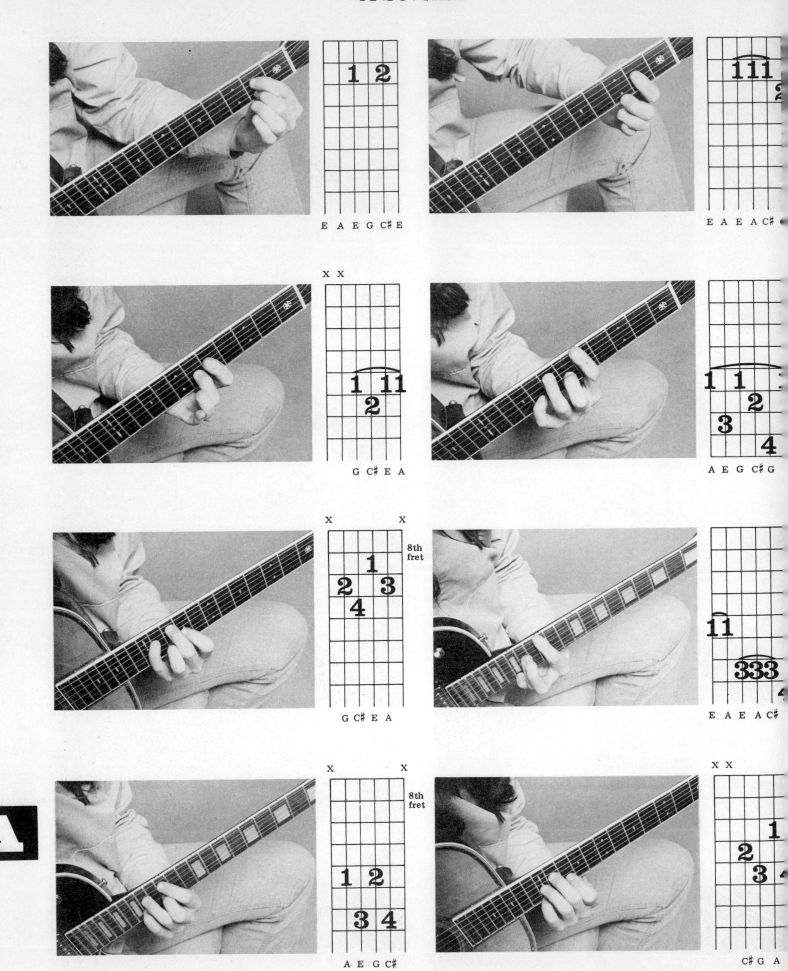

240

A Minor Seventh

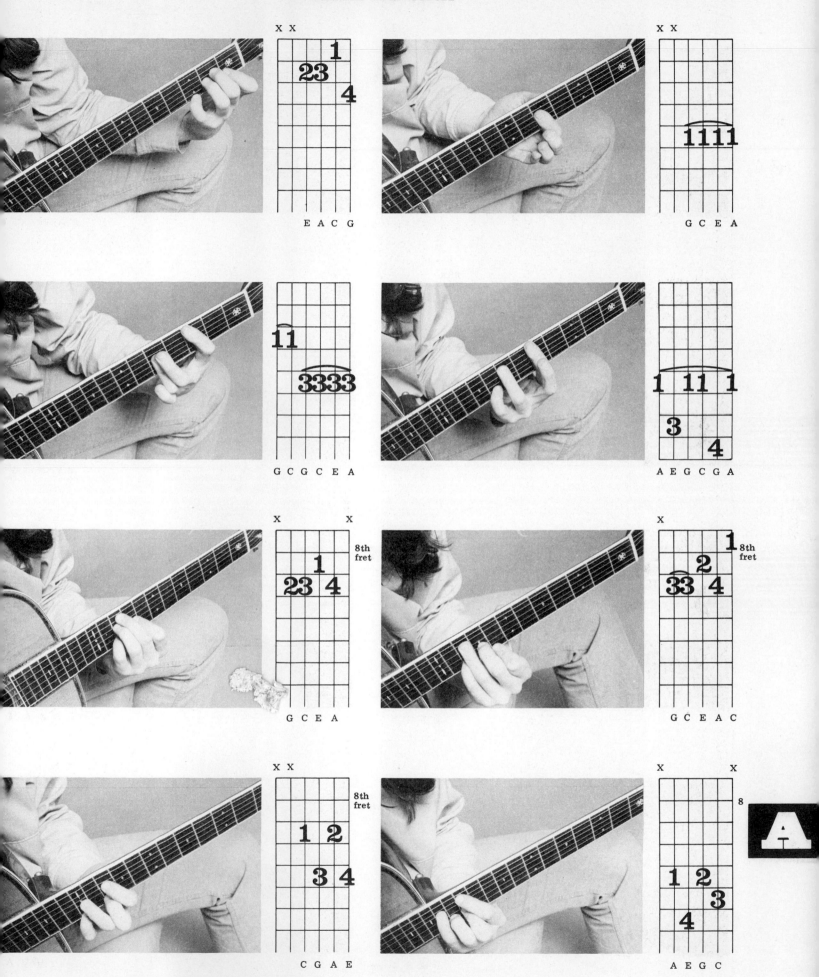

241

A Diminished

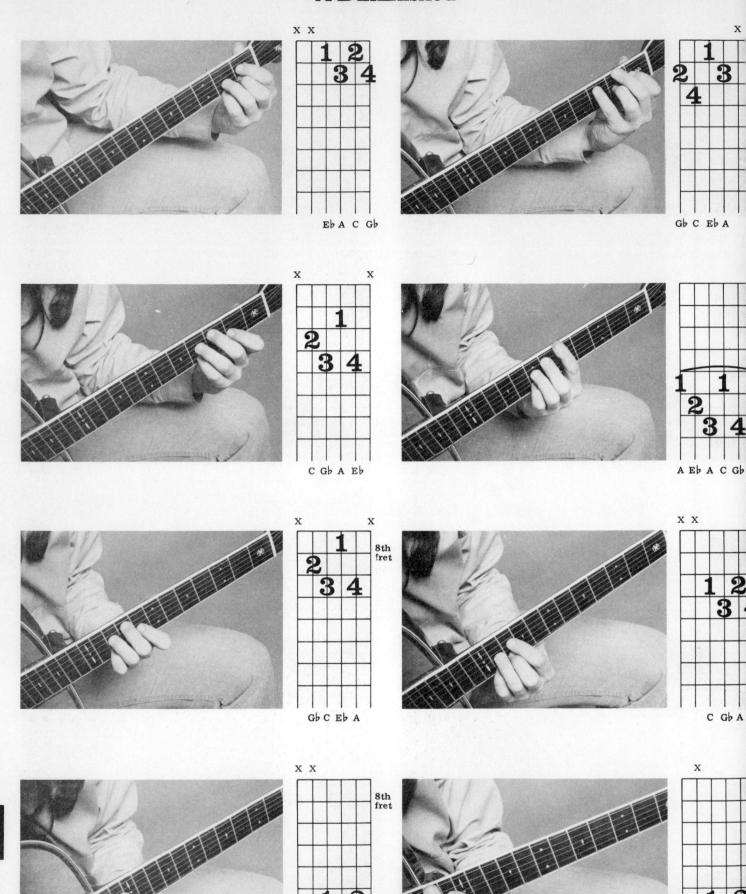

A Augmented

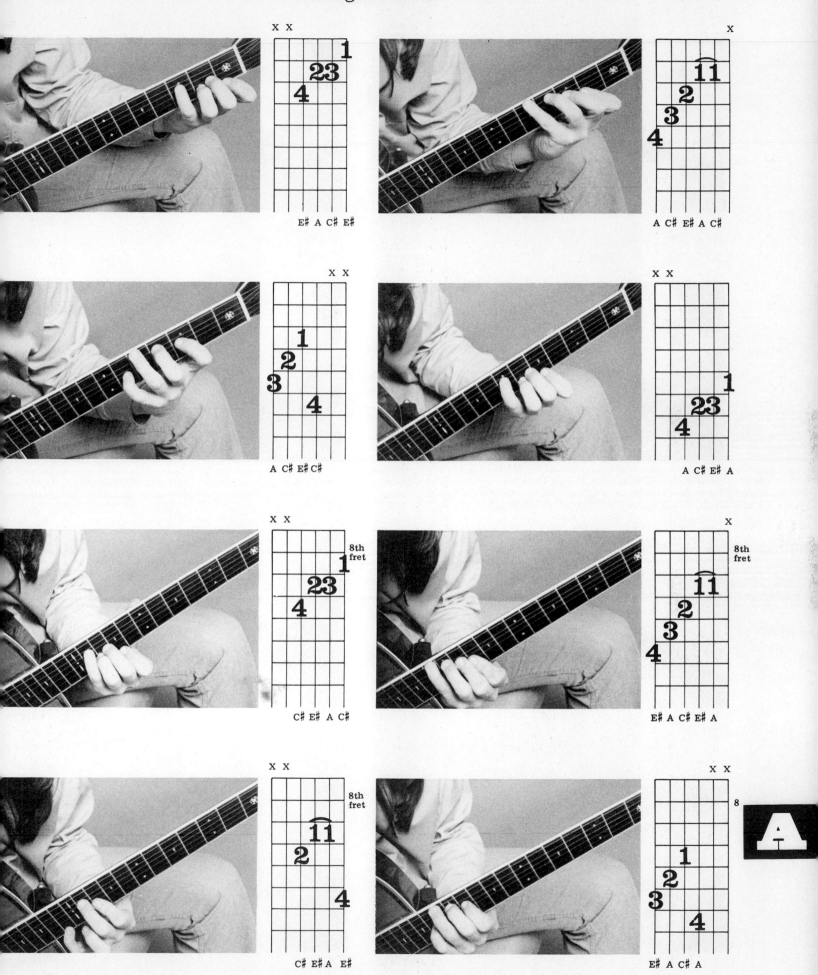

243

A Seventh Augmented Fifth

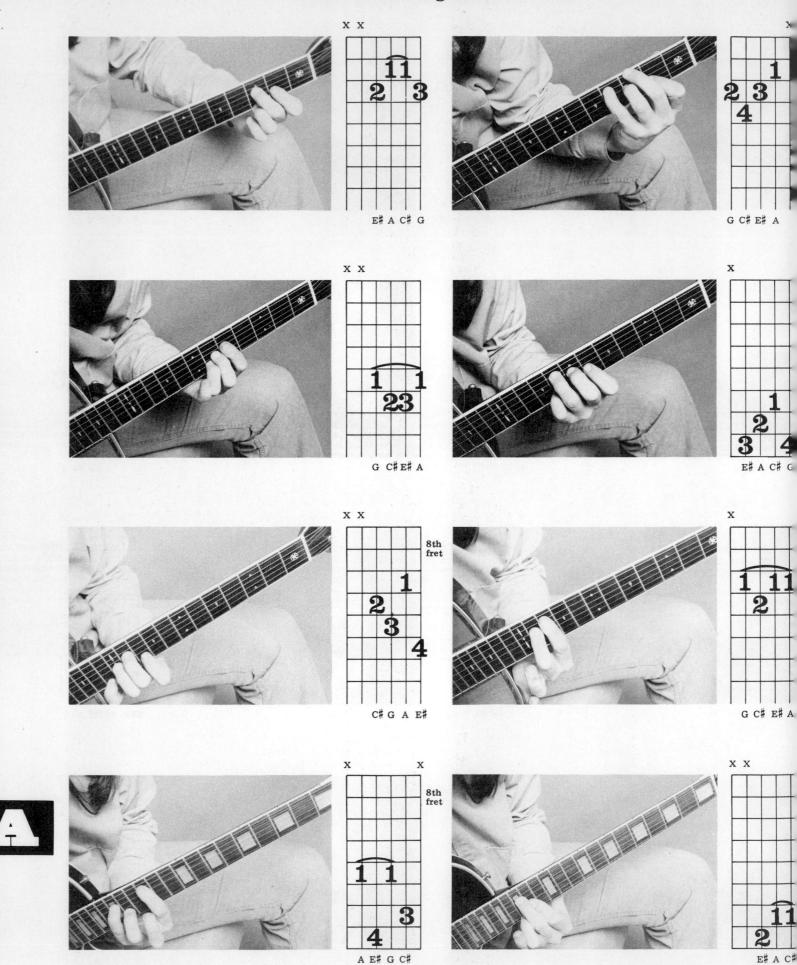

244

A Seventh Flat Five

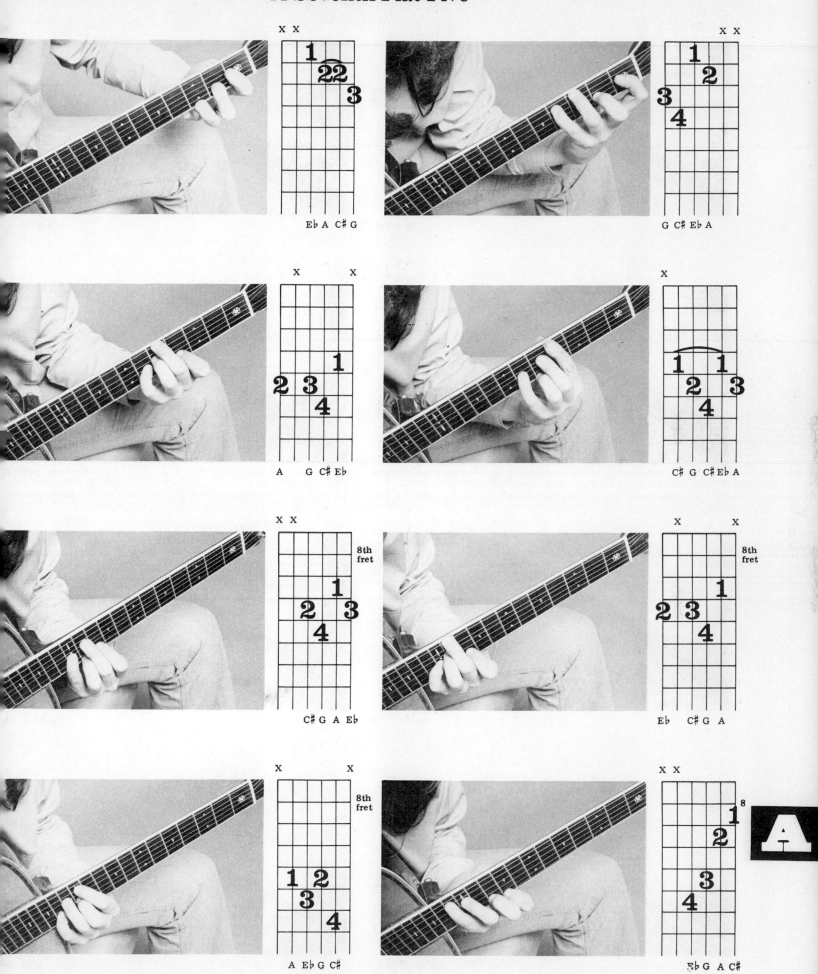

A Seventh Flat Nine

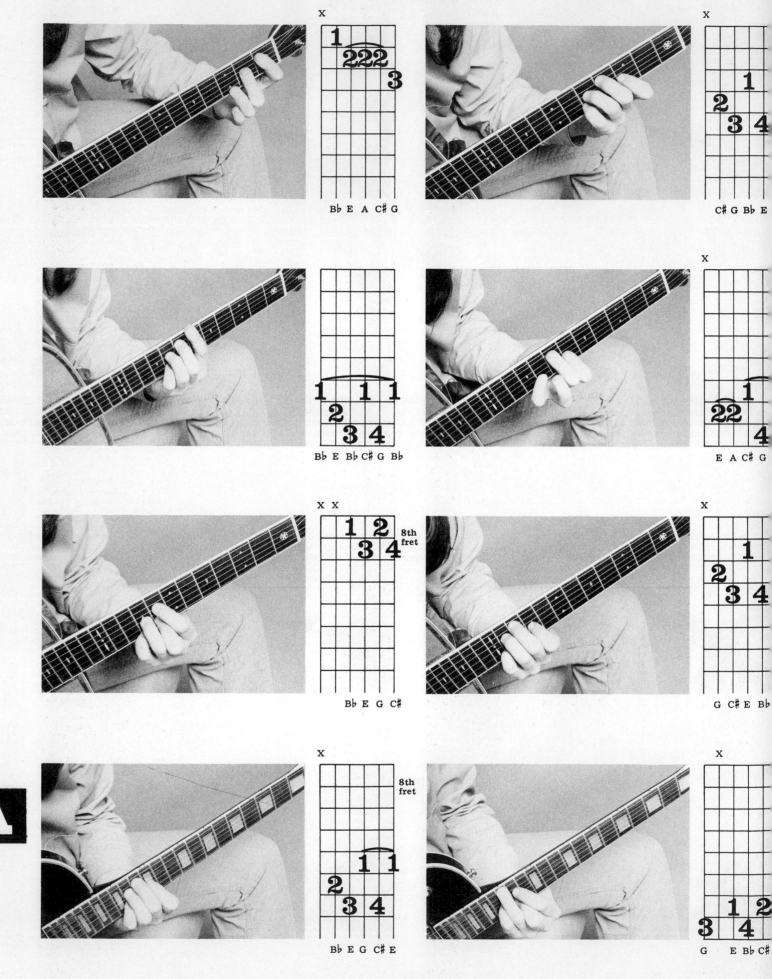

A Major Seventh

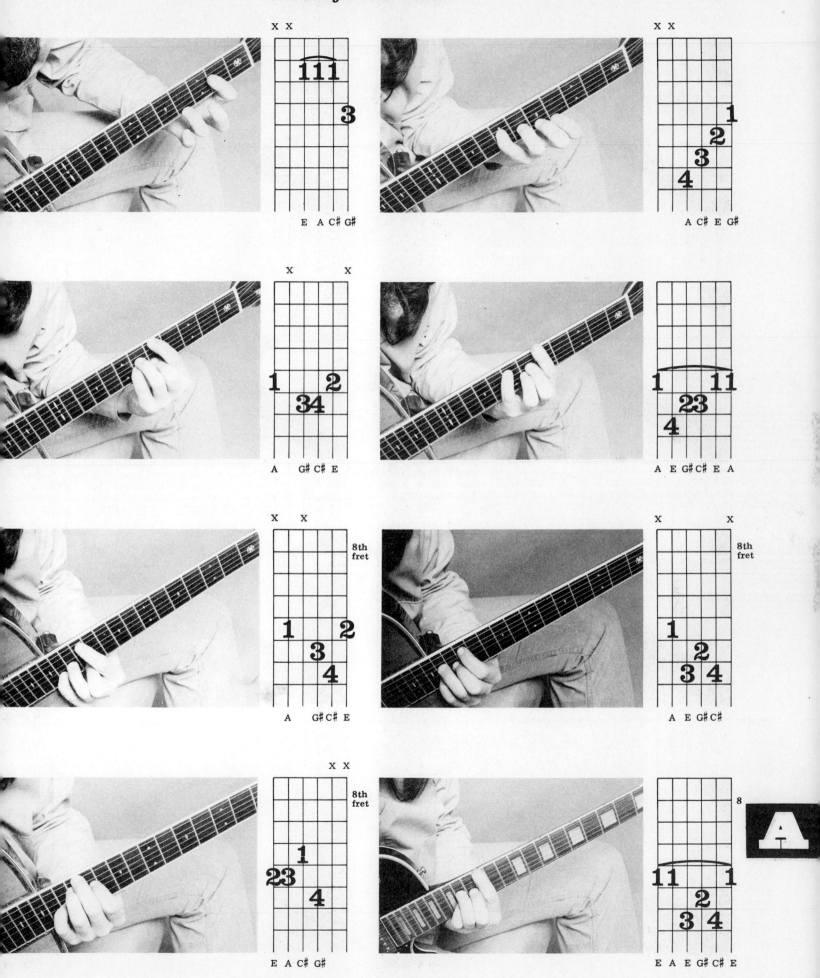

247

A Minor Seventh Flat Five

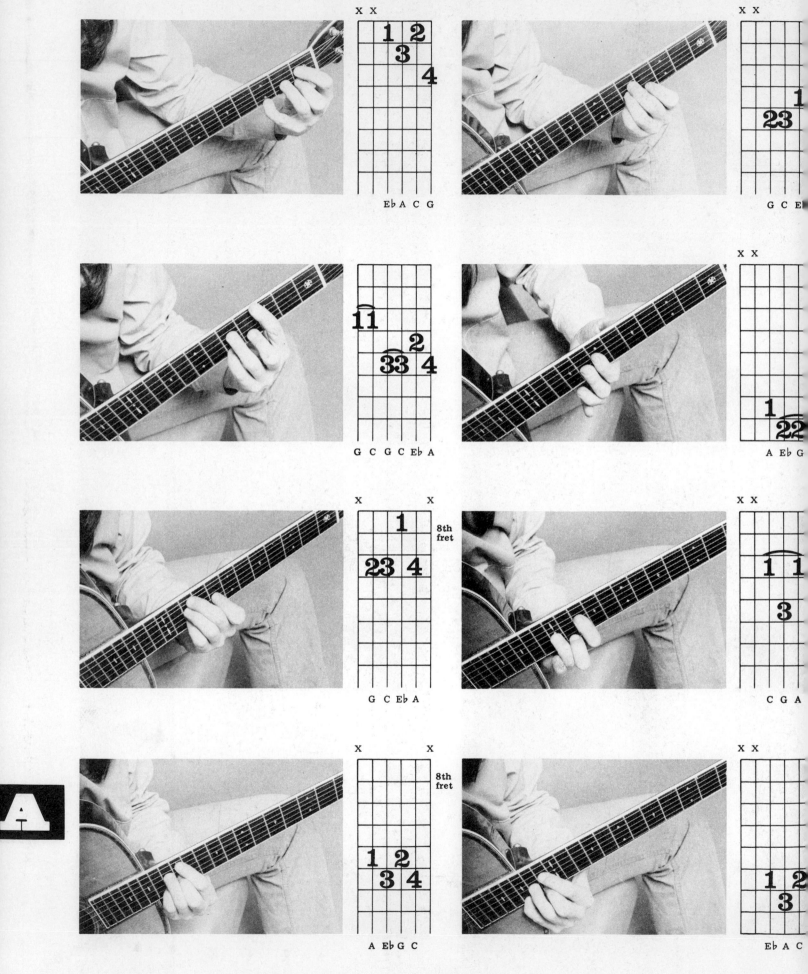

Eb A C G

G C E

G C G Eb A

A Eb G

8th fret

G C Eb A

C G A

A Eb G C

Eb A C

8th fret

248

A Seventh Suspension Four

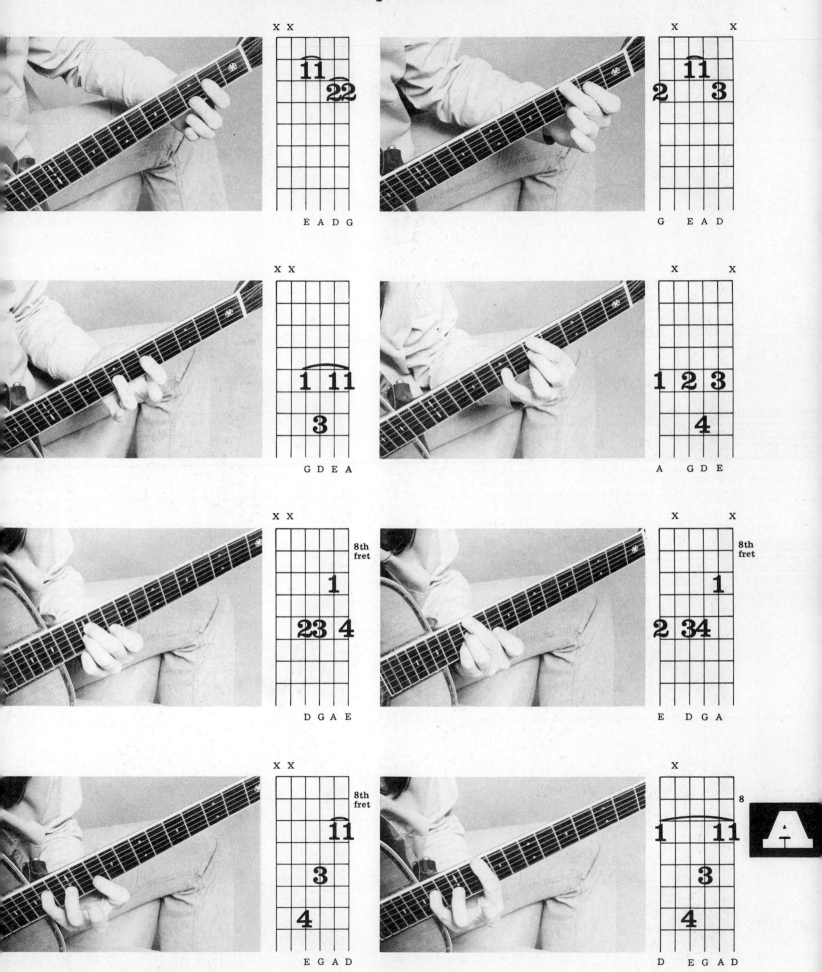

249

A Ninth

250

A Minor Ninth

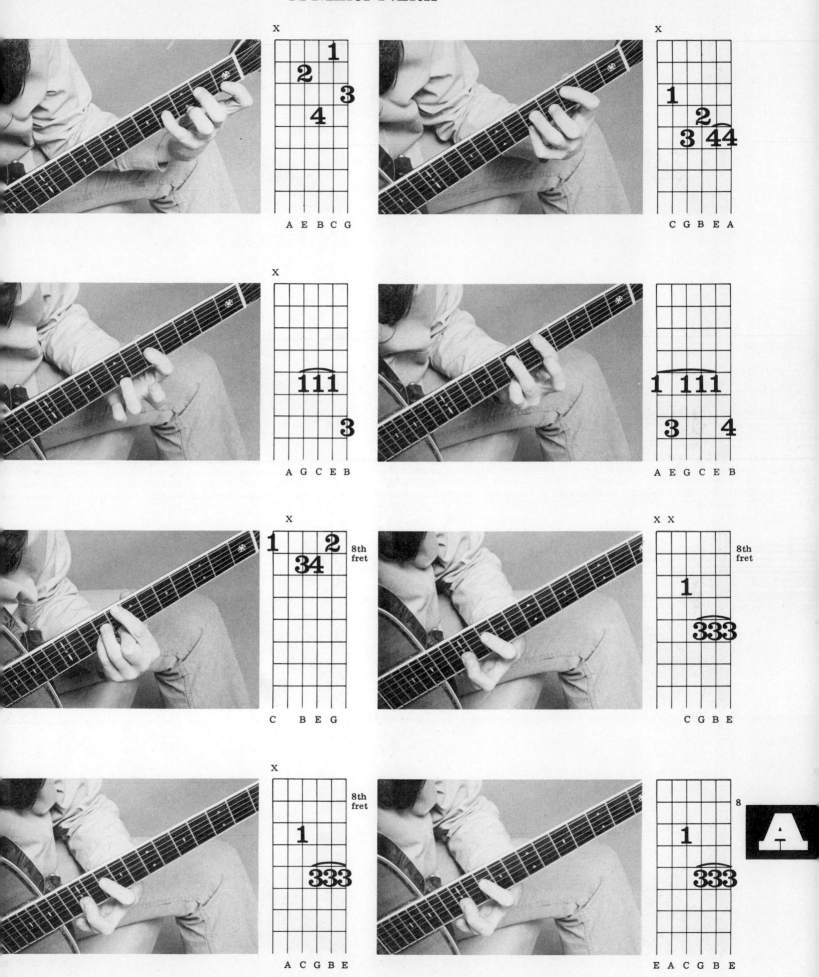

251

A Ninth Augmented Fifth

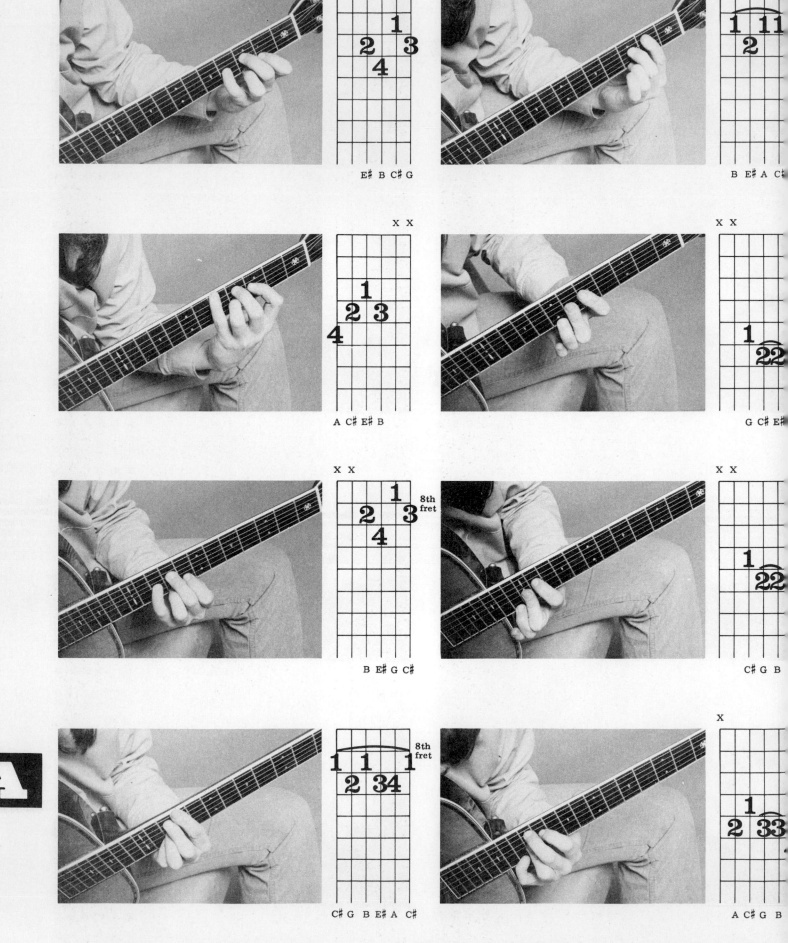

252

A Ninth Flat Five

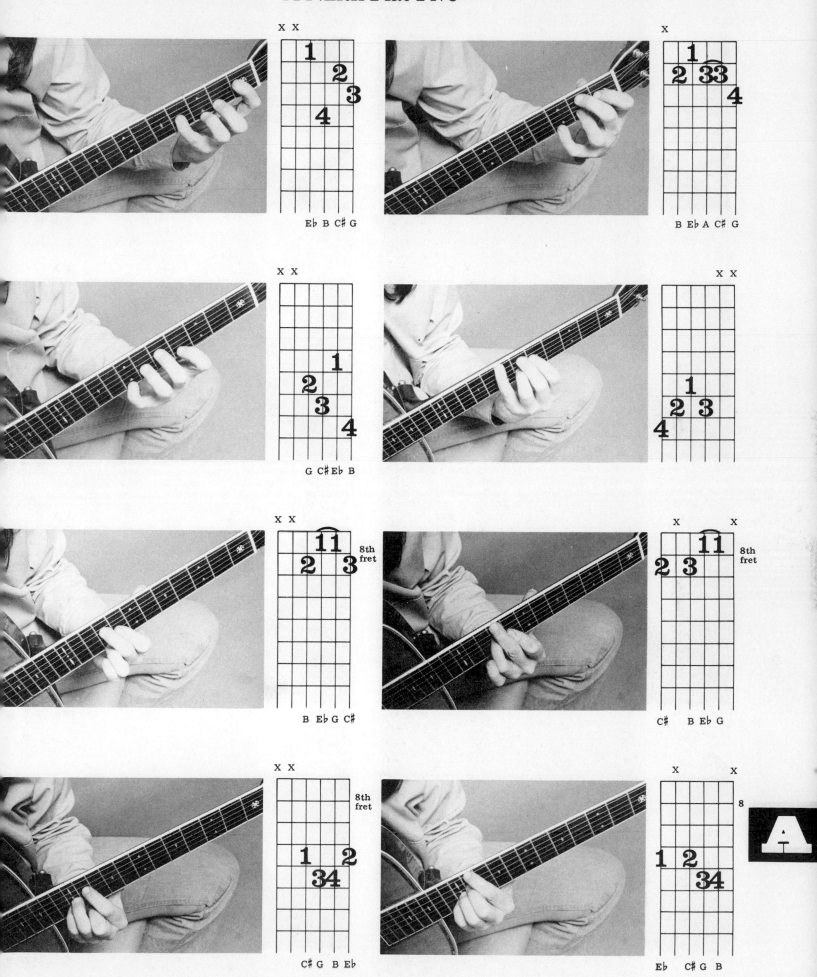

253

A Major Ninth

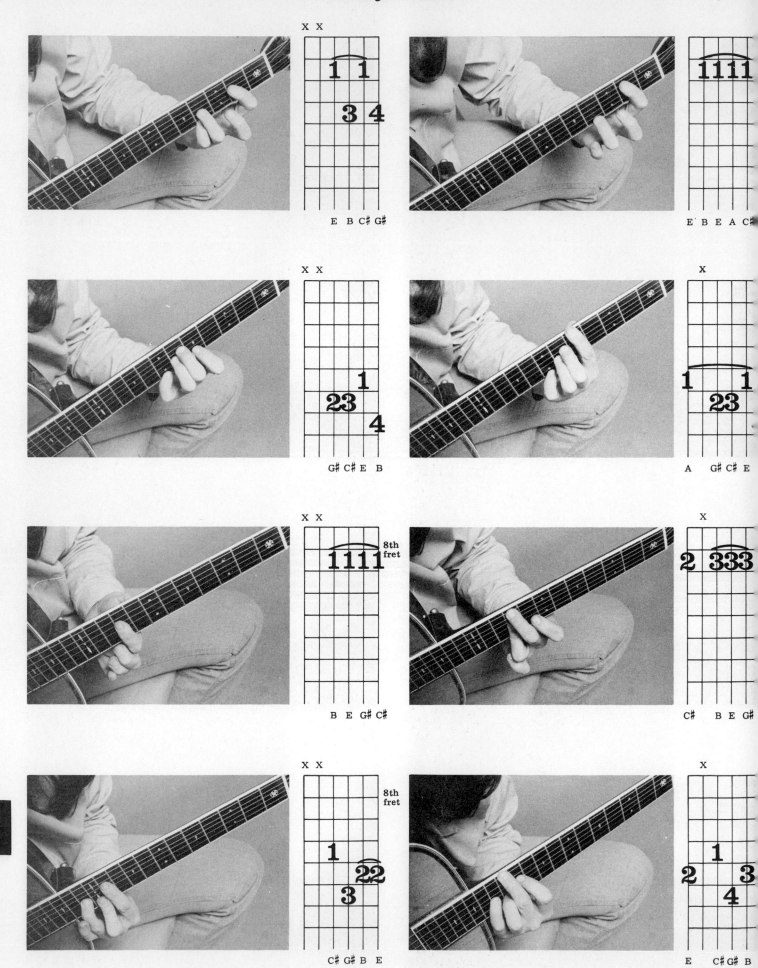

254

A Eleventh

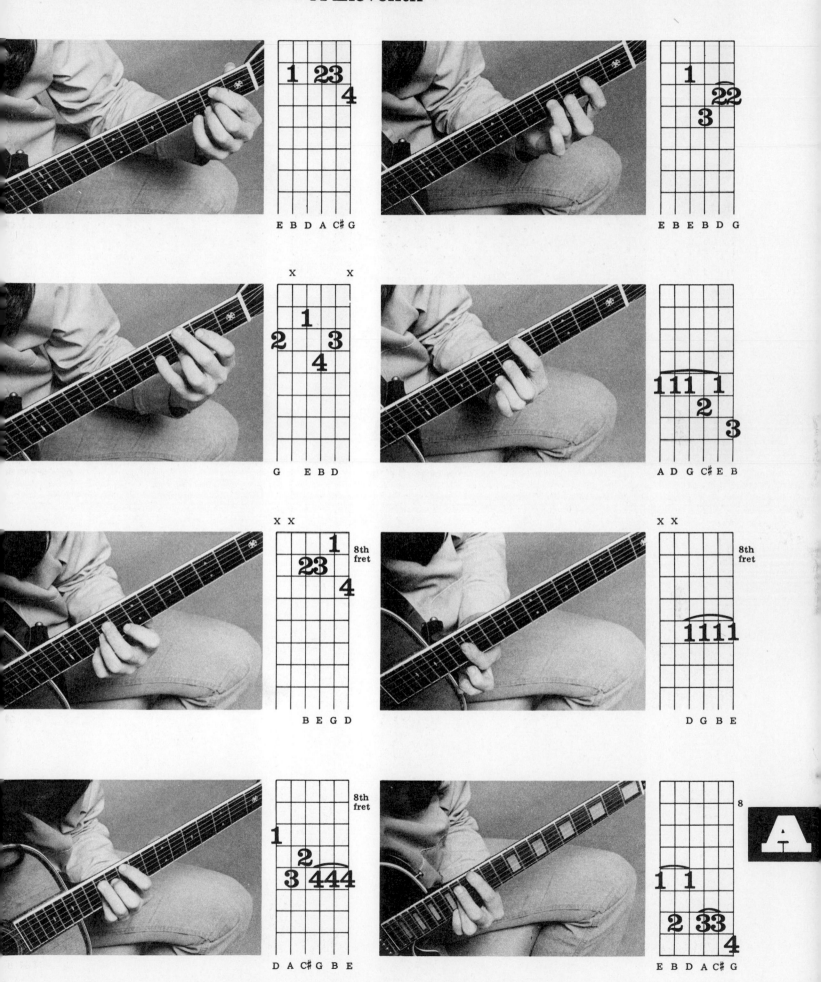

255

A Augmented Eleventh

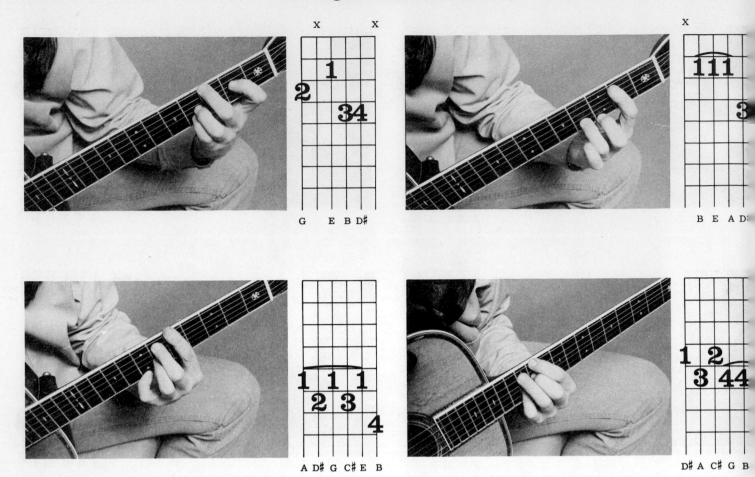

A Thirteenth

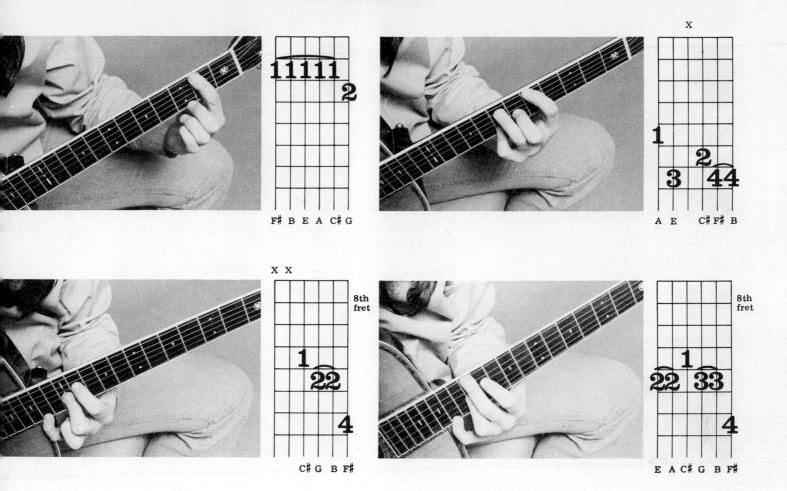

F# B E A C# G

x

A E   C# F# B

x x   8th
fret

C# G B F#

8th
fret

E A C# G B F#

A

257

A Thirteenth Flat Nine

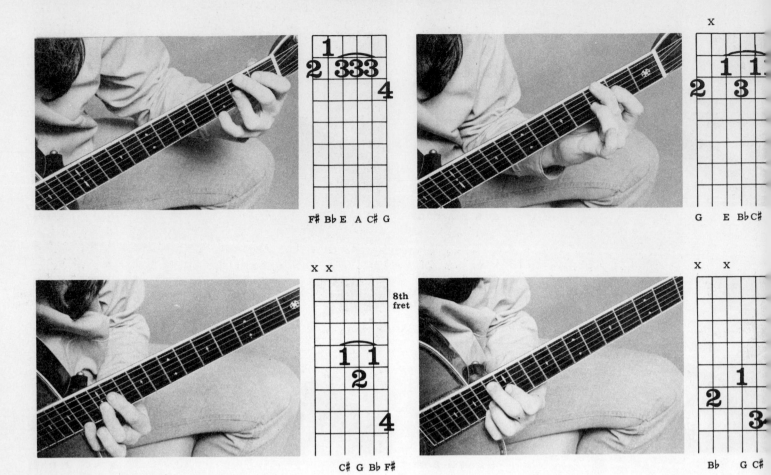

F# Bb E A C# G

G   E Bb C#

C# G Bb F#

Bb   G C#

A Seven Six

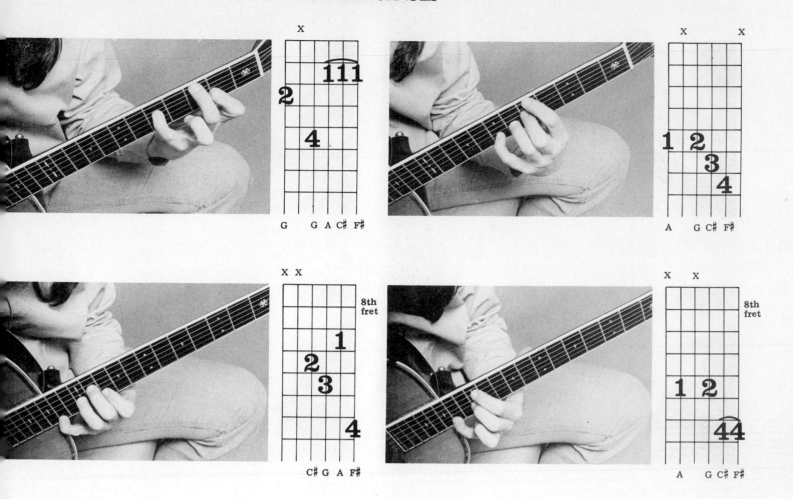

259

A Nine Six

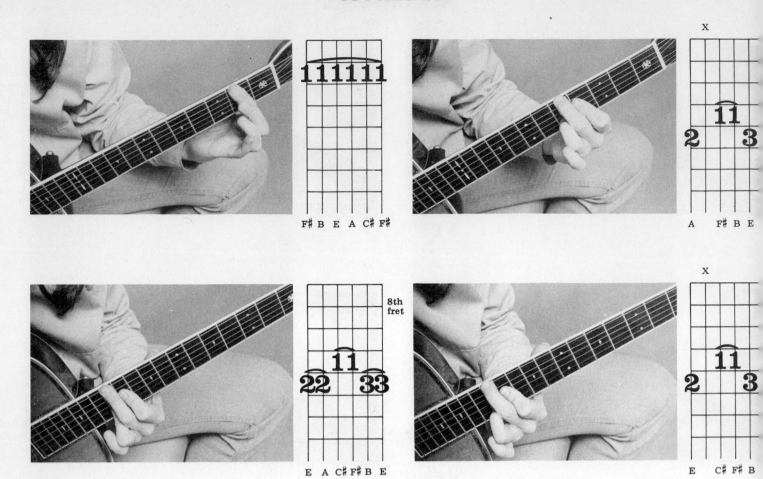

F# B E A C# F#

X

11
2   3

A   F# B E

8th fret

22   11   33

E A C# F# B E

X

11
2   3

E   C# F# B

A#/Bb Major

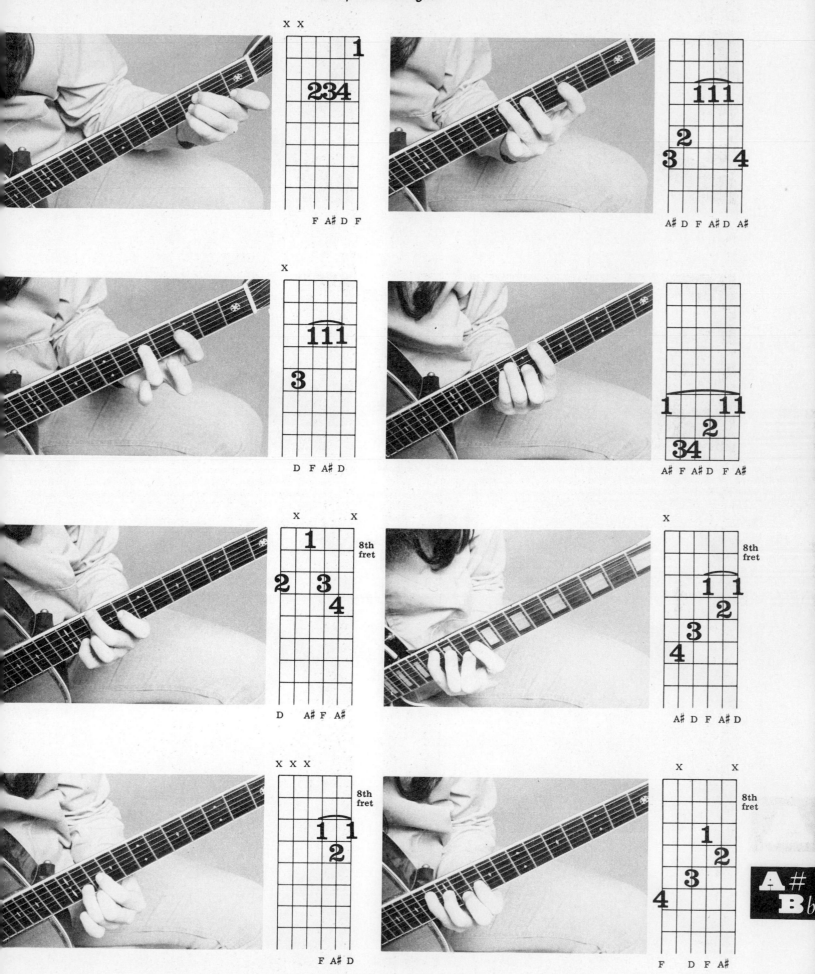

261

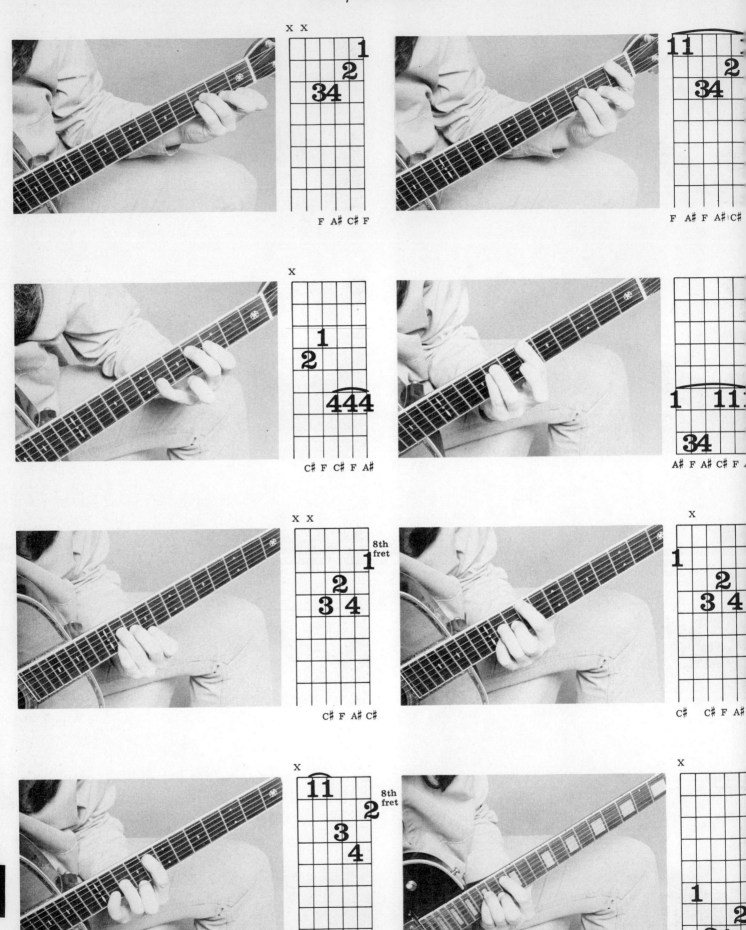

A#/Bb Major Sixth

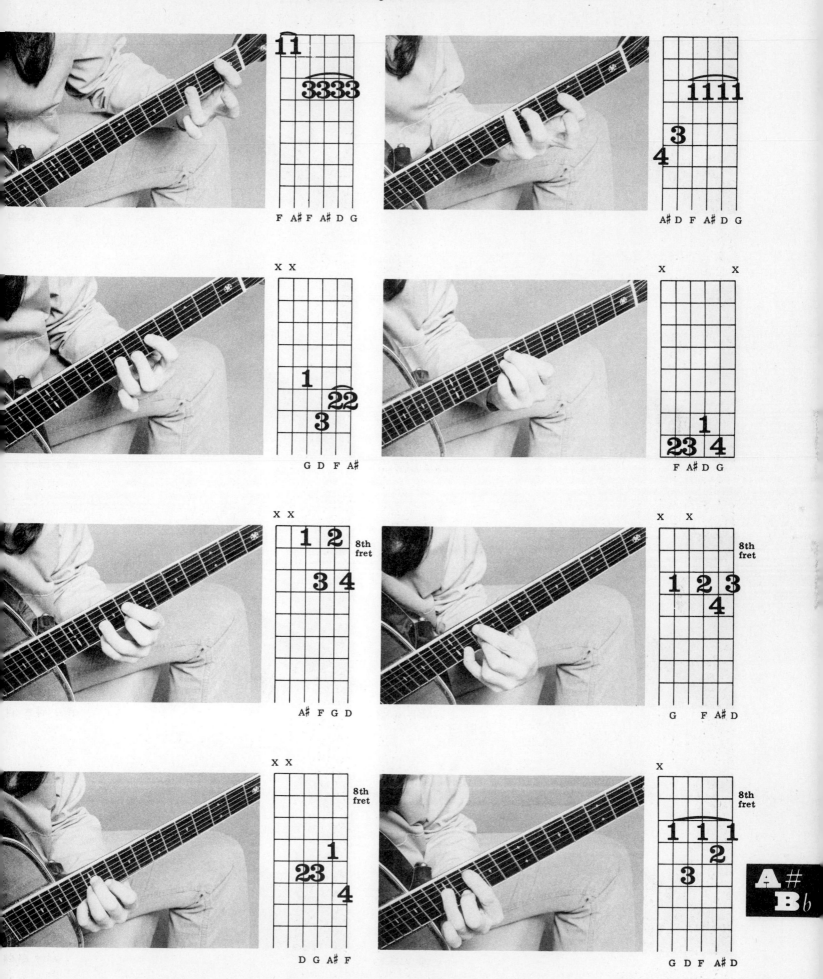

263

A #/Bb Minor Sixth

A#/Bb Seventh

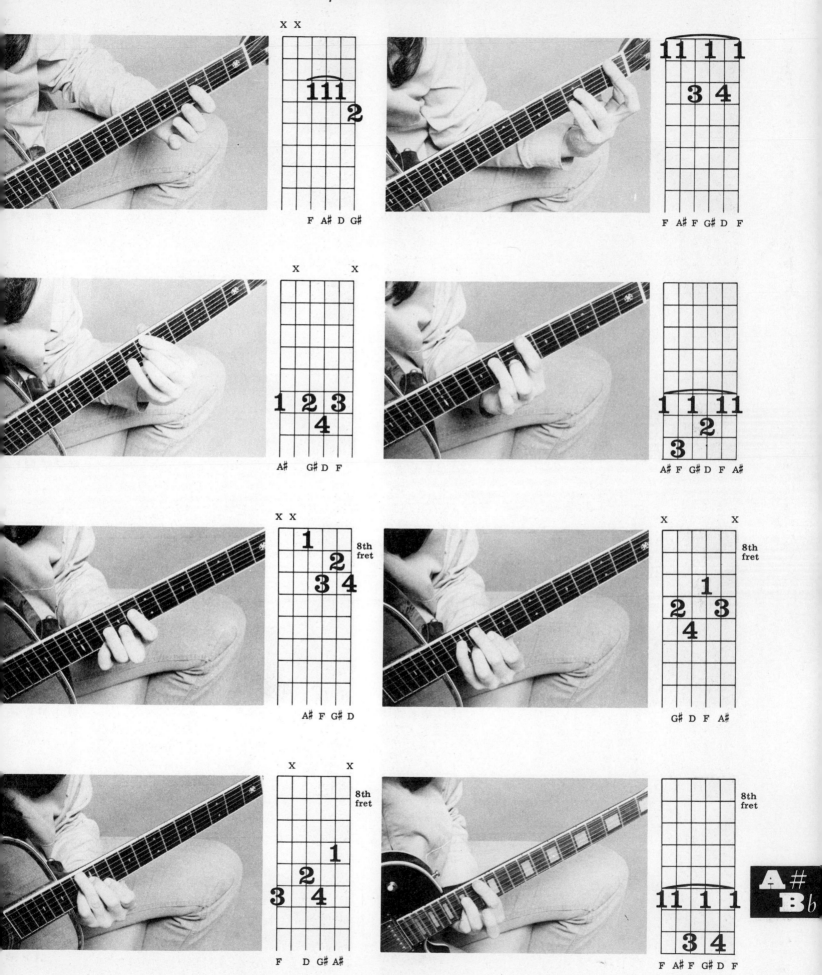

265

A#/Bb Minor Seventh

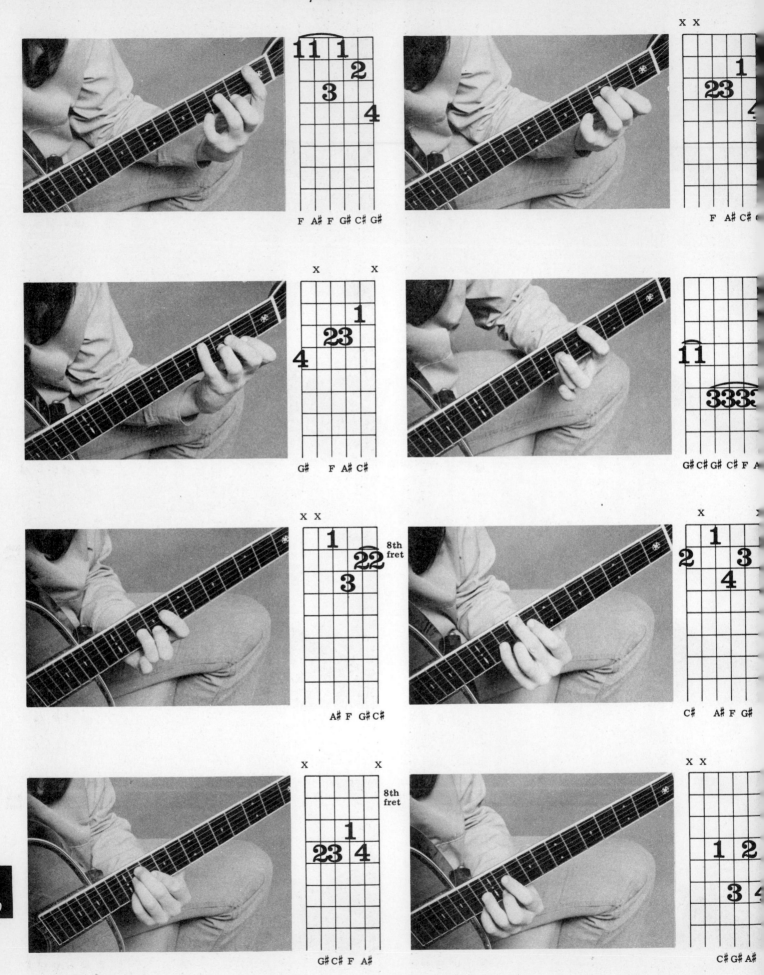

A#/B♭ Diminished

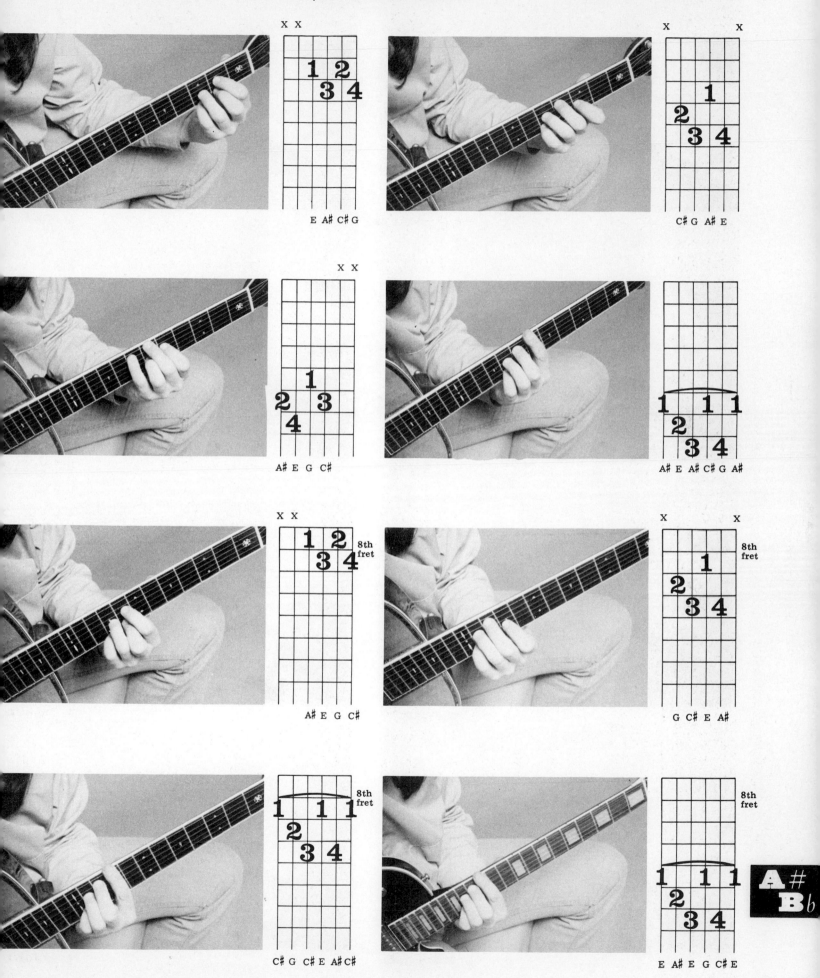

267

A#/Bb Augmented

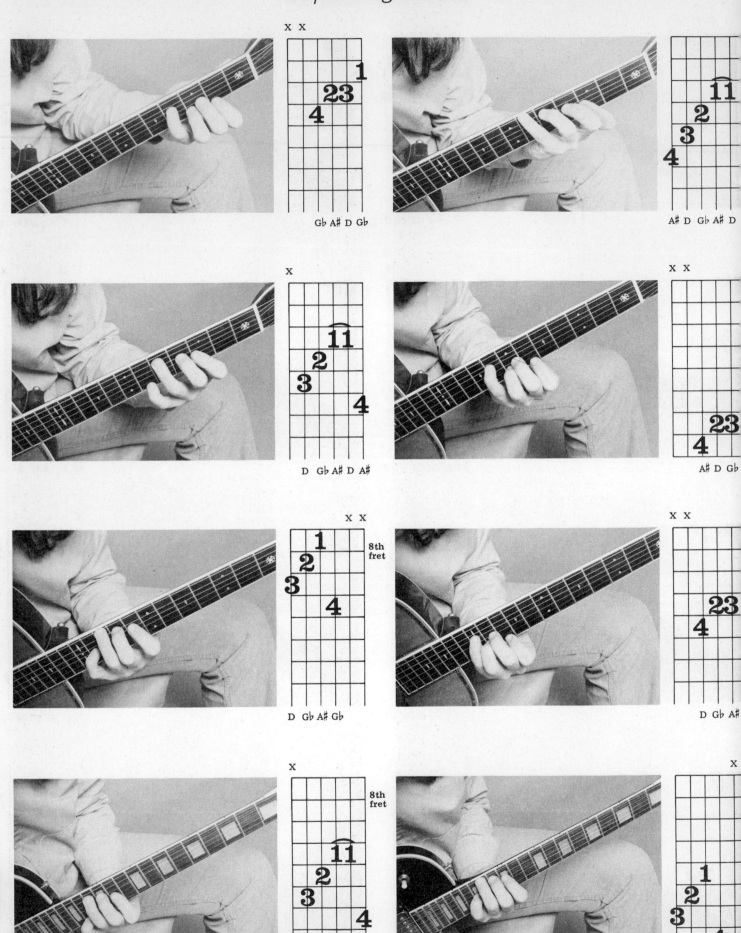

268

A#/Bb Seventh Augmented Fifth

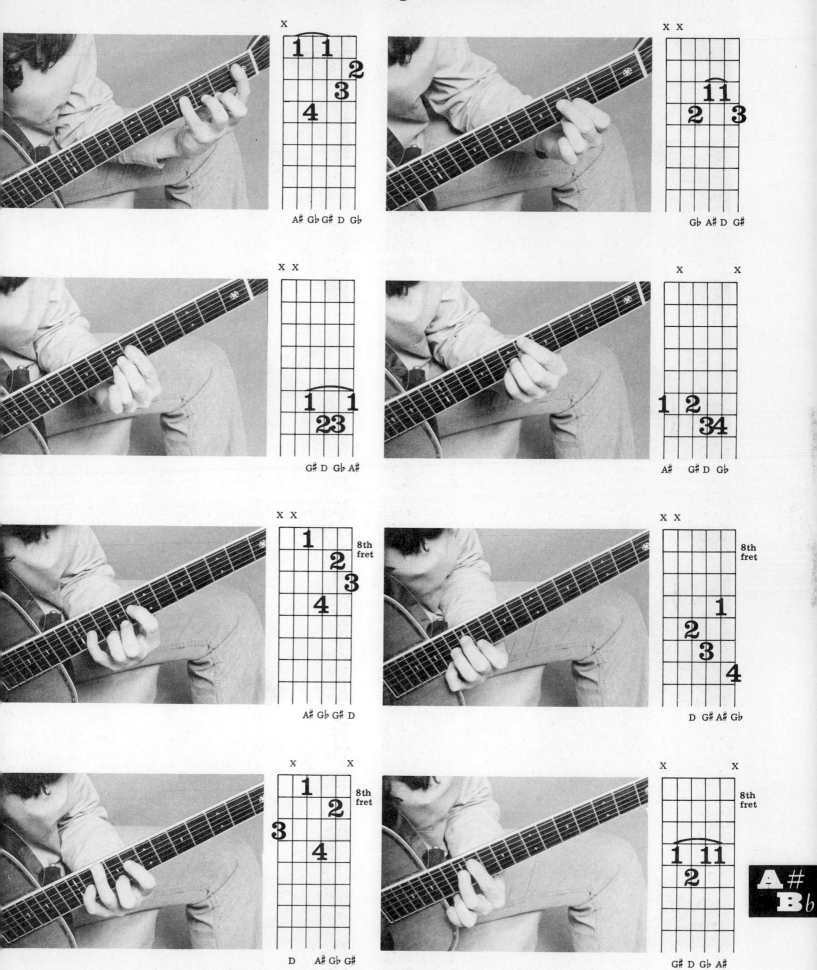

A#/B♭ Seventh Flat Five

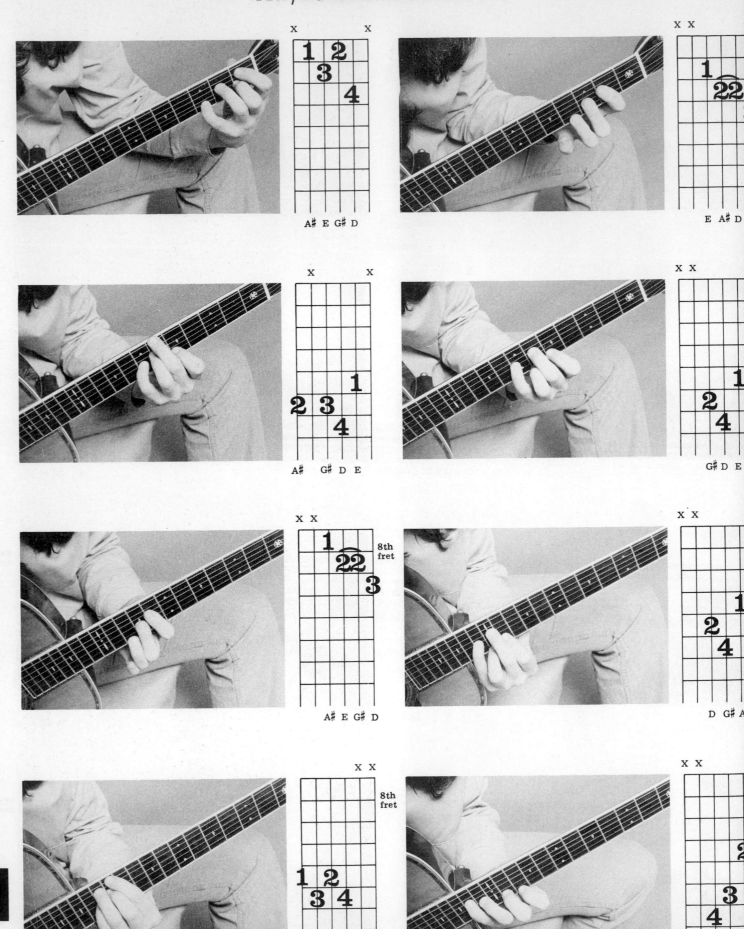

270

A#/Bb Seventh Flat Nine

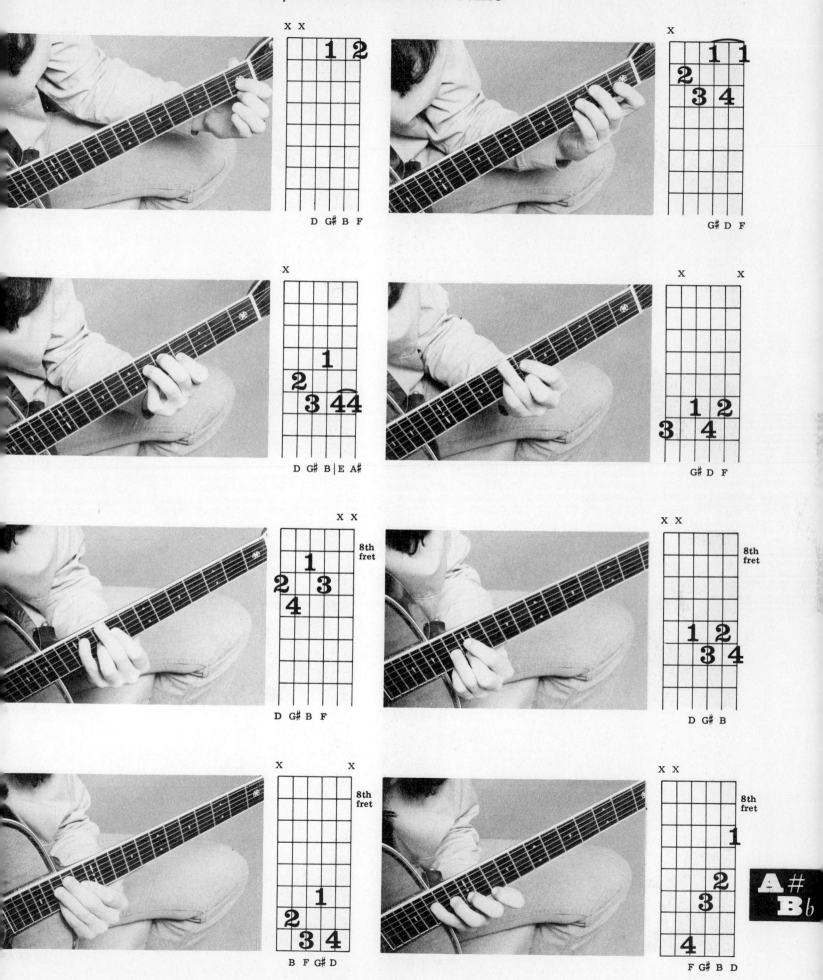

271

A#/B♭ Major Seventh

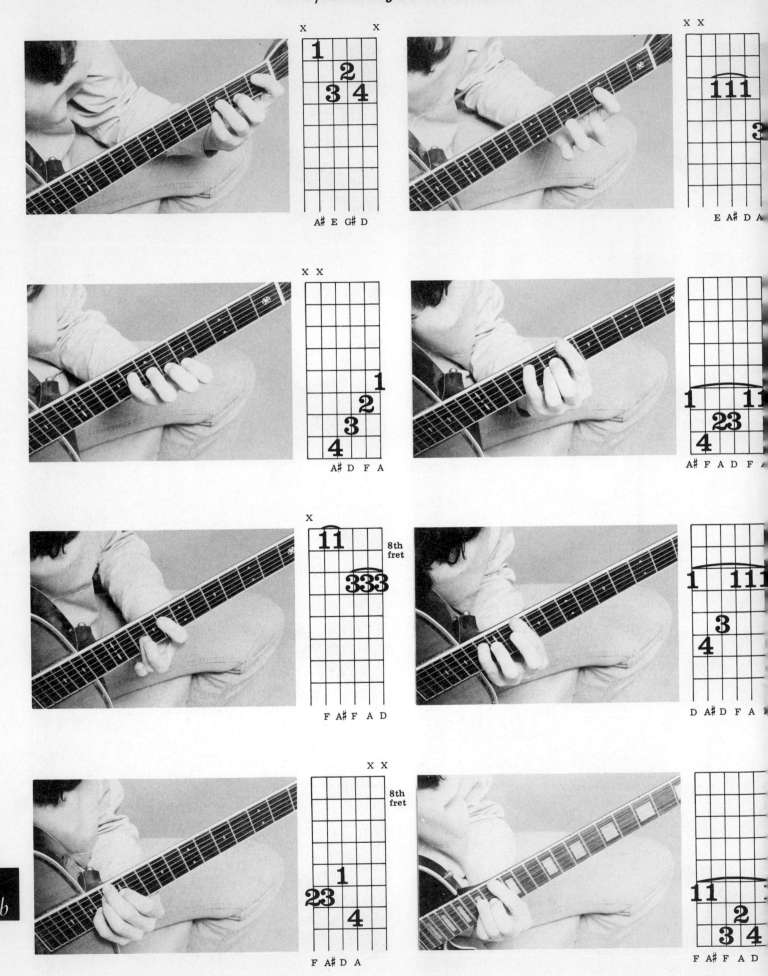

A#/Bb Minor Seventh Flat Five

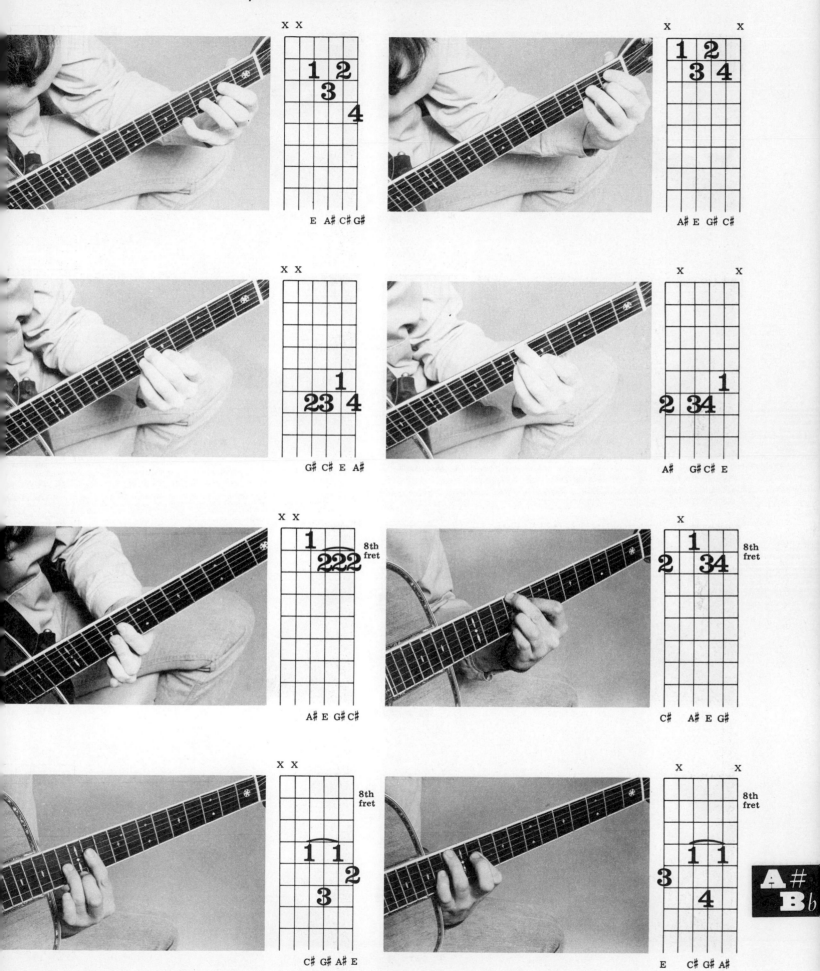

273

A#/Bb Seventh Suspension Four

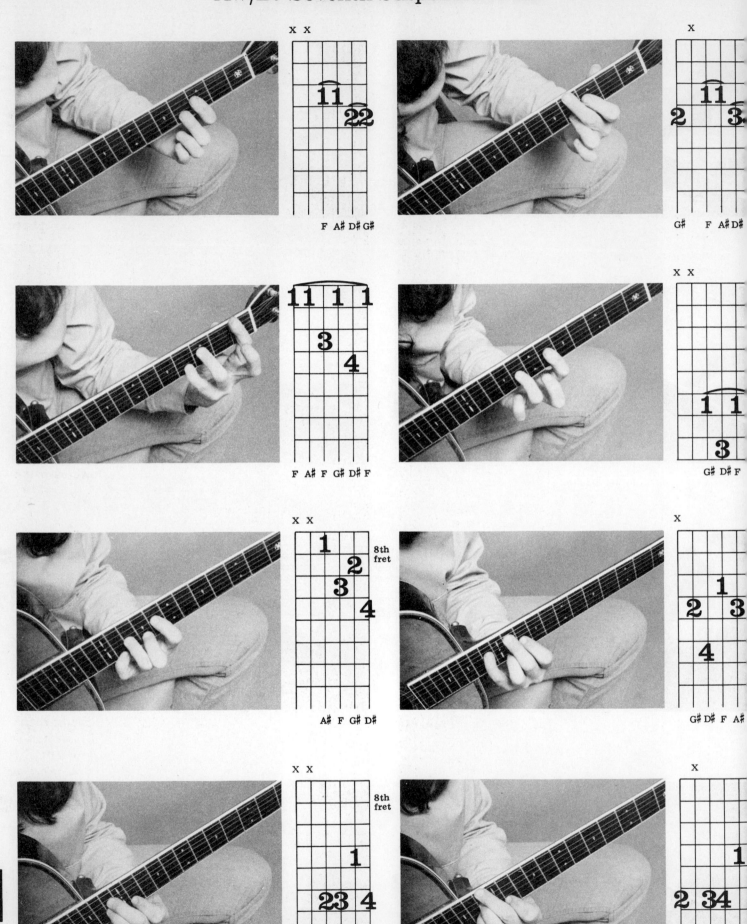

A#/Bb Ninth

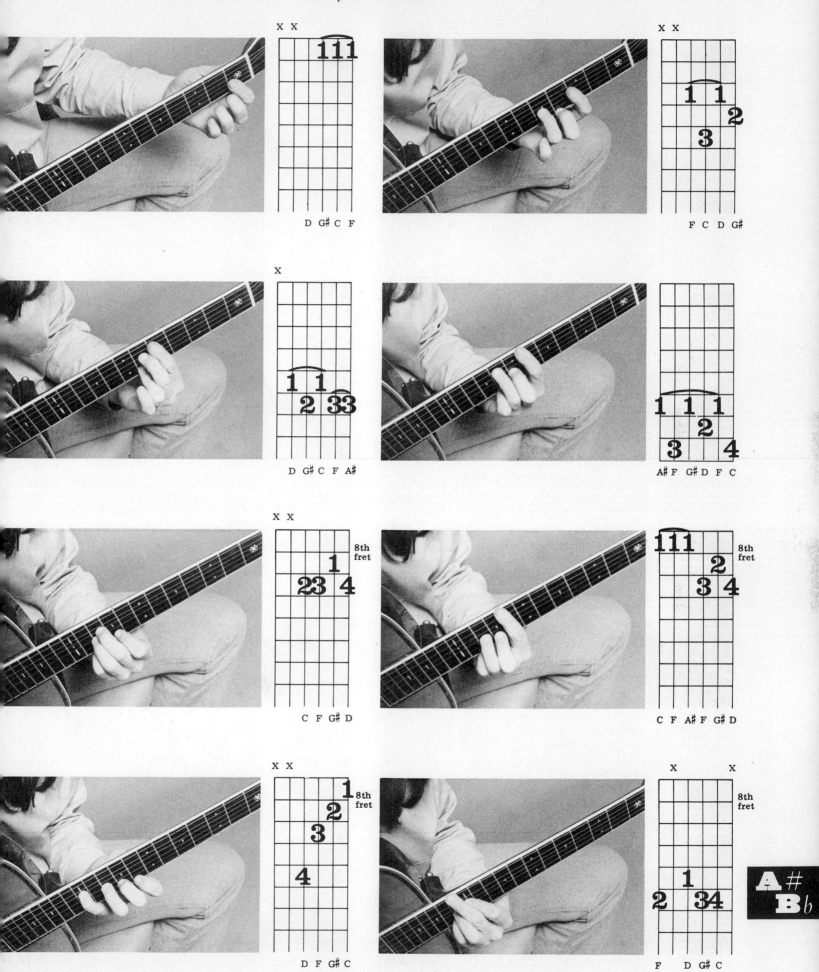

275

A#/Bb Minor Ninth

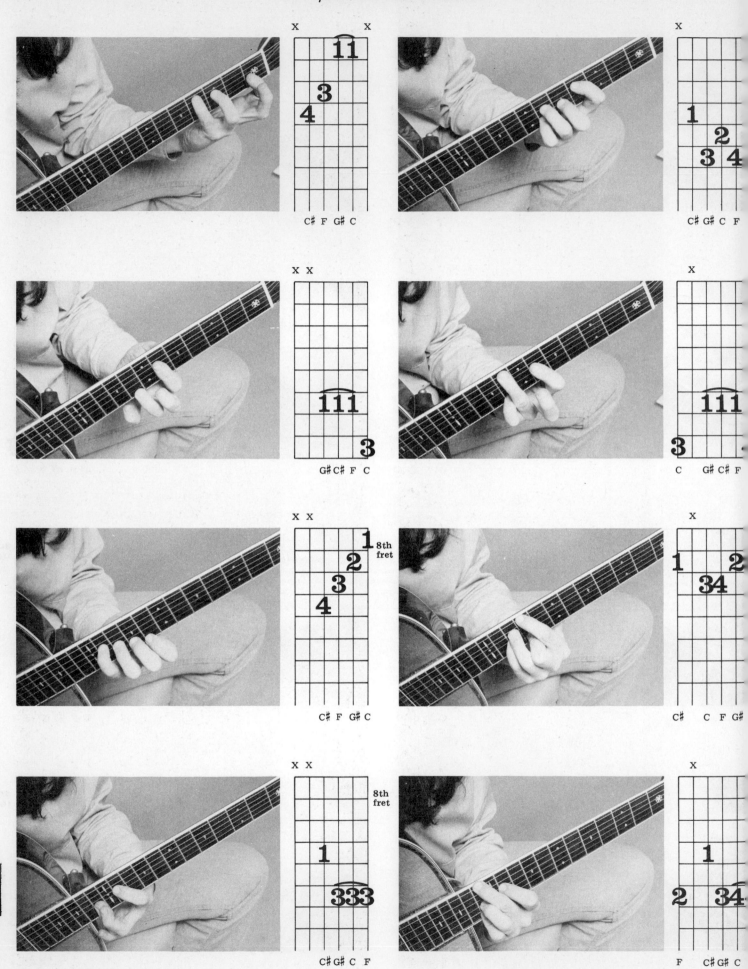

A#/B♭ Ninth Augmented Fifth

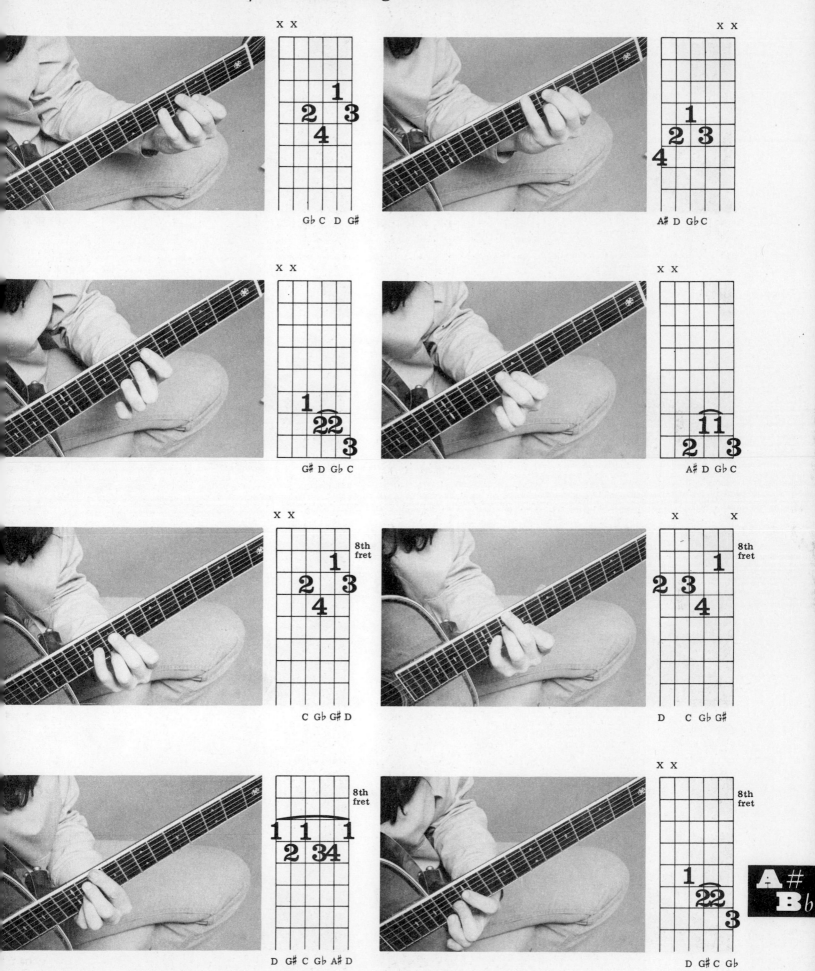

A#/Bb Ninth Flat Five

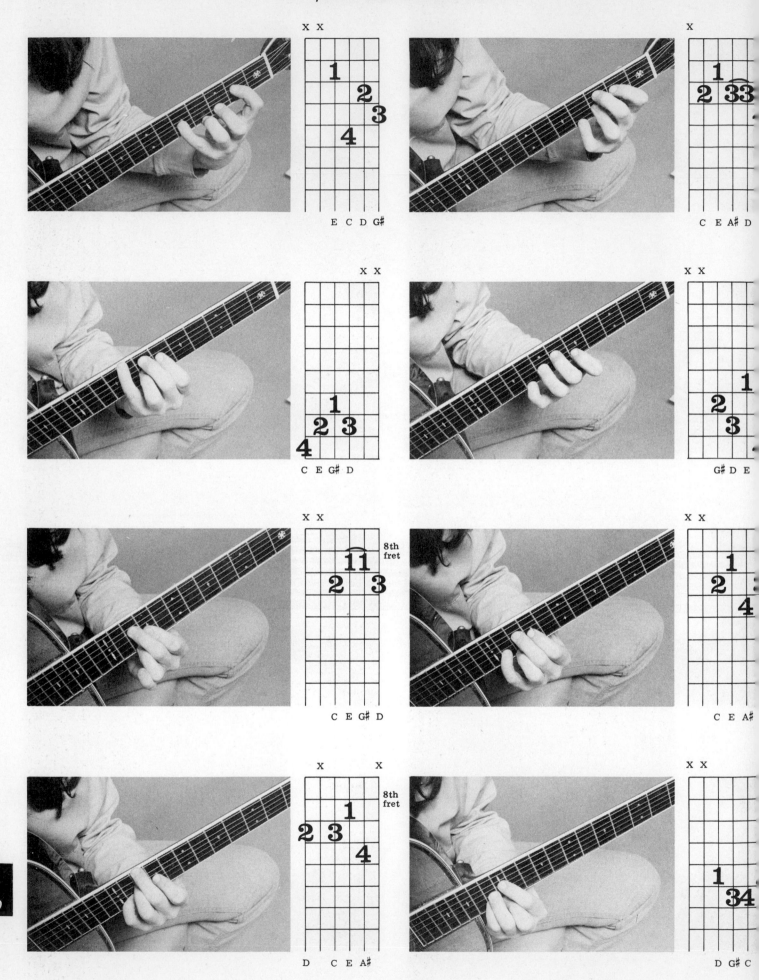

278

A#/B♭ Major Ninth

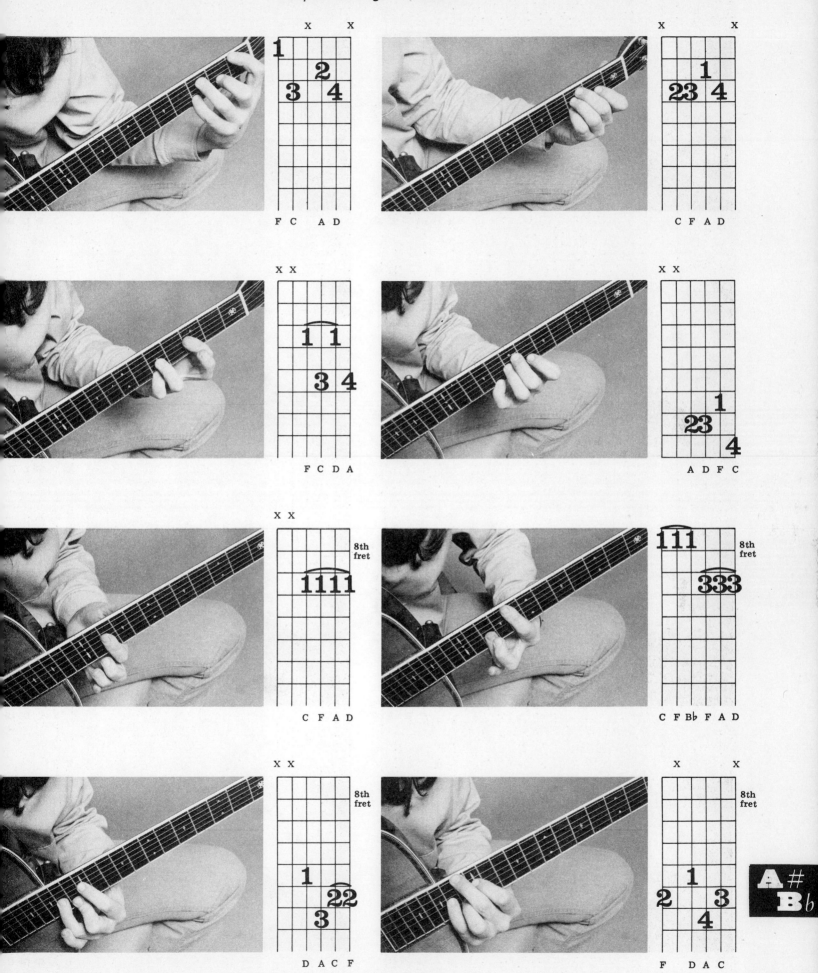

A#/Bb Eleventh

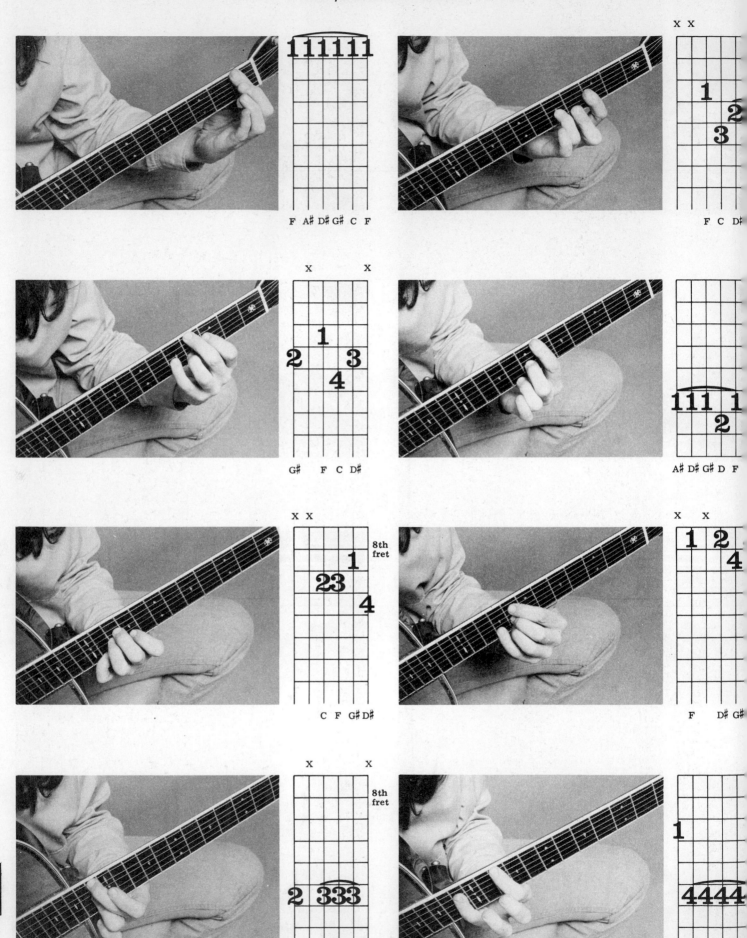

A#/Bb Augmented Eleventh

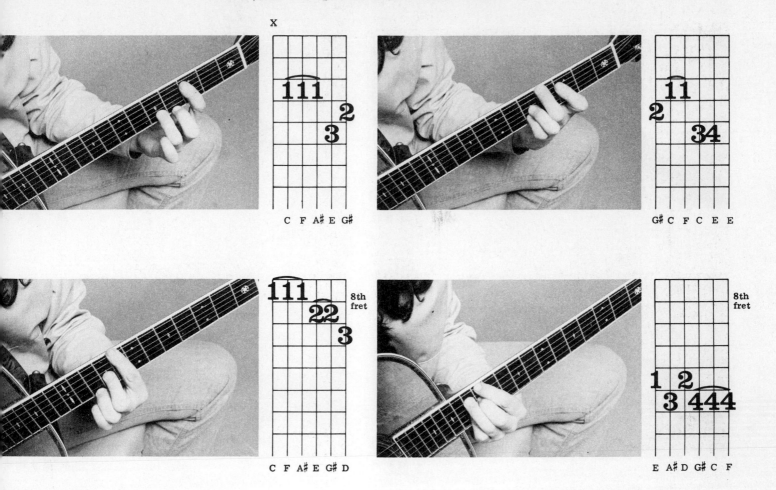

C F A# E G#

G# C F C E E

C F A# E G# D

E A# D G# C F

A#/Bb Thirteenth

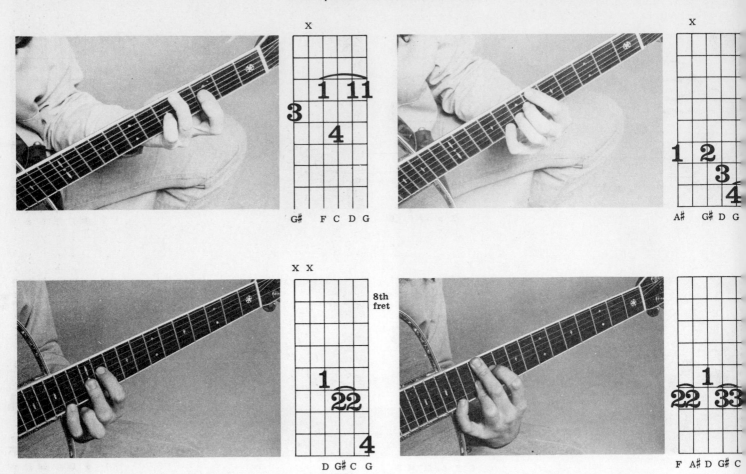

A#/Bb Thirteenth Flat Nine

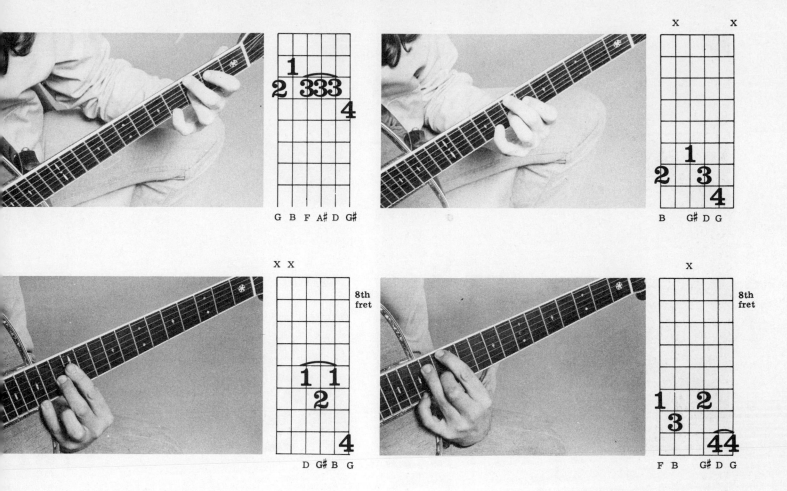

G B F A# D G#

B G# D G

X X

8th
fret

D G# B G

X

8th
fret

F B G# D G

A#/B♭ Seven Six

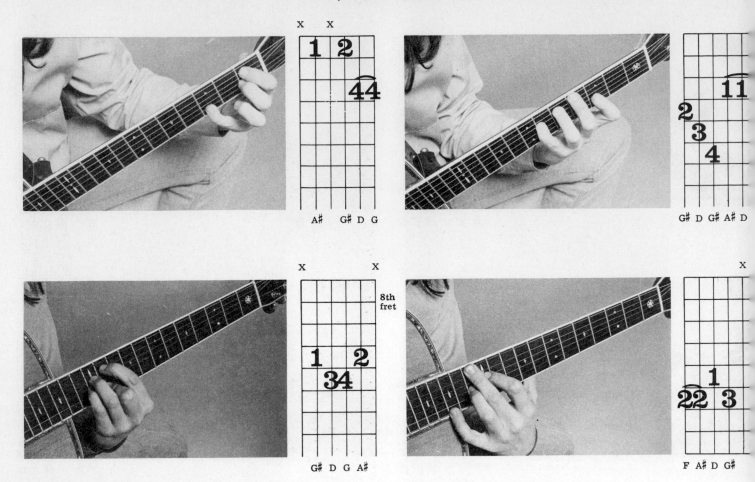

A#/Bb Nine Six

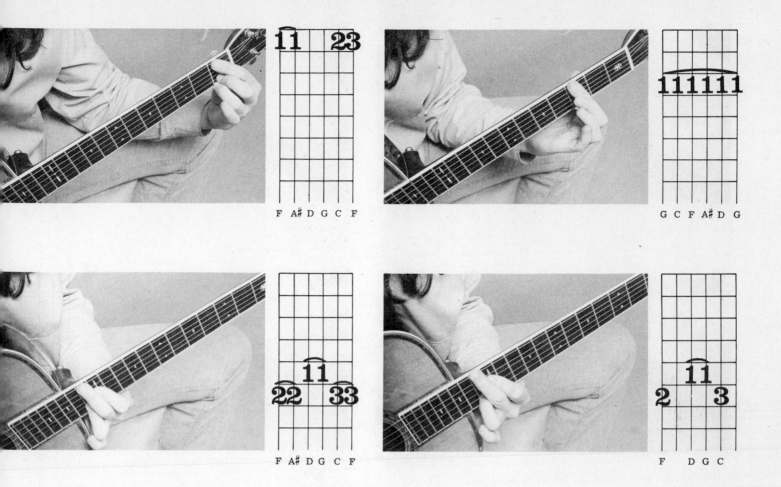

B Major

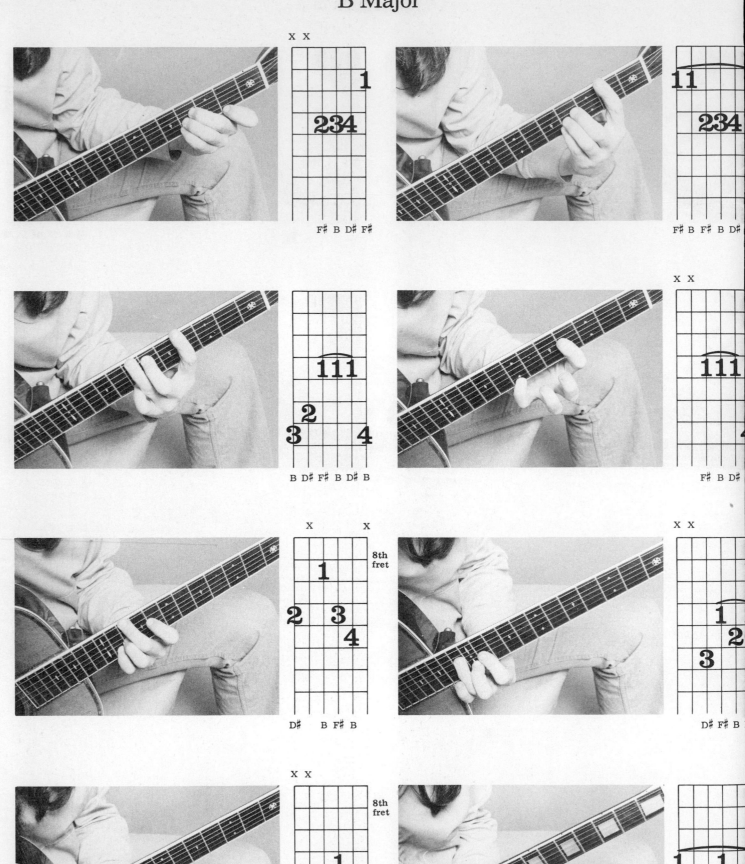

286

B Minor

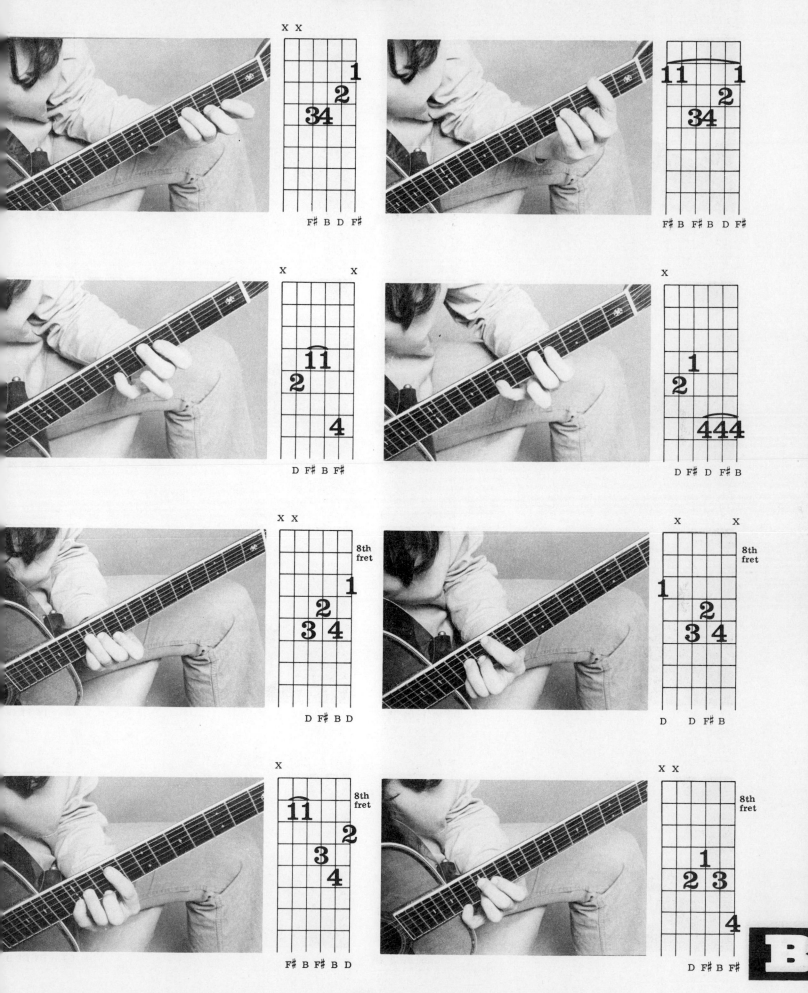

287

B Major Sixth

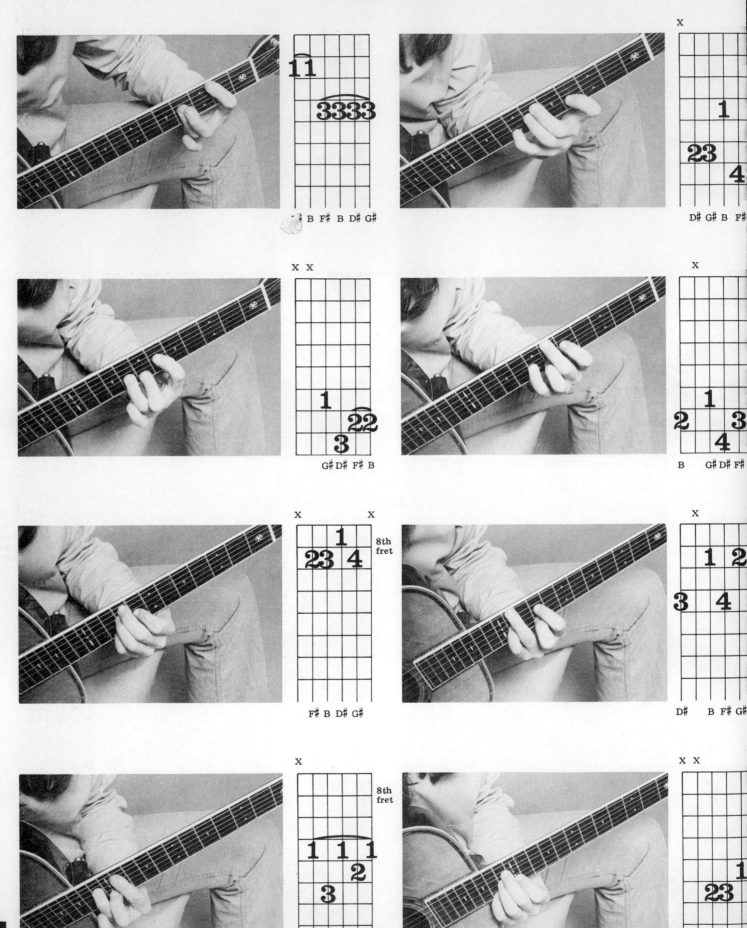

B Minor Sixth

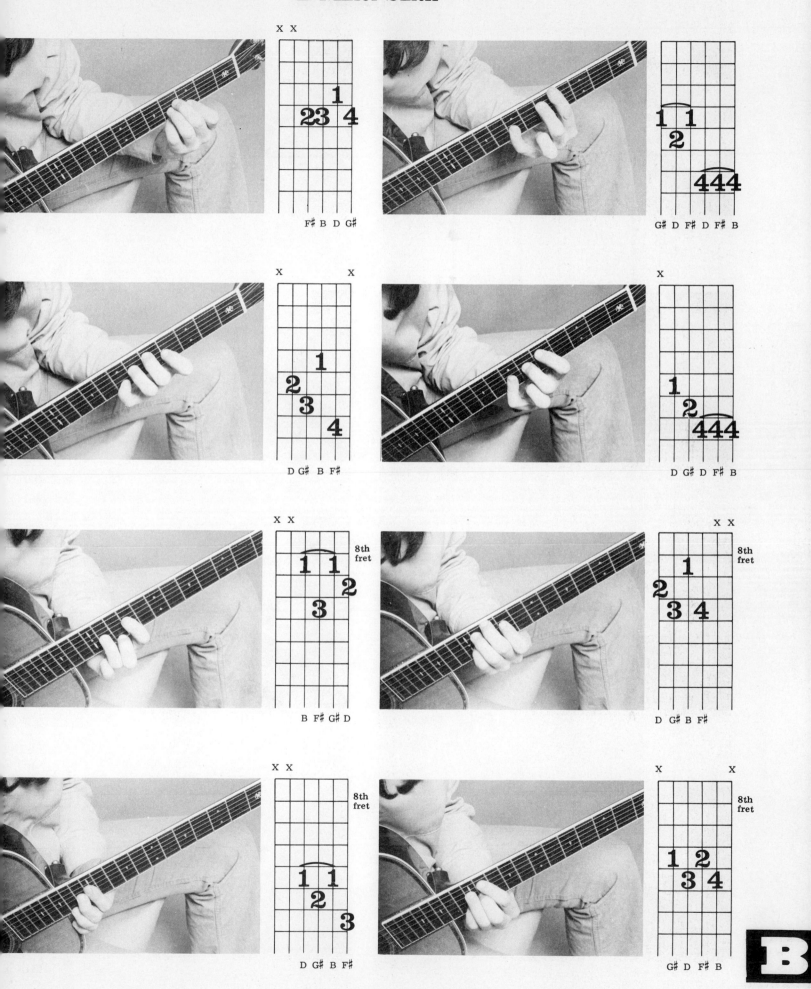

289

B Seventh

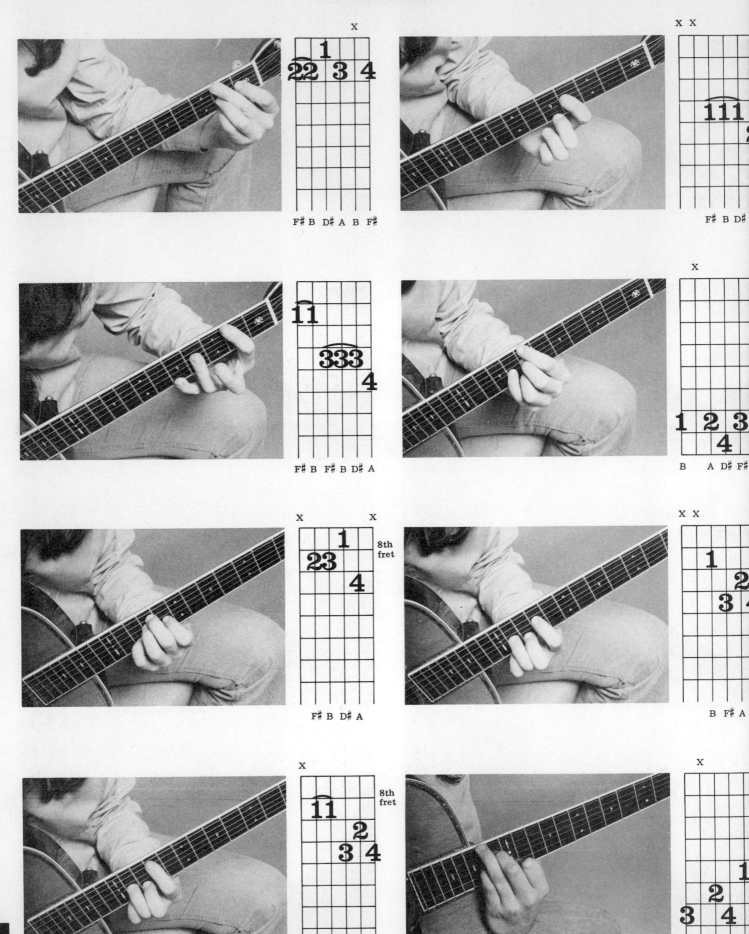

290

B Minor Seventh

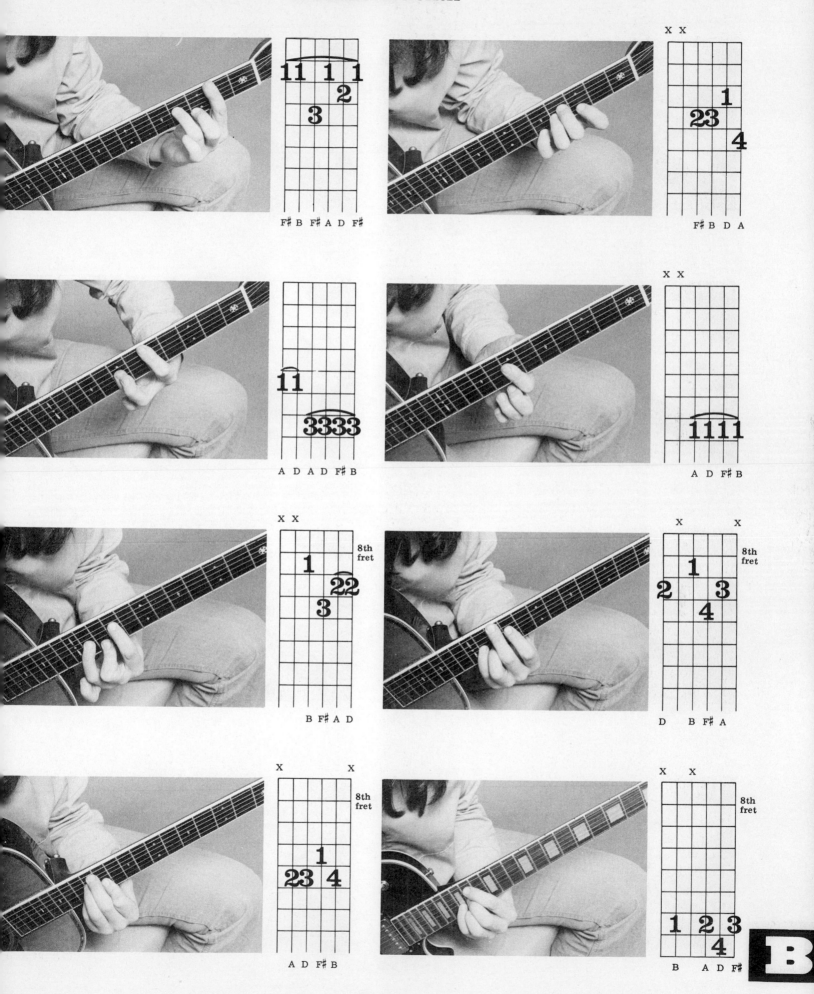

B Diminished

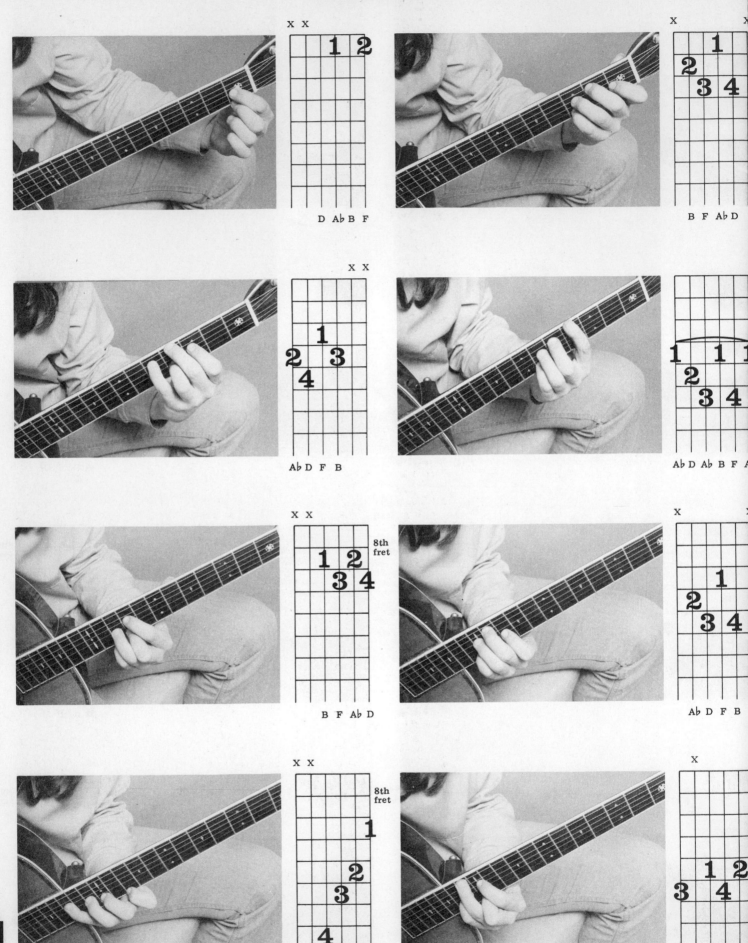

292

B Augmented

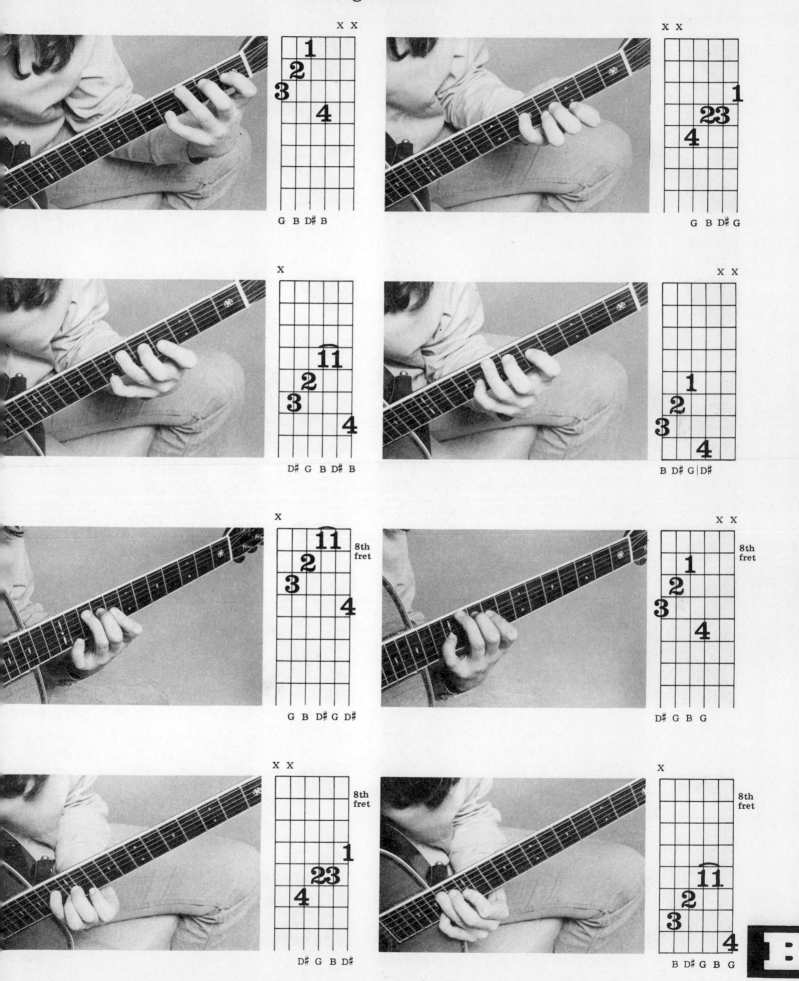

293

B Seventh Augmented Fifth

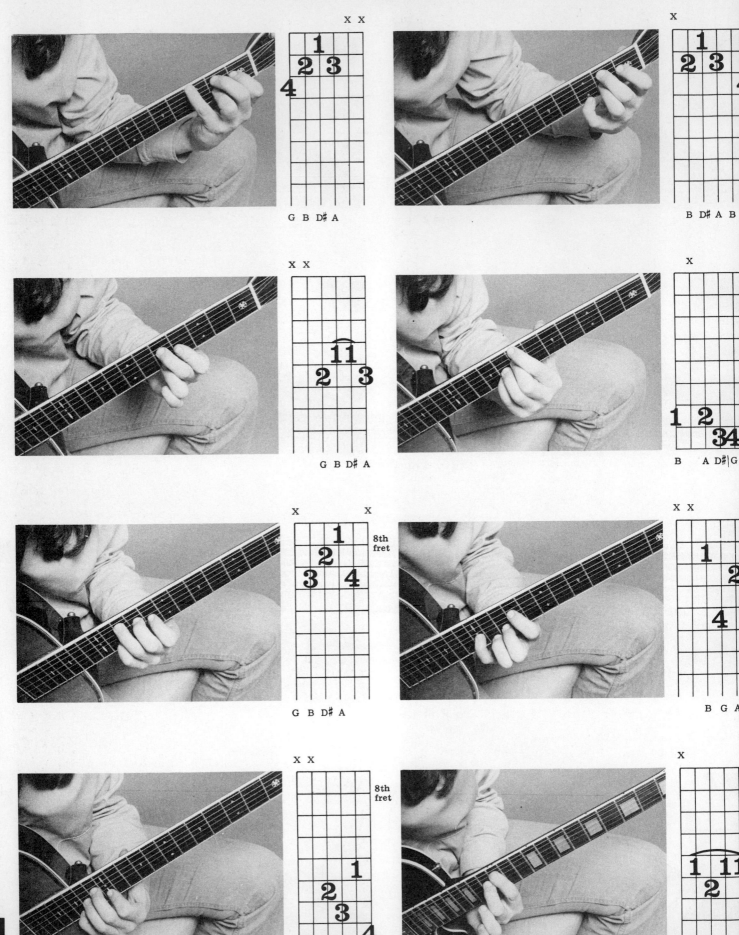

294

B Seventh Flat Five

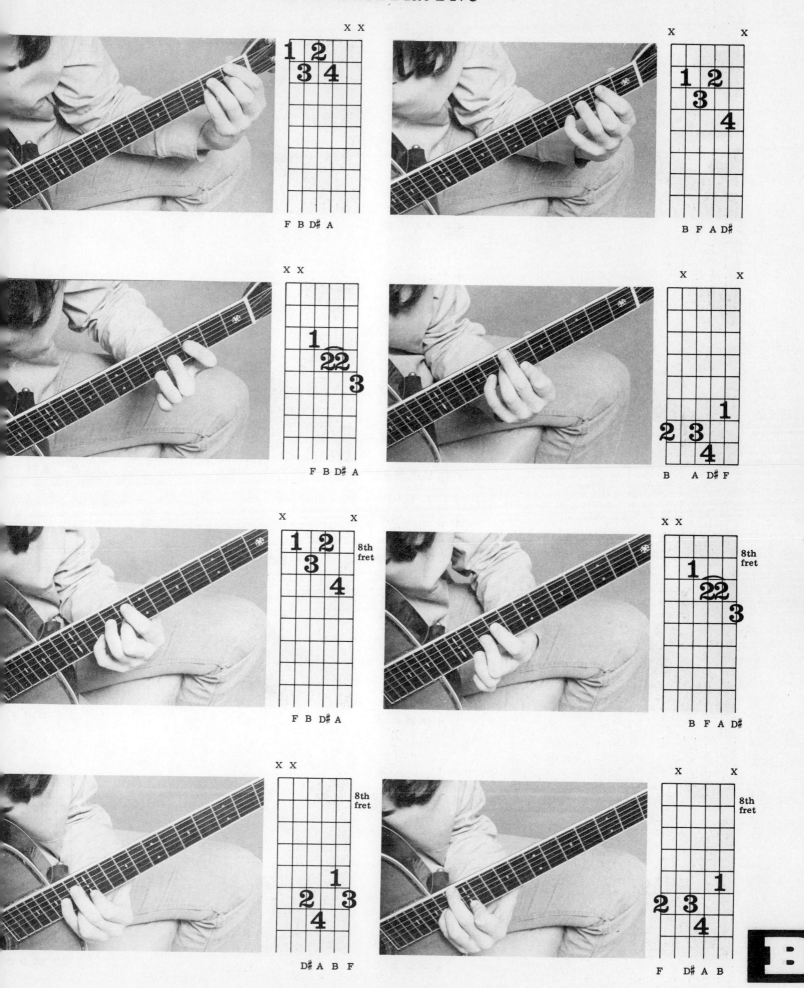

295

B Seventh Flat Nine

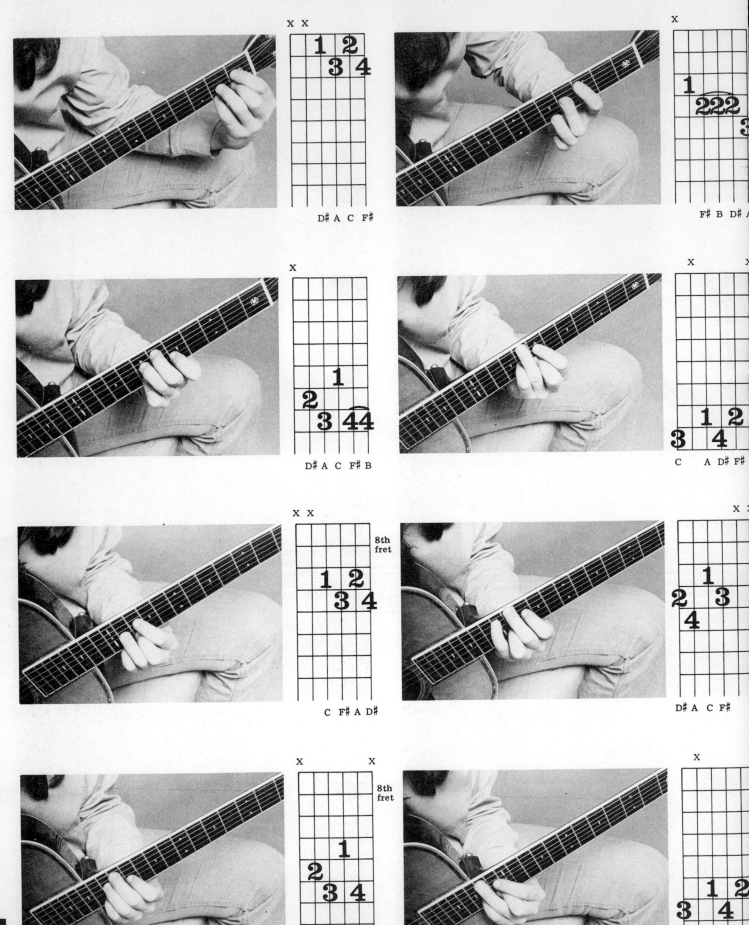

296

B Major Seventh

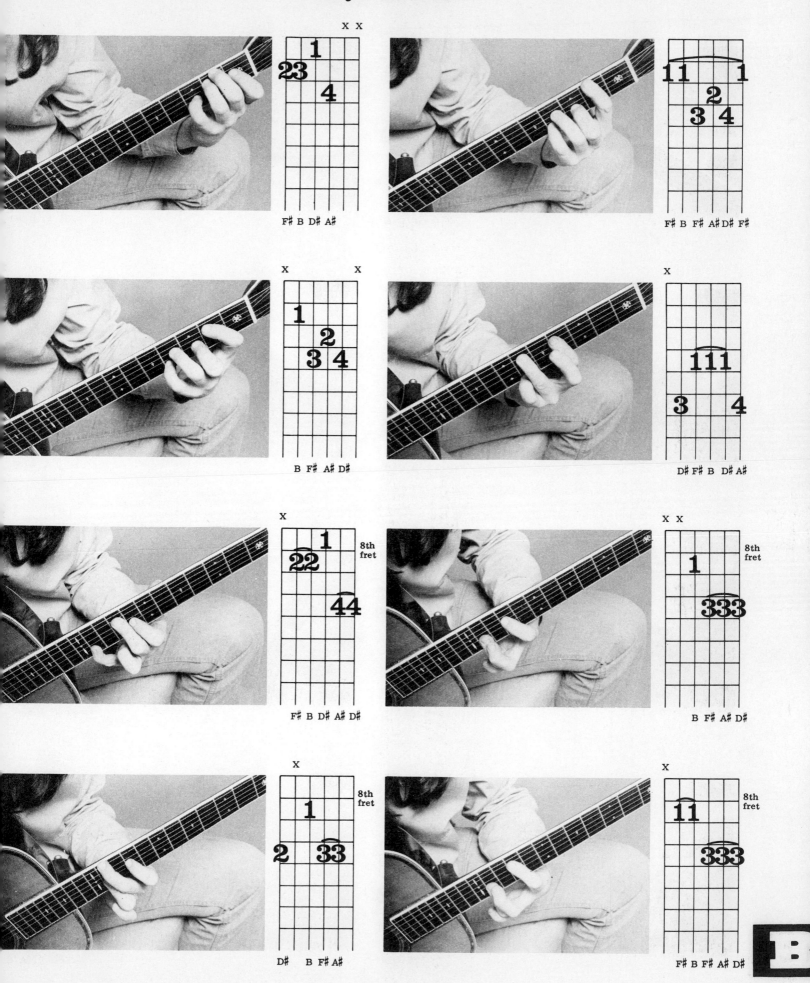

B Minor Seventh Flat Five

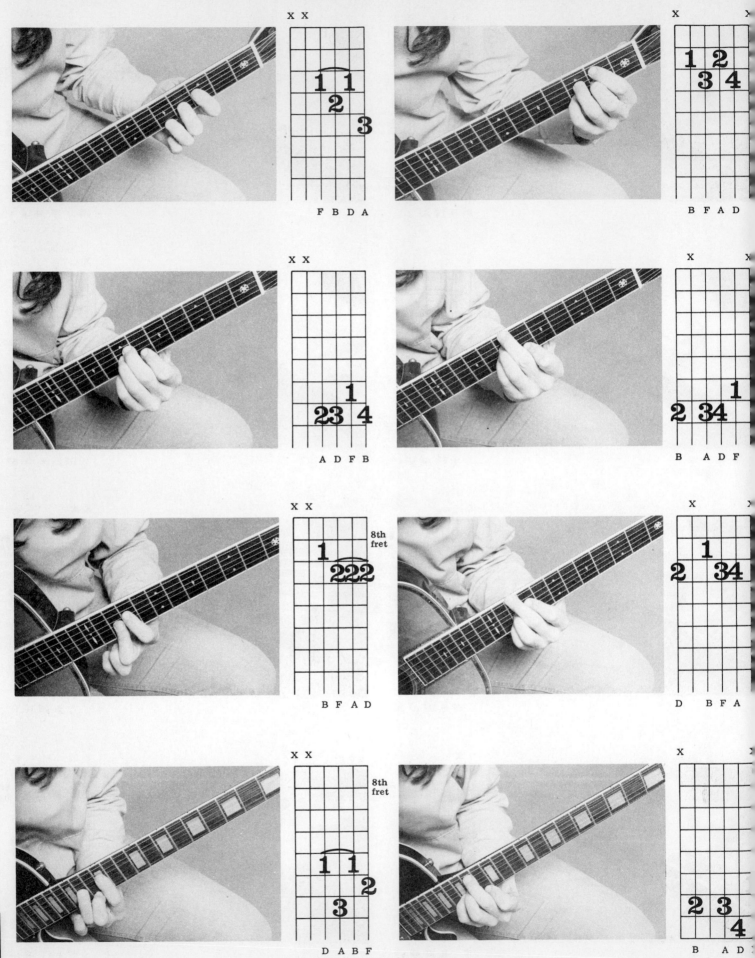

B Seventh Suspension Four

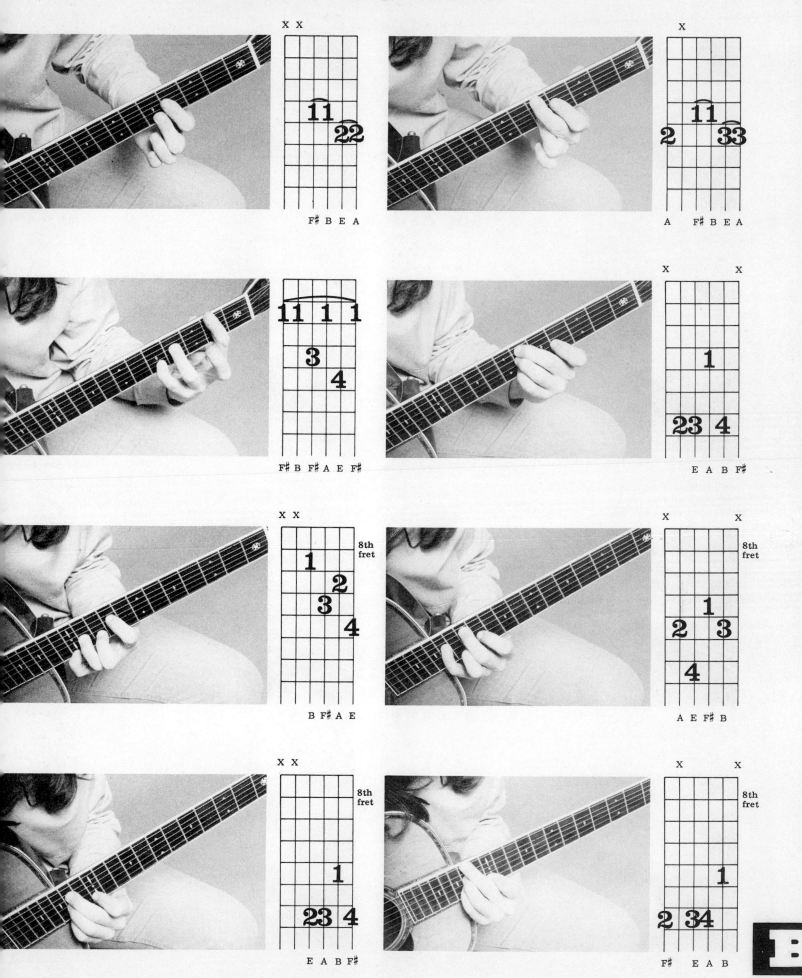

299

B Ninth

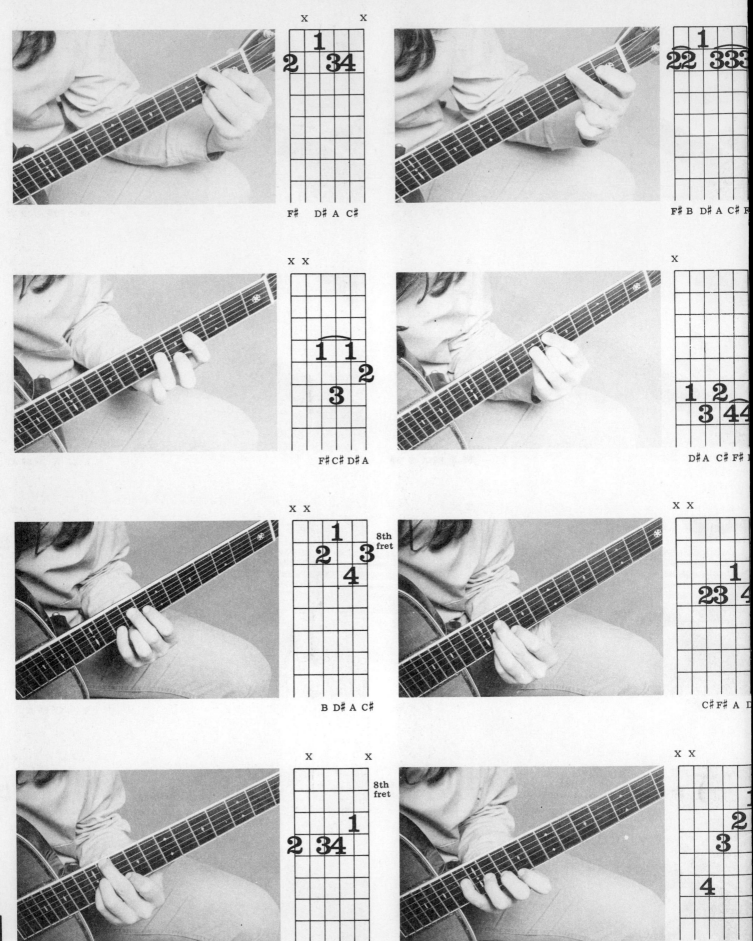

B Minor Ninth

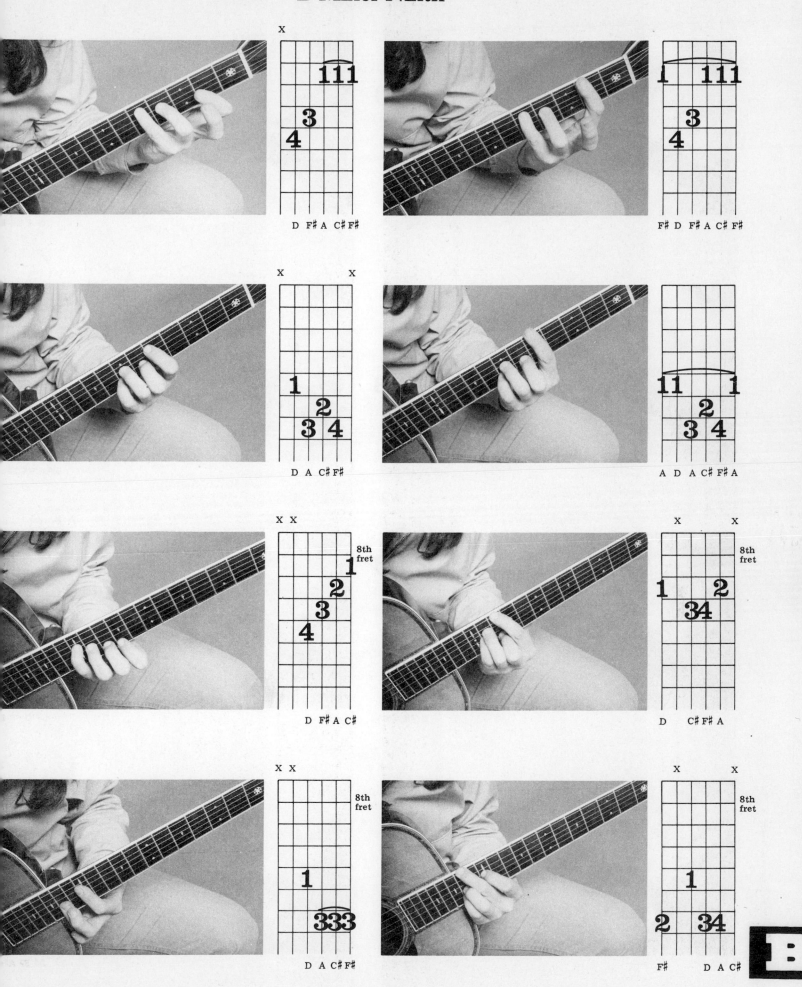

B Ninth Augmented Fifth

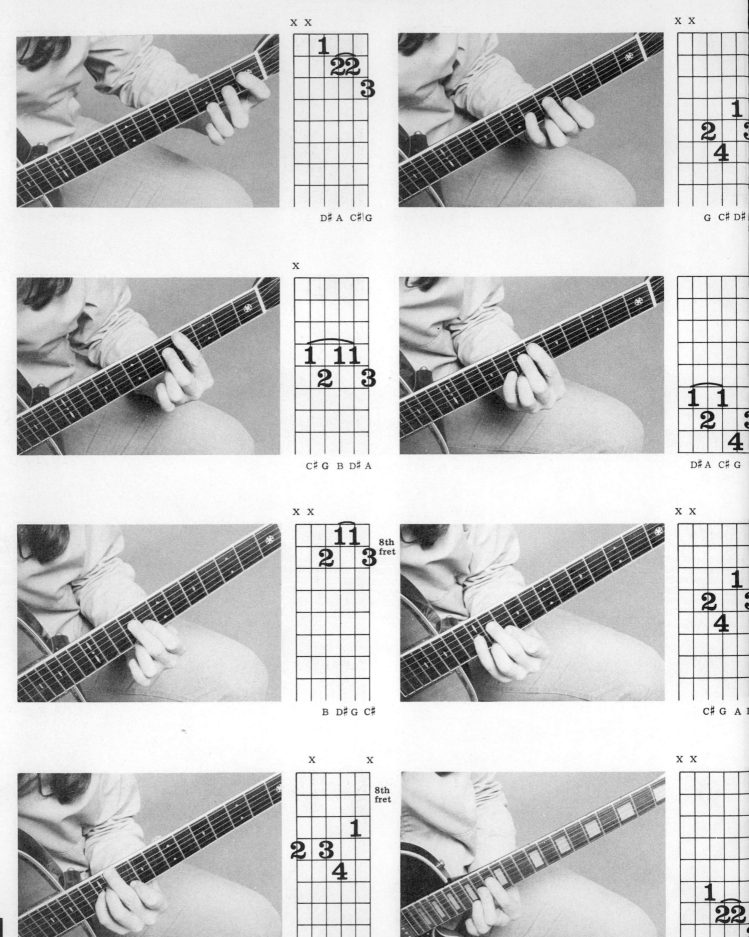

B Ninth Flat Five

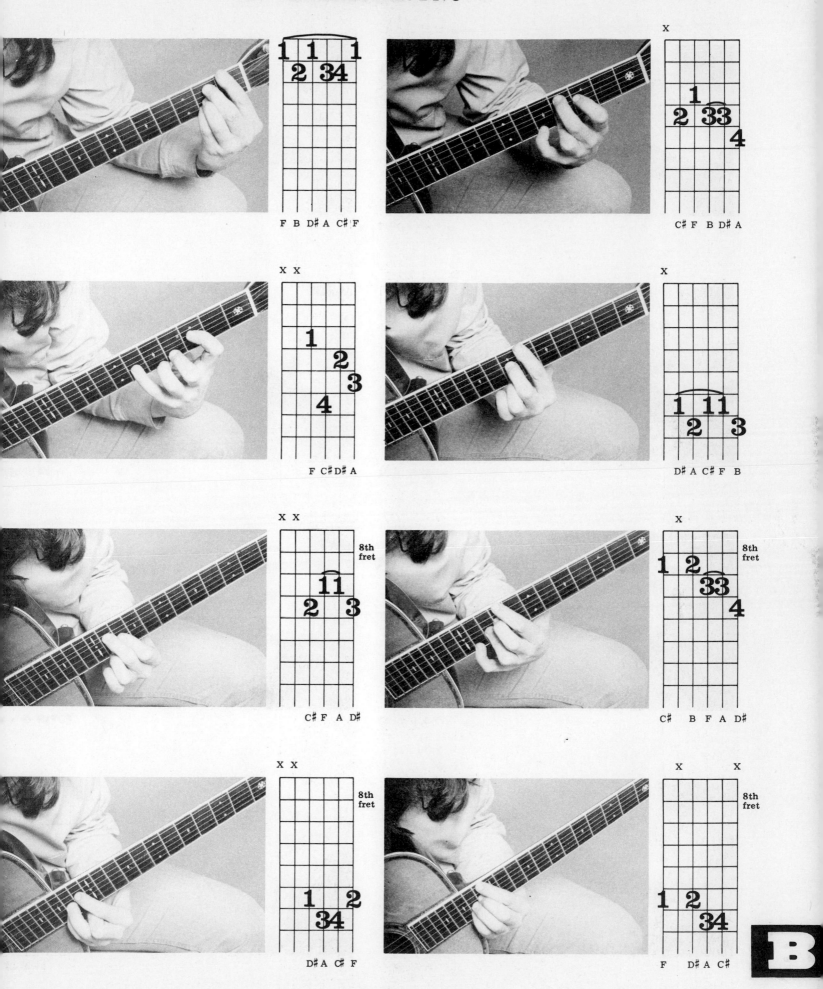

303

B Major Ninth

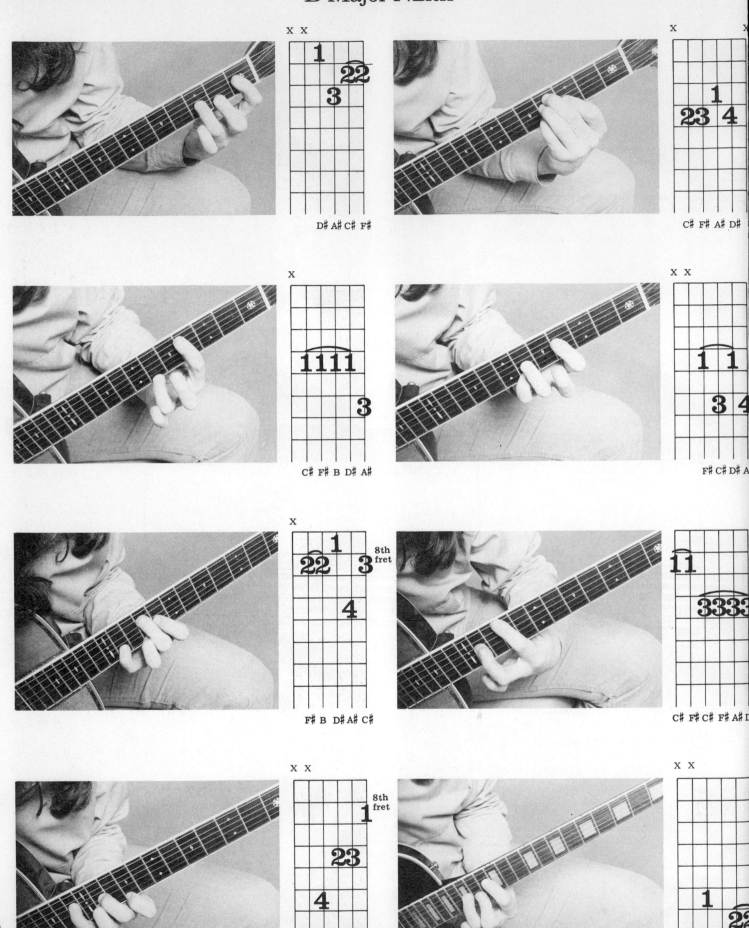

B Eleventh

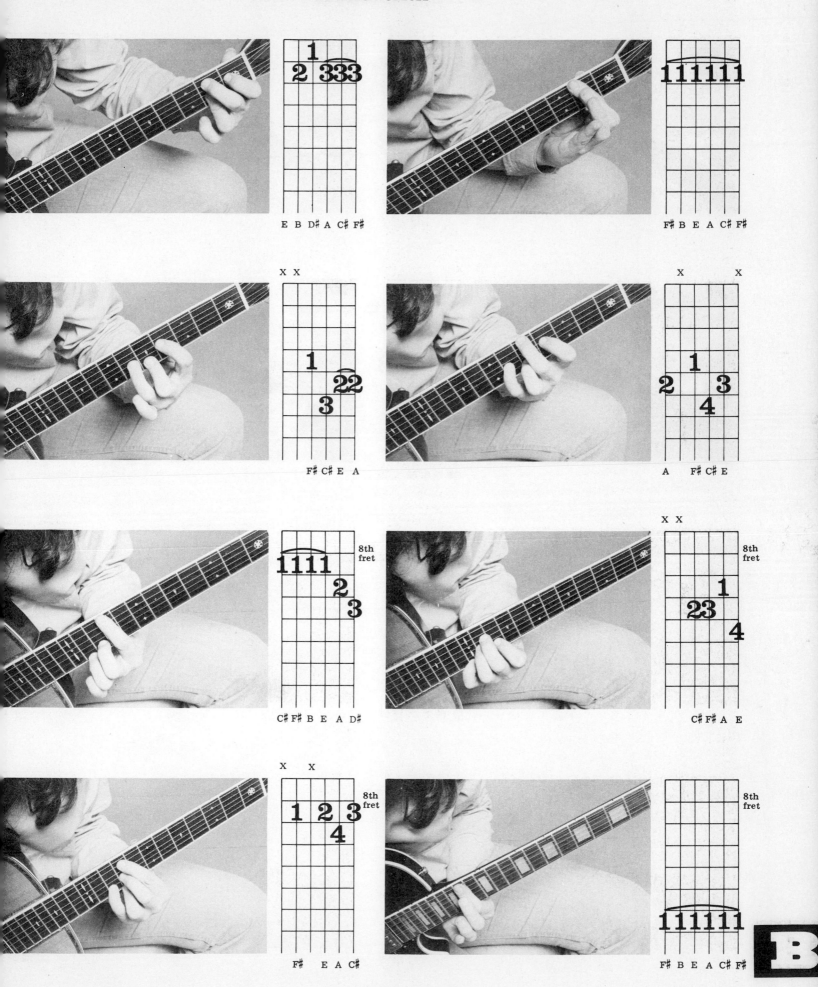

305

B Augmented Eleventh

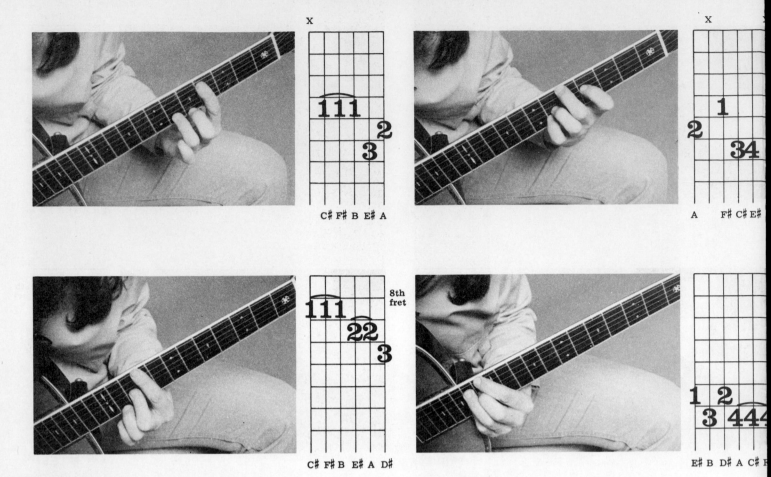

C# F# B E# A

A   F# C# E#

C# F# B E# A D#

E# B D# A C#

B Thirteenth

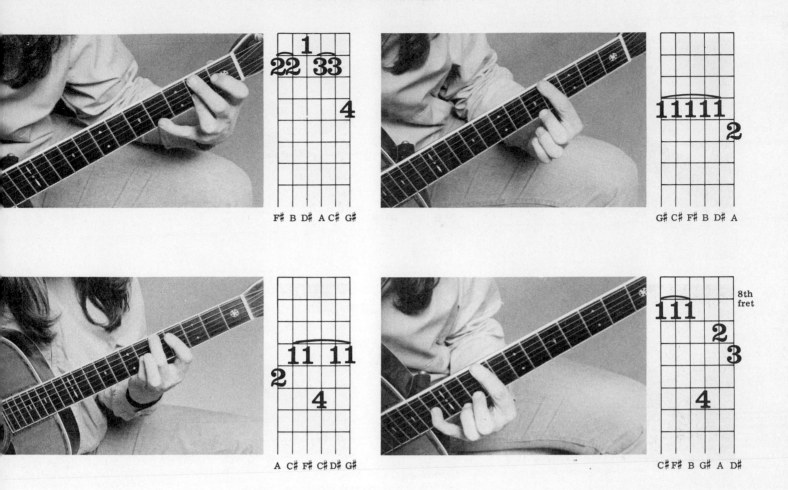

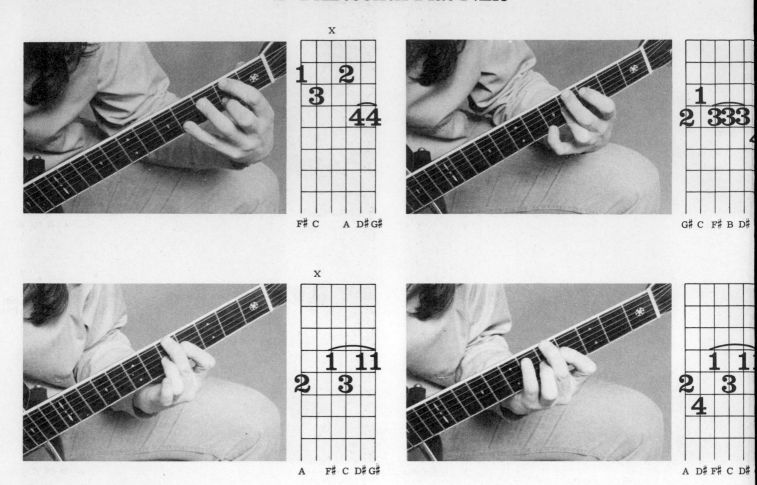

B Seven Six

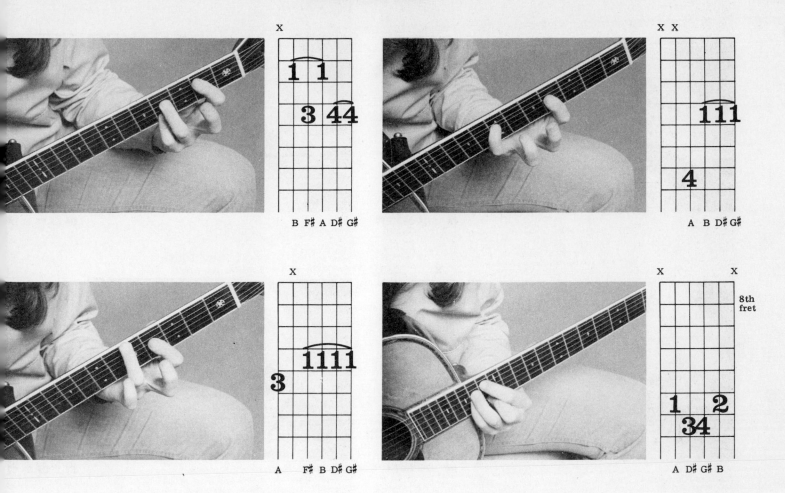

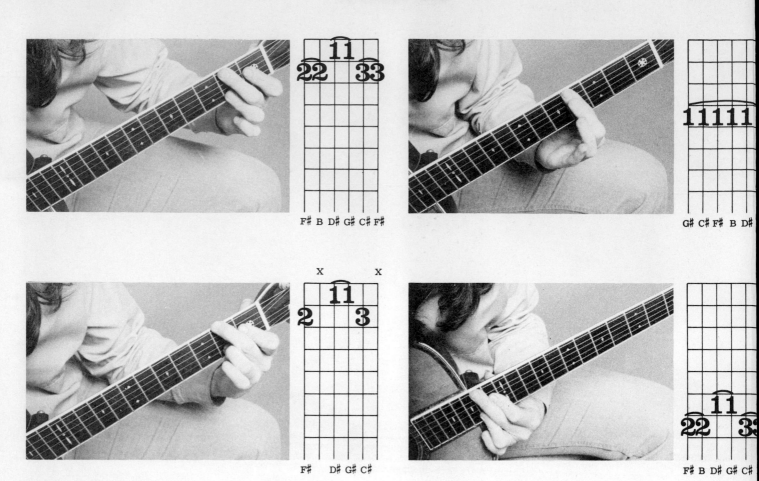